*The Language Demand*

# The Language Demands of School
## Putting Academic English to the Test

*Edited by* ALISON L. BAILEY
*University of California, Los Angeles*

*Yale University Press* New Haven and London

Set in New Aster by Integrated Publishing Solutions.
Printed in the United States of America.

Library of Congress Cataloging-in-Publication Data
The language demands of school : putting academic English to the test / edited by Alison L.
Bailey.
    p.   cm.
Includes bibliographical references and index.
ISBN-13: 978-0-300-10946-7 (pbk. : alk. paper)
ISBN-10: 0-300-10946-6 (pbk. : alk. paper)
1. English language—Study and teaching (Elementary)—United States. 2. English language—
Study and teaching (Secondary)—United States. 3. Language arts—United States—Evaluation.
4. Language arts—United States—Standards. 5. Educational tests and measurements—United
States.   I. Bailey, Alison L.
LB1576.L2967 2006
428.0071—dc22

                                                                                2006003782

A catalogue record for this book is available from the British Library.

The paper in this book meets the guidelines for permanence and durability of the Committee
on Production Guidelines for Book Longevity of the Council on Library Resources.

10   9   8   7   6   5   4   3   2   1

*To my grandparents, Florence Hinchcliffe and Joseph Roberts,*
*Amy Jane Tibbs and Ernest Bailey, and to my parents, Florence*
*and Michael Rex Bailey, with love, as always, from*
*their coal miner's granddaughter*

# Contents

# Foreword

> The ability to use the specialized language of the
> academic sphere is like a gatekeeper: it opens doors
> for those who have it, and fastens them shut for those
> who do not.
>
> —STANFORD TEACHER EDUCATION PROGRAM

Alison Bailey's timely collection of essays related to academic English language (AEL) highlights the growing challenges to all educators of English language learners (ELLs). *The Language Demands of School: Putting Academic English to the Test* reflects the urgency of acting in the current policy environment. Before 1994, federal and state policies addressed the instruction of ELLs in isolation from other student groups. The policies did not require that academic achievement of ELLs be monitored to ensure that their performance was comparable to that of other student groups. Nor did the policies require that ELLs be included in state, district, or school accountability systems.

The reauthorization of the Elementary and Secondary Education Act (ESEA) in 1994, known as the Improving America's Schools Act (IASA), and its reauthorization in 2001, known as the No Child Left Behind Act (NCLB), changed the educational system. The new policies established under NCLB require that content standards, assessments, and accountability be the same for all students, including ELLs. In short, not only must ELLs be taught to speak English, they also must be prepared academically to meet standards in the content areas of English language arts, mathematics, and science. For accountability purposes, these students must take the same state assessments as other students to demonstrate mastery of the content. As a subgroup, ELLs also must meet the adequate yearly progress (AYP) targets set for all students.

This book provides a new perspective on the concept of academic language first put forward by Jim Cummins in the late 1970s.

AEL is defined by Bailey as "a precise and predictable way of using language that places demands on the user not typically encountered in everyday settings." The academic English language framework developed by Bailey and Frances Butler is used to examine language proficiency in three language-use domains: language proficiency tests, content assessments, and instruction.

The chapters in the volume draw attention to three important assessment issues: (1) the need for more refined language proficiency measures to identify ELLs and track their progress in achieving English language proficiency; (2) the need for English language proficiency measures that can be used as tools to predict when students are ready to take content assessments with or without test accommodations; and (3) the need for the refinement or development of content assessments that take into account ELLs' reduced levels of English language proficiency while in the process of learning English as a second language.

Instructional practices also are examined. The volume documents approaches that take academic language into account and highlights the necessity for all teachers, not just teachers who teach English as a second language, to be knowledgeable and explicit in teaching academic language. In the chapters addressing instructional practices, the authors emphasize the need for professional development of teachers and instructional leaders who can take into account the academic and linguistic needs of ELLs in a variety of contexts.

Considering the growing number of ELLs in U.S. schools, nearly every educator is or will soon be confronted with the need to create meaningful instructional contexts in which ELLs are challenged to meet and exceed state content standards. This book serves as a rich resource for all educational leaders. Overall, the volume provides an understanding of the most up-to-date insights related to academic language and its application to testing and instruction. Perhaps most valuable is the fact that the book combines the perspectives of researchers, policy makers, and educational practitioners. While the volume does not provide a final resolution to the important questions related to the assessment and instruction of ELLs, it raises the questions that need to be asked and supplies perspectives for addressing these critical issues.

It is true that the policies of NCLB are challenging to all educators. However, the appropriate implementation of these policies has the potential to level the playing field for ELLs by ensuring that instruction and assessments are of the highest standard. Understanding the nuances and challenges of academic language helps to ensure that educational leaders provide appropriate professional development and implement instructional and assessment practices that support the academic achievement of ELLs.

The ultimate message of the book is that it is necessary to acknowledge the role of academic language proficiency in academic tests and instruction. Using an AEL framework as a tool to refine assessment and instructional practices has the potential to open and expand the doors of academic achievement for ELLs.

Charlene Rivera
Research Professor
The George Washington University

# *Preface*

This book describes both theoretical and empirical bases for forming the definition of academic English language (AEL). This task is undertaken as a fundamental step in developing improved language assessments, instructional materials, and professional development in the area of English language learner (ELL) pedagogy. The book is intended to fill a gap in the current literature by addressing what kind or kinds of English we require of K-12 ELL students from an evidence-based perspective, with a particular emphasis on assessment issues. This goal is timely given the broader context of the No Child Left Behind Act of 2001 (NCLB). Under this act, ELL students must show measurable progress each year in English language development (ELD). Consequently, states are urgently identifying or developing tests of English language proficiency that can help them meet this federal mandate. One of the problems that has surfaced in the search for English language tests for K-12 ELL students is the inadequacy of existing research on the development of the academic English language skills that *all* students—both ELL and native English speaking—must have to be successful in the school setting.

The eight chapters comprise research by me and my colleagues at the National Center for Research on Evaluation, Standards, and Student Testing (CRESST) at UCLA and contributions from the perspectives of policy makers (e.g., how national and local government is interpreting academic English for accountability purposes), test developers (e.g., how language assessment professionals in the publishing arena are operationalizing academic English), and practitioners (e.g., how classroom teachers understand the construct academic English and how the results of formative language assessment can inform their practice). This approach was successfully adopted for a symposium entitled "Academic English Language Proficiency Expectations for English Language Learners: Perspectives from State Administration, Language Development Research, and Language Testing" at the 2003 American Educational Research Association Annual Meeting in Chicago. The CRESST research documenting the academic English language demands placed on school-age learners of English played a central role in the symposium. A policy maker, a teacher, a language development researcher, and a testing specialist responded with presentations providing interpretations of the academic English language construct from their unique perspectives.

The volume is a comprehensive collection of readings for graduate seminars and teacher training and could serve as a reference for researchers, test developers, policy makers, and teachers. Teachers of English to Speakers of Other Languages (TESOL), English as a second language (ESL), and English as a foreign language (EFL) researchers and practitioners will also find the volume of interest.

## Overview

In chapter 1, I provide introductory remarks and the background contexts relevant to research of academic English. The chapter addresses the important U.S. national need for determining the validity of large-scale content assessments in English with students who are in the process of acquiring English as a second language. Often these students have been excluded from such assessments, but there have been recent growing efforts to include them; indeed, ELL students must now be included in large-scale content assessments under the NCLB Act. Language accommodation strategies have been widely used but are coming under increasing scrutiny by language researchers and testing experts for reasons we elaborate on. I examine one alternative to language accommodations for ELL students—the explicit teaching and assessment of AEL. Each subsequent chapter focuses on a different aspect of the research and policy problem around conceptualizing and assessing AEL. Chapters 2 and 3 are ordered to follow the chronology by which the need for new assessments of academic English came about: first the research of the late 1990s that identified the mismatch between current assessment and school language demands, then the federal policy requiring that states be held accountable for annual growth in English proficiency. Specifically, chapter 2, by Frances Butler, Robin Stevens, and Martha Castellon, describes two large-scale studies of student performance on concurrent content-area assessments and language assessments to determine the relationship between academic achievement and language proficiency. The two studies focus attention on the need to broaden the content of language proficiency tests to include academic English. Chapter 3 is written by Jan Mayer, director of learning and curriculum at the California Department of Education and former Title III director for the state. She exemplifies the perspective of those who must implement state and federal policy for English language learners. The chapter provides an overview of the key accountability provisions for English learners in Titles I and III of the NCLB Act, describes California's approach to phasing in the new accountability system, and identifies areas of research that would benefit discussions surrounding policy development and implementation.

In chapter 4, Frances Butler and I provide a framework for operationalizing the AEL construct for educational applications. While the primary focus of this framework is assessment, information on the AEL construct that is derived from this work can and should be seen as applicable to both instructional practices and teacher professional development. In chapter 5, Frances Butler, Robin Stevens, Carol Lord, and I describe the results of our work on classroom discourse and textbook analyses, detailing the language demands placed on students in the upper elementary grades in mainstream classrooms. Chapter 6, written by test development specialists Fred Davidson, Jung Tae Kim, Hyeong-Jong Lee, Jinshu Li, and Alexis López, outlines a set of principles for "auditing" the test development process to help ensure the creation of fair and valid measures. Although the authors illustrate with examples from the development of a new AEL assessment, the WIDA, the principles they elaborate can be applied to other test development situations. However, the guidance the chapter offers is especially pertinent for K-12 language testers in this current climate of intense language test development resulting from the NCLB Act. Chapter 7 is written by Margaret Heritage, a professional development specialist and former school principal; Norma Silva, a school principal; and Mary Pierce, an elementary teacher and assistant principal. Together they provide a view of the academic language construct as it impacts classroom-based assessment. They propose a model of instruction and assessment that requires all teachers, regardless of discipline, to have knowledge of academic language as they formulate judgments of their students' learning. In the eighth and final chapter, I identify specific strands for future research, including the need to document student trajectories of AEL development, the relationship between social language and academic language, and the distinction between discipline-specific academic language and general academic language that may cut across content areas.

It is the hope of all the contributors and myself that our efforts will inspire further empirical research to characterize AEL, and that the conceptual framework will be extended by others to guide the research and development of AEL instructional materials. The catholic approach taken by Heritage, Silva, and Pierce in chapter 7 has, I believe, already begun the crucial extension of the AEL construct into teacher professional development.

# *Acknowledgments*

I gratefully acknowledge the assistance of numerous graduate student researchers who have worked for the Academic English Language Proficiency (AELP) project at the National Center for Research on Evaluation, Standards, and Student Testing (CRESST). Over the years these have included Priya Abeywickrama, Frank Herrera, Becky Huang, Charmien LaFramenta, Christine Ong, and, in the very early stages of this work, Rebeca Fernandez, Mary Dingle, and Ani Moughamian. Thanks also go to Ani for assistance in the preparation of the index. At different times Robin Stevens and Martha Castellon were key project staff, and Carol Lord was a principal consultant for the project. Other current and former CRESST colleagues have also provided analytical assistance or other forms of valuable feedback, including Joan Herman, Seth Leon, Judy Miyoshi, Eva Baker, Christy Kim Boscardin, Zenaida Aguirre-Munoz, Malka Borrego, Morgan Joeck, and Jamal Abedi.

I also acknowledge the continuing support of the AELP project at CRESST by Eva Baker and Joan Herman and the CRESST National Advisory Board. Funding for research reported in chapters 2, 4, and 5 was provided to CRESST by the U.S. Department of Education, Institute of Education Sciences (and the former Office of Educational Research and Improvement) under award #R305B960002. The findings and opinions expressed do not neccessarily reflect the positions or policies of the National Institute on Student Achievement, Curriculum, and Assessment, the Institute of Education Sciences, or the U.S. Department of Education.

Colleagues at UCLA and further afield reviewed much of the work reported here when it was in its infancy, most notably Anne Katz, whom I thank for her careful reading of an early version of this manuscript. Others who provided feedback to the AELP project over the years include Marguerite Ann Snow, Jean Turner, Kathleen Bailey, Richard Durán, Bill Sandoval, Robert Linquanti, Catherine Snow, Melinda Erickson, Noel Enyedy, Margo Gottlieb, Penny McKay, Lilly Wong Fillmore, Maria Seidner, and Mary McGroarty. I want to formally thank them for their input. I wish also to mention a number of colleagues, primarily practitioners in the field of ELL assessment, who have given me tremendous opportunities to think deeply about the intersection of research and practice in this domain. These include Mark Fetler and staff in the California Department of Education; Kent Hinton and staff at the San Joaquim Country Office of Education; Jim Stack at San Francisco Unified School District; the teachers and students in four Southern Californian school districts whose cooperation was invaluable for one of the studies reported in chapter 5; Gary Buck of Lidget Green and the staff of the Minnesota Department of Education; staff of the Mountain West Assessment Consortium; Charlene Rivera and staff of the Region III (Mid-Atlantic States) Comprehensive Center at George Washington University; staff of the Office of English Language Acquisition at the U.S. Department of Education; and Roberta Stathis, Sari Luoma, and staff at Ballard and Tighe Publishers, who truly allowed me to "put academic language to the test" with the new IDEA Proficiency Test (IPT) assessment for pre-K/K ELL students.

Family and friends stayed the course with me. At times my parents became my special assistants (the *Prof's PAs*) and always believed I could do this. Friends who need naming for a myriad of reasons they are all, I hope, well aware of are Jennifer McCormick, Jennifer Obidah, Pablo Stansbery, Joelle Greene, Stan Rubin, Allyssa McCabe, Emily Hayden, Denise Quigley, and last but by no means ever to become least, Frank and Nicky Ziolkowski, who came along in time to inspire me to finish.

At Yale University Press, I thank Mary Jane Peluso, Brie Kluytenaar, Robin DuBlanc, and Ann-Marie Imbornoni for bringing this work to fruition and the reviewers Anne Katz and B. Kumaravadivelu. I am of course deeply grateful to the contributors of the chapters: Robin Stevens, Martha Castellon, Jan Mayer, Carol Lord, Fred Davidson (who suggested the project to Mary Jane), Jung Tae Kim, Hyeong-Jong Lee, Jinshu Li, Alexis López, Margaret Heritage, Norma Silva, and Mary Pierce. Their efforts have translated academic language research into meaningful daily practices for educators and their students.

Finally, there is one name that is up to now conspicuously absent from this list. I wish to extend a particularly heartfelt thank you for all the camaraderie and collaboration provided to me by my dear colleague and friend Frances Butler. She has taught me everything I know about the field of language testing. With this book, I hope to share with a new generation of language researchers and educators the baton she passes to us.

# *Abbreviations*

AEL  academic English language
AELP Academic English Language Proficiency
AERA  American Educational Research Association
ALADIN  Academic Language Assessment and Development of Individual Needs
ALEC  Academic Language Exposure Checklist
AMAO  Annual Measurable Achievement Objective
ANOVA  analysis of variance
APA  American Psychological Association
AYP  adequate yearly progress
BICS  basic interpersonal communication skills
CAHSEE  California High School Exit Examination
CAL  Center for Applied Linguistics
CALLA  Cognitive Academic Language Learning Approach
CALP  cognitive academic language proficiency
CAPA  California Alternate Performance Assessment
CELDT  California English Language Development Test
CHILDES  Child Language Data Exchange System
CI  confidence interval
CLAN  Computer Language Analysis
CRESST  National Center for Research on Evaluation, Standards, and Student Testing
CST  California Standards Test
EFL  English as a foreign language
EL  English learner
ELA  English language arts
ELD  English language development
ELDA  English Language Development Assessment

ELL  English language learner
ELP  English language proficiency
EO  English-only
ESEA  Elementary and Secondary Education Act
ESL  English as a second language
FEP  fluent English proficient
HLM  Hierarchical Linear Modeling
IASA  Improving America's School Act
IFEP  initial fluent English proficient
IMAGE  Illinois Measure of Annual Growth in English
IRE/F  initiate-respond-evaluate/feedback
IPT  IDEA Proficiency Test
ITBS  Iowa Test of Basic Skills
ITELL  Iowa Tests of English Language Learning
LAS  Language Assessment Scales
LEA  local educational agency
LEP  limited English proficient
NCE  normal curve equivalent
NCELA  National Clearinghouse for English Language Acquisition
NCLB  No Child left Behind Act of 2001
NCME  National Council on Measurement in Education
NLLIA  National Languages and Literacy Institute of Australia
NRC  National Research Council
NYSESLAT  New York State English as a Second Language Achieve-
    ment Test
OELA  Office of English Language Acquisition
OTL  opportunity to learn
RE  reverse engineering
RFEP  redesignated (or reclassified) fluent English proficient
SDAIE  Specially Designed Academic Instruction in English
SIOP  Sheltered Instruction Observation Protocol
SLA  second language acquisition
TEAE  Test of Emerging Academic English
TEALS  Test of Emerging Academic Listening and Speaking
TESOL  Teachers of English to Speakers of Other Languages
WIDA  Wisconsin, Delaware, and Arkansas (Assessment Consortium)
ZPD  zone of proximal development

# CHAPTER 1

# Introduction: Teaching and Assessing Students Learning English in School

ALISON L. BAILEY

The subtitle of this book, "Putting Academic English to the Test," is intentionally ambiguous. Each of the two possible meanings serves an important purpose. In the idiomatic use of the phrase *to put to the test,* the subtitle invites a challenge to the authors of many of the chapters: Can the research on academic language be put to service in educationally meaningful ways? What does the operationalization of the academic language concept afford us in terms of fairer and better assessment? Will documenting the hallmarks of academic language lead to greater effectiveness in curriculum and teacher professional development? Answering these questions in any great depth would take far more space than can be allotted in this one volume. Rather, the goal of this book is to illustrate what has been achieved so far and to provide frameworks that our research at the National Center for the Study of Evaluation, Standards, and Student Testing (CRESST) has produced so that others might yet yield what still needs to be achieved.

In its second meaning, *putting academic English to the test* is read literally—adding the construct "academic English language" (AEL) to assessments of English language development (ELD). This meaning captures the major focus of the book on the current state of language assessment for students learning English in schools in the United States. A review of the available ELD assessments in the spring of 2005 as I write this introduction suggests that much is in flux.

Currently, assessments of English language development aimed at the 5–18-year-old population in the United States fall into three main categories: assessments that have been available for the past 15 to 20 years that appear to tap into the language of social settings, new assessments that have partially integrated the academic language construct into their operational definitions, and assessments under development that have embraced the notion of academic language across all four language modalities—listening, speaking, reading, and writing.

Assessment of English language learners (ELLs) in kindergarten through high school is a requirement of the No Child Left Behind Act (NCLB, 2001). This federal law mandated the yearly assessment of English language skills for ELL students beginning in the 2002–3 school year. Many states are still in the process of responding to this mandate. Many are still administering the older generation of assessments that focus on social or general uses of language rather than language aligned with the discourse of the classroom, textbooks, educational standards, and content-area assessments. Those that are in the process of developing or refining new ELD assessments are daily seeking guidance from language researchers and test developers. The chapters in this book have pulled together much of what my colleagues and I have researched and proposed to a variety of states and the assessment consortia who represent them.

In this initial chapter, I will first provide greater detail about the political and educational contexts that have led to the current activity in language assessment and in assessment and instructional practices more broadly for language minority students in the United States. I will then briefly highlight some of the new assessment development efforts across the states and the implications these efforts will have for instruction and teacher professional development. I hope that the articulation of these implications will make self-evident the need for the detailed review of what we currently think academic English language to be. This review reveals large and educationally critical gaps in our knowledge of what students need to know about language in academic settings and how we think they acquire it.

## The Language Mandate

There are major research and policy problems facing the United States and other English-speaking countries with large populations of primary and secondary school students learning English in academic contexts for academic purposes. The problems can be most succinctly articulated as a lack of comprehensive information about what language demands are placed on school-age children in general and how much English language learners can realistically be expected to learn and how quickly. While we have a large literature base about English as a second language (ESL), this research base cannot answer these questions with sufficient specificity to aid policy makers and educators faced with the creation of English language development tests and curricula.

The number of students in U.S. public schools for whom English is a second language has grown steadily during the past two decades. The latest figures show ELL student enrollment at 5.1 million (U.S. Department of Education, 2005). During this period of growth, educators have struggled to implement approaches that help to ensure both quality instruction and valid and reliable assessments of all students. Unfortunately, English language learners often enter school without the requisite English language skills to benefit from the mainstream curriculum, and thus in the past they were often excluded from accountability systems. Now, however, with the No Child Left Behind Act (2001), focus on adequate yearly progress in math, reading, and shortly (2005-6 school year) science for all students (Title I) and special emphasis on ensuring that ELLs make steady progress in acquiring English (Title III) virtually guarantees the inclusion of ELLs in state accountability systems. Under this law, ELL students must show measurable progress each year in the listening, speaking, reading, writing, and comprehension of English (many states are interpreting the fifth element as a combination of the listening comprehension and reading comprehension assessment subsections). Consequently, as already mentioned, states are urgently identifying or developing tests of English language proficiency that can help them meet this federal mandate (Olson, 2002).

Previous research in the area of rate and attainment of ELD has suggested that ELL students can take between four to eight years to achieve the English language proficiency necessary for success on academic content assessments (e.g., Collier, 1995; Cummins, 1981; Hakuta, Butler, and Witt, 2000). Students who start their U.S. schooling in upper elementary grades make more rapid progress than those who start at 12 years and older, often despite the same number of years of exposure to English and years in U.S. schooling (Collier, 1987). Differences in achievement by discipline have also been found, with quicker and greater mathematics attainment (while English language is still developing) than science, social studies (Collier, 1989), or language arts attainment (Butler, Stevens, and Castellon, chapter 2; De Avila, 1997). Relatedly, research on the poorer academic achievement of students who are recent redesignated fluent English proficient (RFEP) students (compared to other students in mainstream classrooms) suggests their difficulties may be due in part to the demands of English in nonsheltered content classes and on standardized content assessments (e.g., Stack, 2002).

While this research base provides estimates of student gains and expectations for ELD performance and its impact on academic achievement, it has limitations for answering questions about the nature of AEL development. These limitations include (1) the appropriateness of existing instruments for measuring forms and uses of school language, as already mentioned above; and (2) the use of primarily cross-sectional design that does not provide longitudinal data on individual student growth and exposure to the language of school. Collectively, these pose a serious challenge to accurate and useful prediction of language and academic outcomes.

Including ELLs in accountability systems is not without challenges. For example, the language demands of content-area assessments may be so great for ELL students as to invalidate the determination of their content knowledge. Ultimately, we often have no way of knowing if the performance of ELL students primarily reflects their language abilities or their content knowledge. Thus, including ELLs in the testing process, knowing that the interpretation of test scores may be invalid, is problematic (August and Hakuta, 1997). However, to exclude ELL students is also unacceptable. If ELL students are not tested, information on their achievement is, in effect, absent from any decision making that impacts their school careers.

## Educate or Accommodate?

One widely used means of achieving the goal of inclusion for all students in academic achievement assessment is the use of test accommodations with students who have not yet mastered English (e.g., Butler and Stevens, 1997; Kopriva, 2000; LaCelle-Peterson and Rivera, 1994; Rivera, Stansfield, Scialdone, and Sharkey, 2000). Test accommodations can consist of modifications made to the test itself or modifications made to the test administration procedures, including the test setting. For example, in terms of modifications to the test, students may receive a mathematics test translated into their native language or rendered into simplified English. Accommodations made to the administration of the test include providing students with extra time to complete a test or allowing students the use of English-native language dictionaries.

Studies that have investigated the effects of language accommodations on both ELL and EO students' academic performance (e.g., Abedi, Courtney, and Leon, 2001; Abedi, Lord, Hofstetter, and Baker, 2000; Abedi, Lord, and Plummer, 1997; Castellon-Wellington, 1999; Rivera and Stansfield, 2001) leave us with mixed results as to the fairer assessment of ELL and EO students (extra time, for example, benefits all students). On the one hand, ELL student language abilities, particularly low levels of reading ability, may be a source of construct-irrelevant variance in assessments of academic achievement, such as in mathematics. That is, the mathematics learning that we hope to capture in the assessment may not be reflected; rather, we are measuring the students' inability to read the test questions. On the other hand, if, as Haladyna and Downing (2004) point out, we need to know if students can handle the complexity of language necessary to learn and convey their learning of mathematical concepts, then assessments should include the language demands typical of the instructional contexts students will encounter. Arguably, no less an assessment will allow us to know if students are ready to cope with the language of mainstream mathematics classes.

The complexities of assessing the academic achievement of ELL students are thus many. We argue that there is still much research needed to determine the effectiveness of using accommodations and even then, as others have stated before us, we need to establish clearer procedures for making accommodation decisions in an informed and systematic way (e.g., August and Hakuta, 1997; Bailey and Butler, chapter 4; Haladyna and Downing, 2004). While accommodation studies all share the same objective—to inform educational policy makers about the equitable inclusion of both ELL students and English proficient students on content-area assessments—we have suggested a change of approach that will require future inclusion efforts to begin first by ensuring equitable exposure to and learning of AEL and second by devising academic English language proficiency assessments to help gauge student readiness for mainstream instruction and content-area testing (Bailey and Butler, 2004; Bailey and Butler, chapter 4).

## New Assessments of ELD

A major issue, then, at this critical policy decision-making juncture, is how to determine if the requisite English language skills for demonstrating content knowledge on assessments have been acquired by ELL students. Many existing English language proficiency tests do not assess the type of language students must understand and be able to use in the mainstream classroom and on standardized content tests. Existing language tests tend to assess social everyday language rather than the more formal academic English language of the classroom and content tests. Unfortunately for current educational testing needs, basic social language has been found to be only minimally correlated with the more demanding language of school (e.g., Collier and Thomas, 1989).

This is not to minimize the importance of social language skills for successful school and personal outcomes. Indeed, the level of linguistic sophistication necessary to navigate everyday informal situations suggests that we also need to foster student growth in the area of social language development (Bailey, in press). However, currently a student may perform well on a general language test and still not have the necessary language skills for academic tasks (see Butler et al., chapter 2 for a discussion of just such findings with eleventh-grade students). There is, then, an important assessment gap between the type of English an ELL student may know and be able to use—that tested on many current ELD tests—and the language critical to school success.

As mentioned, assessments of ELD fall into three main categories: older assessments that appear to primarily measure social language uses, new assessments that have partially integrated the academic language construct into operational definitions of ELD, and assessments still under development that have adopted the AEL construct as critical to the measurement of scholastic uses of English. For example, the Language Assessment Scales (De Avila and Duncan, 1987, 1988, 1989, 1990; Duncan and De Avila, 1990), are widely used older ELD assessments that are found to have fewer language features matching the language demands of content-area assessments (Butler et al., chapter 2; Stevens, Butler, and Castellon-Wellington, 2000) than derived versions of the LAS such as the current California English Language Development Test (CELDT, CTB/McGrawHill, 2004). The CELDT shows the influence of the California ELD standards (California State Board of Education, 1999) and includes characteristics of classroom language on the test blueprint in all four language modalities (listening, speaking, reading, and writing) (see Bailey and Butler, 2005; Sato, Lagunoff, Worth, Bailey, and Butler, 2005).

Other states are following similar initiatives and have new assessments at different stages of development incorporating varying degrees of the AEL construct.[1] For example, Wisconsin, Delaware, and Arkansas have worked together to produce the WIDA (WIDA Consortium, 2005; see also Davidson, Kim, Lee, Li, and López, chapter 6), which has developed new English language proficiency standards. These will be adopted by Teachers of English to Speakers of Other Languages (TESOL) to replace their original K-12 ELD standards (TESOL, 1997), which had served as the national ELD standards and as the foundation of many state ELD standards and test blueprints.

The English Language Development Assessment (ELDA) is the effort of member states of the Council of Chief State School Officers (CCSSO, 2005). The ELDA will include "topics" from the content areas, such as social studies and science, presumably as part of an AEL construct. Presumably the ELDA item writers will use these topics to create school-related scenarios or to provide specifications for vocabulary to be used in test items rather than to measure content-area knowledge itself.

Both the WIDA and ELDA will include all language modalities. Interestingly, one new ELD assessment responding to the NCLB Act mandate does not include all modalities within its AEL construct. The Stanford English Language Proficiency Test (Harcourt Educational Measurement, 2003), while based on the Bailey and Butler conceptual framework for AEL presented in chapter 4, has articulated speaking skills as social uses of language only and not as part of the AEL construct.

The new IPT/PEM (IDEA Proficiency Test/Pearson Educational Measurement) Title III Testing Solution (Ballard and Tighe, 2005) has also adopted the AEL construct framework as the basis for this replacement of the former, more social language-oriented IPT assessments, adding to the empirical database through analysis of videos of classroom teachers talking and various state-level ELD and content-standards documents following Bailey and Butler (2002/3; see also chapter 4) (Bailey and Luoma, 2003; Luoma, Cho, and Buck,

2004). This new suite of IPT assessments also includes K-2 reading and writing forms as well as a pre-K/K language and early literacy assessment (Bailey, Luoma, and Cho, 2005), whereas a number of the new ELD assessments being developed do not include assessment of literacy skills earlier than the second- or third-grade levels. There is some debate in the field as to what constitutes a reading and writing test with ELL students when English-only (EO) and fluent English proficient (FEP) students have also yet to learn to read and write. This, together with a concern that young children are excessively assessed, has led some states (e.g., California) to eschew the assessment of literacy skills in young ELL students (see Mayer, chapter 3 for further discussion). However, for a successful school experience, four- to five-year-old ELL students will no doubt need to participate in all aspects of their preschool or kindergarten curriculum, engaging with both teachers and peers to acquire and demonstrate knowledge of both social skills *and* nascent academic demands. Indeed, goal 1 of the National Educational Goals Panel (NEGP, n.d.) focuses on having all children start school "ready to learn." This goal specifically includes language development in its five dimensions of early development and learning.

If test developers take young children's social and cognitive developmental needs into account, then assessing both their oral and early literacy abilities can be possible. For example, using manipulatives (objects, not pictures) to engage the young ELL student during assessment allows children this age to do better on both production and comprehension tasks (e.g., Cocking and McHale, 1981), and providing verbal and gestural supports or scaffolding allows a young child to demonstrate to the assessor at what level of assistance he or she can and cannot complete a task. The latter, of course, is also information to the assessor as to what kind of instructional supports a very young ELL student may require in a preschool program.

Differences in the operationalization of language constructs found in the ELD tests outlined above may impact how students are instructed in ELD and how teachers themselves understand the construct of AEL. So what exactly is the AEL construct that these and other test developers now purport to tap with the new assessments? The next section of this chapter attempts to shed some light on this question by reviewing studies of English language acquisition and showing how these have informed our research on academic language at CRESST.

## What English Language Demands Do We Place on K-12 Students?

As an entry point to understanding the AEL construct, we have found the following definition by Chamot and O'Malley (1994) to be both widely accessible and inspiring in its simplicity. Academic language is "the language that is used by teachers and students for the purpose of acquiring new knowledge and skills . . . imparting new information, describing abstract ideas, and developing students' conceptual understanding" (p. 40).

Cummins (1980, 2000) first made the crucial distinction between what is known as basic interpersonal communication skills (BICS), acquired and used in everyday interactions, and cognitive academic language proficiency (CALP), acquired and used in the academic context. BICS, or social, everyday language, most often occurs in the "here and now" of a shared conversation, allowing for use of less demanding indexical modes of communication, such as gestures and pronominalization (Schleppegrell, 2001, 2004). It is on the construct CALP that Chamot and O'Malley (1994; Chamot, 2005) based their definition of AEL and their curriculum for teaching it—the Cognitive Academic Language Learning Approach (CALLA).

As I have stressed elsewhere (Bailey, in press), we should guard against believing that there is something inherent in social language that makes it less sophisticated or less cognitively demanding than language used in an academic context. Think about the complex and highly sophisticated social applications of language that are needed to woo or deceive a loved one; and conversely, there are contexts in which AEL can be as simple as responding with a head nod to a yes or no question. Thus it is perhaps most accurate to speak of the difference between BICS and CALP as differences in the relative frequency of complex grammatical structures, specialized vocabulary, and uncommon language functions.

In some regard, it is not meaningful to conceive of *language* as either social or academic, rather it is the *situation* that is either predominantly social or academic. Even this distinction is problematic. Dewey's pedagogic creed (1897) serves as a good reminder that schools are simply one more social context or "community" and that language is always "a social instrument." Sociolinguistic studies of the language production of school-age children in both formal and informal settings (e.g., Gumperz and Cook-Gumperz, 1980; Hymes,

1974; Labov, 1972) have documented the social context of scholastic settings whereby becoming a member of a discourse community, such as that of mathematicians, is signaled by the use of certain discourse and linguistic features most commonly found in settings where "mathematics" is spoken (Pimm, 1987). Elsewhere, Johns (1997) identifies a register of English used in professional books and characterized by the specific linguistic features associated with the different academic disciplines.

While current cognitive theory has also increasingly argued that cognition and discourse are often specific to a discipline or context (e.g., Lave and Wenger, 1991), in our own work and in the literature we have found some remarkable similarities across the disciplinary discourses for teaching mathematics, science, and social studies. For example, current reform in each of these disciplines calls for students to engage in academic arguments and debates that may share the same underlying organizational structures (e.g., Bazerman, 2003). This has led us to hypothesize discipline-specific AEL as well as a common core or general AEL that cuts across disciplines (see Bailey and Butler, chapter 4 for further discussion).

We can add two additional features to Chamot and O'Malley's (1994) definition of academic language cited above. First, language as it is used in academic contexts requires students to demonstrate their knowledge by using recognizable verbal and written academic formats. For example, students must learn norms for presenting information to the teacher so that the teacher can successfully monitor their learning. The opportunity to display knowledge may also be as important as the opportunity to learn (OTL) new information, as it not only confirms acquisition for a teacher but may consolidate learning for a student (Cazden, 2001). Second, students receive fewer opportunities to negotiate meaning or to use contextual cues in the classroom setting than in many social settings. This is the decontextualized use of language that has been recognized as a key discourse-level feature of language used in school (e.g., Cazden, 2001; Menyuk, 1995; Snow, 1991).

Bailey (in press) has summarized the ability to be *academically* proficient in either a first or second language as knowing and being able to "use general and content-specific vocabulary, specialized or complex grammatical structures, and multifarious language functions and discourse structures—all for the purpose of acquiring new knowledge and skills, interacting about a topic, or imparting information to others." Short (1994) and Lemke (1990), in particular, have documented the range of language functions found in social studies classes and science classes respectively. Most commonly language is used in service of *explanation* and *description,* and, in the case of social studies, *justification.* These findings are largely replicated in the analyses of language use in science classrooms and social studies and science textbooks reported by Bailey, Butler, Stevens, and Lord in chapter 5.

Students must be able to integrate all aspects of language that they hear and use in school and do so across all language modalities. That is, teachers often set tasks and activities that rely on students being able to process information in both the oral (speaking and listening modalities) and the print (reading and writing modalities) domains. It is the integration of the modalities themselves that Gibbons (1998) has termed *intertextual.* This use of language requires students to shift the same information back and forth across the modalities, perhaps first reading about a new science topic, then participating as both speaker and attentive audience member in a whole-group discussion, ultimately individually authoring an essay on the new information they have acquired. Oral language skills, however, are not only critical for signaling classroom participation, they also serve as a foundation upon which reading and writing skills are based, both in the initial acquisition of print skills (e.g., Allen, 1976; Dickinson, McCabe, Anastasopoulos, Peisner-Feinberg, and Poe, 2003; Stauffer, 1980) and in the ongoing process of reading and writing about new ideas and knowledge.

While there is much research on the second language acquisition process and differential outcomes for learners (see Larsen-Freeman, 2000 for review), this work has focused primarily on the development of language as a broad construct, only recently articulating the notion of English for specific purposes—for example, as the medium for acquiring discipline-specific knowledge (e.g., Douglas, 2000). However, this research has been conducted almost exclusively at the higher education level with already-educated adult ESL learners. In contrast, researchers appear to have largely ignored the K-12 arena, finding it difficult to articulate norms for even first language development in school-age children. The potential for and causes of individual variation in first and second language development are great. Students are exposed to a wide variety of different language settings, not least by their own choice of content classes once they enter the higher grades (Nippold, 1995).

Collectively, the research cited here has documented the existence of an AEL phenomenon. However, there have been few attempts to operationalize the concept sufficiently for utilization in assessment, curriculum, or professional development. To achieve further specificity, therefore, academic language is defined in our work as language that stands in contrast to the everyday informal speech that students use outside the classroom environment. AEL can be distinguished from English in other settings on at least three key levels: the lexical, grammatical, and discourse levels, each described below.

## Lexical Features of AEL

At the lexical level, following Scarcella and Zimmerman (1998), we suggest that academic vocabulary, as one component of the broader academic language construct, comprises both a general academic lexicon (e.g., containing words such as *evidence, demonstrate,* and *represent*) and specialized ones (e.g., containing content-related words such as *diameter, condense,* and *abolitionist*), each of which students must acquire in order to become fully proficient in English in the academic setting.[2] According to Nation (2001), at the tertiary education level, general academic vocabulary covers on average 8.5% of words in academic texts, and specialized or technical vocabulary covers about 5% of words in academic texts (see also Nation and Coxhead, 2001).

Beck et al. (2002), Cunningham and Moore (1993), and Stevens, Butler, and Castellon-Wellington (2000) add a third category of vocabulary to this mix—high-frequency general words used regularly in everyday contexts that contrast with the often more morphologically complex vocabulary of school, though they may have equivalent meanings in some cases (e.g., *gather* vs. *collate*) (Corson, 1997). Conversely, a single word can have multiple meanings, which helps in efficiently expanding a child's lexicon, adding one new word form but many different meanings. The English language, it is argued, is comprised of more than 60%-70% of such polysemous words (e.g., McLaughlin, August, and Snow, 2000). ELL students especially may have constrained English vocabularies in that they may know just one or two of the most frequently encountered meanings of an English word (e.g., McLaughlin et al., 2000), and the importance of vocabulary breadth and depth is further underscored by the finding that the vocabulary knowledge of fifth and sixth-grade Latino students can be the most important predictor of performance on a reading assessment (Garcia, 1991).

The primary distinction in the coding schema developed for the study of textbooks reported in Bailey et al. in chapter 5 was between academic and nonacademic usage of words. Within academic usage we further distinguished between specialized academic vocabulary and general academic vocabulary that cuts across disciplines. This distinction is important for future test development efforts that will attempt to target a broad cross-section of academic language and may therefore need to treat specialized vocabulary separately. During the course of coding we considered the sense intended in the selections and rated the form and usage of words only in the context of the given selections. Specifically, we had to be sure that the word sense intended in the textbook selections was referring to an academic concept (e.g., "Determine the centrifugal *force*" versus "Don't *force* him to do it"). This includes the specialized word sense often used in mathematics for some of the most common words in English. Prepositions, for instance, take on very precise and often unfamiliar usage in the mathematics register (e.g., Pimm, 1987, 1995). For example, the preposition *in* used in a phrase like "three in four" makes the relationship between the two numbers proportional, in this case, three-quarters or 75%. Even in the earliest grades use of a simple preposition like *by* can take on the unfamiliar meaning of *according to* in a phrase like *sort by color* (Bailey, in press).

In the analysis reported in chapter 5, if the intended meaning of a word was the same both in and out of the classroom setting, we considered the word usage to be nonacademic. Throughout this process we were careful to avoid equating unfamiliar words with academic vocabulary. While we did not classify the use of seemingly arbitrary proper names (such as *Peter* and *Anne*), most often found in mathematics word problems, as academic vocabulary, proper names related to content learning or crucial to the academic concepts of a topic were rated as specialized (e.g., *Continental Congress*, *Newton*, and *John Adams*). Similarly, measurement vocabulary and abbreviations for measurement and formulas were also rated as a subcategory of specialized academic vocabulary (e.g., *kilometer, km,* and *km/hr*). Colloquialisms and idiomatic expressions (e.g., *half-joked* and *twister*) and verbatim speech formed their own separate sub-categories if used to convey content information.

## Grammatical Features of AEL

Turning to the grammatical or syntactic features of AEL, there are features of English grammar that are often only encountered during formal discourse or in print and for that reason are key components of the articulation of the AEL construct. In mathematics, for example, certain syntactic structures are required for conveying notions of comparative size (*X is greater/less than Y, as X as Y*) and conditional relationships (*if X, then Y*), among others (e.g., Spanos, Rhodes, Dale, and Crandall, 1988). Snow (1990) has argued that a syntactic skill that often cuts across specific content areas—writing formal definitions—requires students to combine the copula *to be*, a superordinate category, and a complement clause (e.g., *A rabbit is an animal with long ears*).

Oral and printed language often differ syntactically and place different demands on users of the language (e.g., Reppen, 2001; Schleppegrell, 2001, 2004). For example, passive voice constructions in English such as "The British were trounced by the colonials" occur less frequently in everyday conversation than in academic writing (Celce-Murcia and Larsen-Freeman, 1983), and children have been found to have more difficulty understanding passive verb forms than active verb forms (Bever, 1970; de Villiers and de Villiers, 1973; Fraser, Bellugi, and Brown, 1963). Eighth-grade students in one study, for example, were given equivalent mathematics test items with and without passive voice constructions and scored higher on the items without passive constructions (Abedi and Lord, 2001; Abedi et al., 1997).

Other syntactic features are also characteristic of written language and may increase the demands of classroom language (Halliday and Martin, 1993).[3] Relative clauses, for example, are less frequent in spoken English than in written English, so some students may have had limited exposure to them before entering school. Furthermore, relative clauses in print differ from those in spoken language (Pauley and Syder, 1983). In general, dependent clauses that embed information may make sentences more complex and difficult than coordinate clauses that do not (Botel and Granowsky,

1974; Hunt, 1965, 1977; Kemper, Jackson, Cheung, and Anagnopoulous, 1993; Lord, 2002; Wang, 1970). Conditional clauses also contribute to text difficulty, and noun phrases with several modifiers can be sources of difficulty, as Spanos et al. (1988) found in student comprehension of math test items.

## Discourse Features of AEL

Turning to classroom discourse, students are required to convey the content knowledge they acquire using organizational features recognizable to teachers (Hicks, 1994). That is, academic success involves a combination of discipline-specific practices (e.g., knowing the conventions for multidigit division) and cross-cutting general academic discourse practices (e.g., knowing how to clearly present and justify an idea in any content area). This requires not only a knowledge of discourse conventions but also pragmatic knowledge that may be applied in both spoken and written contexts. The linguistic registers of the different disciplines and the uses to which language is put in content-area classrooms have also been a focus of increasing study (e.g., Bailey, Butler, LaFramenta and Ong, 2001/4; Johns, 1997; Lemke, 1990; Short, 1993). These studies show not only a wide range of functions language serves in the academic setting (e.g., *explaining, describing, comparing*) but also how the content areas are differentiated by language function (see Bailey et al., chapter 5).

Closely coupled with issues of discourse are the notions of academic language as a sociocultural and psychological phenomenon (e.g., Cazden, 2001; Corson, 1997; Erickson, 1987; Gee, 1996; Gutiérrez, 1995; Kern, 2000; Philips, 1972; Scarcella, 2003). The development of a deep conceptual understanding of discipline-specific concepts is tied to participation in the particularistic discourse practices of disciplinary communities (Greeno and Hall, 1997; Lave and Wenger, 1991; Roth, 2001) such as mathematics (Cobb, Stephan, McClain, and Gravemeijer, 2001; Lampert and Ball, 1998), science (Lehrer, Schauble, Carpenter, and Penner, 2000; Roth and Bowen, 1995), and English language arts (Cazden, 1988, 2001; Gutiérrez, 1994; Lee, 2001; Palinscar and Brown, 1984; Smagorinsky, 2001). Different disciplines have their own accepted norms for what constitutes a good argument during discourse. For example, in mathematics it is demonstration of a logical proof (Lehrer, Randle, and Sancilio, 1989; Kazami, 1999), in science it is often modeling to explain a process (White and Frederiksen, 1998), and in English language arts it is the appropriate citation of primary and secondary texts (Lee, 2001). Such norms for each discipline need to be acquired to meet teacher expectations.

Participation frameworks or structures (Erickson, 1992; Goffman, 1981) influence who can say what and to whom, which also affects the nature of discourse in classroom activities. A common participation framework for discourse in the classroom is the initiate-respond-evaluate/feedback (IRE/F) script (Lemke, 1990; Mehan, 1979), which is a framework in which the teacher asks questions that can be answered briefly and quickly by the students. The teacher then simply evaluates the response as correct or incorrect or provides feedback to students regarding the accuracy and completeness of their answers (Mehan, 1979; O'Connor and Michaels, 1996). The social configuration of a classroom is also important to classroom discourse because it too can constrain the types of activities and communication that take place. For example, a study of a seventh-grade mathematics classroom found that after whole-class discussions, forming small-scale problem-solving groups afforded opportunities for peer-to-peer teaching (Enyedy, 2003). This is a common type of informal learning that occurs in classrooms and is largely outside a teacher's control, which may have an eventual impact on the rate and attainment of AEL for some ELL students. Opportunities to learn or missed opportunities to learn, as these cases may be, could impact AEL acquisition along with academic achievement.

## Assessing Academic English Language: The Next Steps

It is critical that we have a greater understanding of the nature of language—its complexity and usage in academic settings—if we are to effectively teach and assess ELL students. The necessary next steps, particularly for the improved assessment of AEL, are documented in the ensuing chapters. The current chapter has reviewed the language and discourse literature to help determine what we know already of AEL and what aspects we must research further. From this review we learn a lot about AEL, but we also learn that it will be necessary to create a more complete picture both across the grade spans and as regards the entire school curriculum. We learn in addition that we must render this and all new information into a usable form for educational applications. Particularly in the case of our main focus, AEL assessment, this will need to be in the form of detailed specifications about the lexical, syntactic, and discourse demands at different grade levels and in different content areas.

The next chapter will document the first empirical studies that went into a *needs analysis* to show the mismatch between the language skills that have traditionally appeared on ELD assessments and the language demands that are truly expected in school. Chapter 3 details the next critical step—government policy to hold states accountable for the development of English language proficiency and to guide state efforts in the creation of assessments better aligned to the language demands of school. The remaining steps described in chapters 4 to 7 involve the development of a conceptual framework within which to conduct empirical research of AEL, devising state-of-the-art test development procedures, and extending the AEL construct into classroom-based assessment practices. Always an iterative process, the final step in this test development process, and the subject of chapter 8, is to ask: What new steps must we then still take?

## Notes

1. This brief review is designed to provide an illustration of the range of test development efforts in the K-12 arena and is not intended to be exhaustive of all the tests that have been recently developed or are currently under development. At the time of writing, other well-known test development initiatives include the New York State English as a Second Language Achievement Test (NYSESLAT, Harcourt Assessment, 2005), commissioned by the New York State Education Department; the Test of Emerging Academic English (TEAE,MetriTech, 2001); and the Test of Emerging Academic Listening and Speaking (TEALS, Lidget Green and Language Learning Solutions, in preparation), developed by the State of Minnesota; the Iowa Tests of English Language Learning (ITELL, University of Iowa, in preparation), developed by the State of Iowa Department of Education and designed in part to correspond to the content areas represented on the Iowa Test of Basic Skills (Riverside Publishing, 2001); and the Illinois Measure of Annual Growth in English (IMAGE, Illinois State Board of Education, Division of Standards and Assessment, 2005). This final test was first created to assess the English reading and writing skills of ELL students until they are sufficiently proficient in English to meaningfully take the Illinois aca-

demic achievement tests. (For further details, see also www.nysed.gov, education.state.mn.us, www.state.ia.us, and www.ccsd15.net.)
2. These are roughly analogous to tier 2 and tier 3 words in the taxonomy devised by Beck, McKown, and Kucan (2002) for instructional purposes.
3. For examples of these syntactic structures, see table 5.2 in Bailey et al., chapter 5.

## References

Abedi, J., Courtney, M., and Leon, S. (2001). *Language accommodations for large-scale assessment in science* (Final Deliverable to OERI, Contract No. R305B960002). Los Angeles: University of California, National Center for Research on Evaluation, Standards, and Student Testing (CRESST).

Abedi, J., and Lord, C. (2001). The language factor in mathematics tests. *Applied Measurement in Education,* 14(3), 219–234.

Abedi, J., Lord, C., Hofstetter, C., and Baker, E. (2000). Impact of accommodation strategies on English language learners' test performance. *Educational Measurement: Issues and Practice, 19*(3), 16–26.

Abedi, J., Lord, C., and Plummer, J. (1997). *Final report of language background as a variable in NAEP mathematics performance* (CSE Tech. Rep. No. 429). Los Angeles: University of California, National Center for Research on Evaluation, Standards, and Student Testing (CRESST).

Allen, R. V. (1976). *Language experience activities.* Boston: Houghton Mifflin.

August, D., and Hakuta, K. (1997). *Improving schooling for language-minority children: A research agenda.* Washington DC: National Academy Press.

Bailey A. L. (in press). From Lambie to Lambaste: The conceptualization, operationalization, and use of academic language in the assessment of ELL students. In K. Rolstad (Ed.), *Rethinking school language.* Mahwah, NJ: LEA.

Bailey, A. L., and Butler, F. A. (2002/3). *An evidentiary framework for operationalizing academic language for broad application to K-12 education: A design document* (CSE Tech. Rep. No. 611). Los Angeles: University of California, National Center for Research on Evaluation, Standards, and Student Testing (CRESST).

Bailey, A. L., and Butler, F. A. (2004). Ethical considerations in the assessment of the language and content knowledge of English language learners, K-12. *Language Assessment Quarterly, 1,* 177–193.

Bailey, A. L., and Butler, F. A. (2005, April). *ELD standards linkage and test alignment under Title III.* Paper presented at the American Educational Research Association Annual Conference, Montreal, Canada.

Bailey, A. L., Butler, F. A., LaFramenta, C., and Ong, C. (2001/4). *Towards the characterization of academic language in upper elementary science classrooms* (CSE Tech. Rep. No. 621). Los Angeles: University of California, National Center for Research on Evaluation, Standards, and Student Testing (CRESST).

Bailey, A. L., and Luoma, S. (2003, July). *Defining the construct "academic language" through empirical research.* Paper presented at the Language Testing Research Conference, Reading, UK.

Bailey, A. L., Luoma, S., and Cho, Y. (2005). *Pre-K-K IDEA proficiency test.* Brea, CA: Ballard and Tighe.

Ballard and Tighe Publishers. (2005). *IPT/PEM (IDEA proficiency test/Pearson Educational measurement) Title III testing solution.* Brea, CA: Author.

Bazerman, C. (2003, May). *What does it mean to think, read, and write analytically?* Berkeley: University of California Literacy Consortium.

Beck, I. L., McKown, M. G., and Kucan, L. (2002). *Bringing words to life: Robust vocabulary instruction.* New York: Guilford.

Bever, T. (1970). The cognitive basis for linguistic structure. In J. R. Hayes (Ed.), *Cognition and the development of language* (pp. 279–353). New York: John Wiley.

Botel, M., and Granowsky, A. (1974). A formula for measuring syntactic complexity: A directional effort. *Elementary English, 1,* 513-516.

Butler, F. A., and Stevens, R. (1997). *Accommodation strategies for English language learners on large-scale assessments: Student characteristics and other considerations* (CSE Tech. Rep. No. 448). Los Angeles: University of California, National Center for Research on Evaluation, Standards, and Student Testing (CRESST).

California State Board of Education. (1999). *English-language development standards for California public schools: Kindergarten through grade twelve.* Sacramento: California Department of Education.

Castellon-Wellington, M. (1999). *The impact of preference for accommodations: The performance of English learners on large-scale academic achievement tests* (CSE Tech Rep. No. 524). Los Angeles: University of California, National Center for Research on Evaluation, Standards, and Student Testing (CRESST).

Cazden, C. B. (1988). Environmental assistance revisited: Variation and functional equivalence. In F. Kessel (Ed.), *The development of language and language researchers: Essays in honor of Roger Brown* (pp. 281–297). Hillsdale, NJ: Lawrence Erlbaum.

Cazden, C. (2001). *Classroom discourse: The language of teaching and learning* (2nd ed.). Portsmouth, NH: Heinemann.

CCSSO (2005). *The English Language Development Assessment.* Retrieved December 1, 2005, from http://www.ccsso.org/projects/SCASS/Projects/Assessing_Limited_English_Proficient_Students/

Celce-Murcia, M., and Larsen-Freeman, D. (1983). *The grammar book: An ESL/EFL teacher's course.* Rowley, MA: Newbury House.

Chamot, A. U. (2005). The Cognitive Academic Language Learning Approach (CALLA): An update. In P. Richard-Amato and M. A. Snow (Eds.), *Academic Success for English Language Learners* (pp. 87–102). White Plains, NY: Longman.

Chamot, A. U., and O'Malley, J. M. (1994). The CALLA handbook: Implementing the cognitive academic language learning approach. Reading, MA: Addison-Wesley.

Cobb, P., Stephan, M., McClain, K., and Gravemeijer, K. (2001). Participating in classroom mathematical practices. *Journal of the Learning Sciences, 10*, 113–163.

Cocking, R. R., and McHale, S. (1981). A comparative study of the use of pictures and objects in assessing children's receptive and productive language. *Journal of Child Language, 8*, 1–13.

Collier, V. (1987). Age and rate of acquisition of second language for academic purposes. *TESOL Quarterly, 21*(4), 617–641.

Collier, V. (1989). How long? A synthesis of research on academic achievement in a second language. *TESOL Quarterly, 23*(3), 509–531.

Collier, V. (1995). *Acquiring a second language for school: Directions in Language and Education,* 1:4. Washington, DC: National Clearinghouse for Bilingual Education.

Collier, V., and Thomas, W. (1989, Fall). How quickly can immigrants become proficient in school English? *Journal of Educational Issues of Language Minority Students*, 5, 26–38.

Corson, D. (1997). The learning and use of academic English words. *Language Learning, 47*(4), 671–718.

CTB/McGraw-Hill. (2004). *California English language development test: Form D.* Monterey, CA: Author.

Cummins, J. (1980). The construct of proficiency in bilingual education. In J. E. Alatis (Ed.), *Georgetown University Round Table on Languages and Linguistics: Current issues in bilingual education, 1980* (pp. 81–103). Washington, DC: Georgetown University.

Cummins, J. (1981). The role of primary language development in promoting educational success for language minority students. In California State Department of Education (Ed)., *Schooling and language minority students: A theoretical framework* (pp. 3-49). Los Angeles: National Dissemination and Assessment Center.

Cummins, J. (2000). *Language, power, and pedagogy: Bilingual children in the crossfire.* Clevedon, UK: Multilingual Matters.

Cunningham, J. W., and Moore, D. W. (1993). The contribution of understanding academic vocabulary to answering comprehension questions. *Journal of Reading Behaviors, 25*, 171–180.

De Avila, E. (1997). Setting expected gains for non and limited English proficient students. *NCBE Resource Collection Series No.8.* Washington, DC: National Clearinghouse for Bilingual Education.

De Avila, E. A., and Duncan, S. E. (1987, 1988, 1989, 1990). *Language assessment scales, oral administration manual, English: Forms 2c and 2d.* Monterey, CA: CTB MacMillan McGraw-Hill.

de Villiers, J., and de Villiers, P. (1973). Development of the use of word order in comprehension. *Journal of Psychological Research, 2,* 331–341.

Dewey, J. (1897). My pedagogic creed. *School Journal, 54,* 77–88.

Dickinson, D. K., McCabe, A., Anastasopoulos, L., Peisner-Feinberg, E. S., and Poe, M. D. (2003). The comprehensive language approach to early literacy: The interrelationships among vocabulary, phonological sensitivity, and print knowledge among preschool-aged children. *Journal of Educational Psychology, 95*(3), 465–481.

Douglas, D. (2000). *Assessing language for specific purposes.* Cambridge: Cambridge University Press.

Duncan, S. E., and De Avila, E. A. (1990). *Language assessment scales (LAS) reading and writing English: Forms 1a and 3a.* Monterey, CA: CTB/McGraw-Hill.

Enyedy, N. (2003). Knowledge construction and collective practice: At the intersection of learning, talk, and social configurations in a computer-mediated mathematics classroom. *Journal of the Learning Sciences, 12*(3), 361–407.

Erickson, F. (1987). Transformation and school success: The politics and culture of educational achievement. *Anthropology and Education Quarterly, 18*(4), 335–356.

Erickson, F. (1992). Ethnographic microanalysis of interaction. In M. D. LeCompte, W. L. Millroy, and J. Preissle (Eds.), *The handbook of qualitative research in education* (pp. 201-225). Burlington, MA: Academic Press.

Fraser, C., Bellugi, U., and Brown, R. (1963). Control of grammar in imitation, comprehension, and production. *Journal of Verbal Learning and Verbal Behavior, 2,* 121–135.

Garcia, G. R. (1991). Factors influencing the English reading test performances of Spanish-speaking Hispanic children. *Reading Research Quarterly, 26,* 371–391.

Gee, J. P. (1996). *Social linguistics and literacies: Ideology in discourse.* London: Falmer Press.

Gibbons, P. (1998). Classroom talk and the learning of new registers in a second language. *Language and Education, 12*(2), 99–118.

Goffman, E. (1981). *Forms of talk.* Philadelphia: University of Pennsylvania Press.

Greeno, J. G., and Hall, R. P. (1997). Practicing representation: Learning with and about representational forms. *Phi Delta Kappan,* 361–367.

Gumperz, J. J., and Cook-Gumperz, J. (1980). *Beyond ethnography: Some uses of sociolinguistics for understanding classroom environments.* Los Angeles: National Dissemination and Assessment Center, California State University, Los Angeles.

Gutiérrez, K. D. (1994). How talk, context, and script shape contexts for learning: A cross-case comparison of journal sharing. *Linguistics and Education, 5,* 335–365.

Gutiérrez, K. (1995). Unpackaging academic discourse. *Discourse Processes, 19*(1), 21–37.

Hakuta, K., Butler, Y., and Witt, D. (2000). *How long does it take English learners to attain proficiency?* Santa Barbara, CA: UC Linguistic Minority Research Institute.

Haladyna, T. M., and Downing, S. M. (2004). Construct-irrelevant variance in high-stakes testing. *Educational Measurement: Issues and Practice, 23,* 17–27.

Halliday, M. A. K., and Martin, J. R. (1993). *Writing science: Literacy and discursive power.* Pittsburgh: University of Pittsburgh Press.

Harcourt Assessment Inc. (2005). *New York State English as a Second Language Achievement Test (NYSESLAT).* San Antonio, TX: Author.

Harcourt Educational Measurement (2003). *Stanford English language proficiency test (Stanford ELP).* San Antonio, TX: Author.

Hicks, D. (1994). Individual and social meanings in the classroom: Narrative discourse as a boundary phenomenon. *Journal of Narrative and Life History, 4*(3), 215–240.

Hunt, K. W. (1965). *Grammatical structures written at three grade levels* (Research Report No. 3). Urbana IL: National Council of Teachers of English.

Hunt, K. W. (1977). Early blooming and late blooming syntactic structures. In C. R. Copper and L. Odell (Eds.), *Evaluating writing: Describing, measuring, judging.* Urbana, IL: National Council of Teachers of English.

Hymes, D. (1974). *Foundations in sociolinguistics: An ethnographic approach.* Philadelphia: University of Pennsylvania Press.

Illinois State Board of Education, Division of Standards and Assessment. (2005). *Illinois measure of annual growth in English (IMAGE).* Springfield, IL: Author.

Johns, A. M. (1997). *Text, role, and context: Developing academic literacies.* Cambridge: Cambridge University Press.

Kazami, E. (1999, Spring). Mathematical discourse that promotes conceptual understanding. *Connections.* Los Angeles: UC Regents.

Kemper, S., Jackson, J. O., Cheung, H., and Anagnopoulous, C. A. (1993). Enhancing older adults' reading comprehension. *Discourse Processes, 16,* 405-428.

Kern, R. (2000). *Literacy and language teaching.* Oxford: Oxford University Press.

Kopriva, R. (2000). *Ensuring accuracy in testing for English language learners.* Washington, DC: Council of Chief State School Officers.

Labov, W. (1972). *Language in the inner city: Studies in the black English vernacular.* Philadelphia: University of Pennsylvania Press.

LaCelle-Peterson, M., and Rivera, C. (1994). Is it real for all kids? A framework for equitable assessment policies for English language learners. *Harvard Educational Review, 64* (1), 55–75.

Lampert, M., and Ball, D. (1998). *Teaching, multimedia, and mathematics: Investigations of real practice.* New York: Teachers College Press.

Larson-Freeman, D. (2000). Second language acquisition and applied linguistics. *Annual Review of Applied Linguistics, 20,* 165–181.

Lave, J., and Wenger, E. (1991). *Situated learning: Legitimate peripheral participation.* Cambridge: Cambridge University Press.

Lee, O. (2001). Culture and language in science education: What do we know and what do we need to know? *Journal of Research in Science Teaching, 38*(5), 499–501.

Lehrer, R., Randle, L., and Sancilio, L. (1989). Learning preproof geometry with LOGO. *Cognition and Instruction, 6*(2), 159–184.

Lehrer, R., Schauble, L., Carpenter, S., and Penner, D. (2000). The interrelated development of inscriptions and conceptual understanding. In P. Cobb, E. Yackel, and K. McClain (Eds.), *Symbolizing and communicating in mathematics classrooms: Perspectives on discourse, tools, and instructional design* (pp. 325–360). Mahwah, NJ: Lawrence Erlbaum.

Lemke, J. (1990). *Talking science: Language, learning, and values.* Norwood, NJ: Ablex. (ERIC Document Reproduction Service No. Ed362379)

Lidget Green and Language Learning Solutions. (In preparation). *Test of emerging academic listening and speaking (TEALS).* Eugene, OR: Author.

Lord, C. (2002). Are subordinate clauses more difficult? In J. Bybee and M. Noonan (Eds.), *Complex sentences in grammar and discourse: Essays in honor of Sandra A. Thompson.* Philadelphia: John Benjamins.

Luoma, S., Cho, Y., and Buck, G. (2004, March). *From needs analysis to test development in a test for ELLs.* Paper presented at the Language Testing Research Colloquium, Temecula, CA.

McLaughlin, B., August, D., and Snow, C. (2000). *Vocabulary knowledge and reading comprehension in English language learners* (Final Performance Report to OERI, Award No. R306F60077–97). Washington, DC: U.S. Department of Education.

Mehan, H. (1979). *Learning lessons: Social organization in the classroom.* Cambridge, MA: Harvard University Press.

Menyuk, P. (1995). Language development and education. *Journal of Education, 177*(1), 39–62.

MetriTech Inc. (2001). *Test of emerging academic English (TEAE).* Champaign, IL: Author.

Nation, I. S. P. (2001). *Learning vocabulary in another language.* Cambridge: Cambridge University Press.

Nation, I. S. P., and Coxhead, A. (2001). The specialised vocabulary of English for academic purposes. In J. Flowerdew and M. Peacock (Eds.),

*Research perspectives on English for academic purposes* (pp. 252–267). Cambridge: Cambridge University Press.

National Educational Goals Panel. (n.d.). *Reconsidering children's early development and learning: Toward common views and vocabulary.* Retrieved June 20, 2004, from http://www.negp.gov/Reports/child-ea.htm.

Nippold, M. A. (1995). Language norms in school-age children and adolescents: An introduction. *Language, Speech, and Hearing Services in Schools, 26,* 307–308.

No Child Left Behind Act. (2001). Pub. L. No. 107-110, 115 Stat. 1425, December 13.

O'Connor, M. C., and Michaels, S. (1996). Shifting participant frameworks: Orchestrating thinking practices in group discussion. In D. Hicks (Ed.), *Discourse, learning, and schooling* (pp. 63–103). New York: Cambridge University Press.

Olson, L. (2002, December). States scramble to rewrite language-proficiency exams. *Education Week.* Available from http://www.edweek.com/ew/ew_printstory.cfm?slug=14lep.h22.

Palinscar, A., and Brown, A. (1984). Reciprocal teaching of comprehension-fostering and comprehension monitoring activities. *Cognition and Instruction, 1*(2), 117–175.

Pauley, A., and Syder, F. H. (1983). Natural selection in syntax: Notes on adaptive variation and change in vernacular and literary grammar. *Journal of Pragmatics, 7,* 551–579.

Philips, S. U. (1972). Participant structures and communicative competence: Warm Springs children in community and classroom. In C. B. Cazden, V. P. John, and D. Hymes, (Eds.), *Functions of language in the classroom* (pp. 370–394). New York: Teachers College Press.

Pimm, D. (1987). *Speaking mathematically: Communication in mathematics classrooms.* London: Routledge and Kegan Paul.

Pimm, D. (1995). *Symbols and meanings in school mathematics.* London: Routledge.

Reppen, R. (2001). Register variation in student and adult speech and writing. In S. Conrad and D. Biber (Eds.), *Variation in English: Multi-dimensional studies* (pp. 187–199). Harlow, Essex, UK: Pearson Education.

Rivera, C., and Stansfield, C. W. (2001, April). *The effects of linguistic simplification of science test items on performance of limited English proficient and monolingual English-speaking students.* Paper presented at the annual meeting of the American Educational Research Association, Seattle, WA.

Rivera, C., Stansfield, C., Scialdone, L., and Sharkey, M. (2000). *An analysis of state policies for the inclusion and accommodation of English language learners in state assessment programs during 1998–1999.* Arlington, VA: George Washington University, Center for Equity and Excellence in Education.

Riverside Publishing. (2001). *Iowa tests of basic skills (ITBS)*. Itasca, IL: Author.

Roth, W. M. (2001). Situating cognition. *Journal of the Learning Sciences, 10,* 27–61.

Roth, W. M., and Bowen, G. M. (1995). Knowing and interacting: A study of culture, practices, and resources in a Grade 8 open-inquiry science classroom guided by a cognitive apprenticeship metaphor. *Cognition and Instruction, 13*(1), 73–128.

Sato, E., Lagunoff, R., Worth, P., Bailey, A. L., and Butler, F. A. (2005). *ELD standards linkage and test alignment under Title III: A pilot study of the CELDT and the California ELD and content standards.* Deliverable to California Department of Education.

Scarcella, R. (2003). *Academic English: A conceptual framework* (Tech. Rep. No. 2003-1). Santa Barbara UC Linguistic Minority Research Institute.

Scarcella, R., and Zimmerman, C. (1998). Academic words and gender: ESL student performance on a test of academic lexicon. *Studies in Second Language Acquisition, 20,* 27–49.

Schleppegrell, M. J. (2001). Linguistic features of the language of schooling. *Linguistics and Education, 12*(4), 431–459.

Schleppegrell, M. J. (2004). *Language of schooling: A functional linguistics perspective.* Mahwah, NJ: Lawrence Erlbaum.

Short, D. J. (1993). *Integrating language and culture in middle school American history classes* (Report to OERI). Washington, DC: Center for Applied Linguistics and the National Center for Research on Cultural Diversity and Second Language Learning.

Short, D. (1994). Expanding middle school horizons: Integrating language, culture, and social studies. *TESOL Quarterly, 28*(3), 581–608.

Smagorinsky, P. (2001). If meaning is constructed, what is it made from? Toward a cultural theory of reading. *Review of Educational Research, 17*(1), 133–169.

Snow, C. (1990). The development of definitional skill. *Journal of Child Language, 3,* 697–710.

Snow, C. (1991). Diverse conversational contexts for the acquisition of various language skills. In J. Miller (Ed.), *Research on child language disorders* (pp. 105–124). Austin, TX: Pro-Ed.

Spanos, G., Rhodes, N. C., Dale, T. C., and Crandall, J. (1988). Linguistic features of mathematical problem solving: Insights and applications. In R. R. Cocking and J. P. Mestre (Eds.), *Linguistic and cultural influences on learning mathematics* (pp. 221–240). Hillsdale, NJ: Erlbaum.

Stack, J. (2002, September). *California English language development test (CELDT): Language proficiency and academic achievement.* Paper presented at the annual conference of the National Center for the Study of Evaluation, Standards, and Student Testing, UCLA, Los Angeles.

Stauffer, R. (1980). *The language-experience approach to the teaching of reading.* New York: Harper Row.

Stevens, R. A., Butler, F. A., and Castellon-Wellington, M. (2000). *Academic language and content assessment: Measuring the progress of ELLs* (Final Deliverable to OERI, Contract No. R305B960002). Los Angeles: University of California, National Center for Research on Evaluation, Standards, and Student Testing (CRESST).

TESOL. (1997). *ESL standards for pre-K-12 students.* Alexandria, VA: Author.

University of Iowa. (In preparation). *Iowa tests of English language learning (ITELL).* Iowa City: Author.

U.S. Department of Education. (2005). *FY 2002–2004 biennial report to Congress on the implementation of NCLB, Title III, the State Formula Grant Program.* Washington, D.C. Retrieved March 31, 2005, from http://www.ncela.gwu.edu/oela/biennial05/index.htm.

Wang, M. D. (1970). The role of syntactic complexity as a determiner of comprehensibility. *Journal of Verbal Learning and Verbal Behavior, 9,* 398–404.

White, B. Y., and Frederiksen, J. R. (1998). Inquiry, modeling, and metacognition: Making science accessible to all students. *Cognition and Instruction, 16*(1), 3–118.

WIDA Consortium. (2005). Retrieved January 31, 2005, from http://www.wida.us.

# CHAPTER 2

# *ELLs and Standardized Assessments: The Interaction between Language Proficiency and Performance on Standardized Tests*

FRANCES A. BUTLER, ROBIN STEVENS,
AND MARTHA CASTELLON

Within the context of accountability at the local and state levels, the growing need during the past decade to assess both the English language proficiency of English language learners (ELLs) and their understanding of subject matter across content areas has created challenges for educators. In this chapter, three critical issues regarding the assessment of ELLs are presented and discussed—first, the heterogeneity of ELLs, that is, the notion that ELLs are not all alike and that awareness and documentation of their differing needs should be a part of any decision-making process; second, the mismatch between the language assessed on English language proficiency tests and the language used on content tests; and third, the importance of operationalizing the language of school (academic English) for test development purposes and for broad educational applications. Data from two studies (Butler and Castellon-Wellington, 2000/5; Stevens, Butler, and Castellon-Wellington, 2000) that examine student concurrent performance on a test of English proficiency and tests of academic achievement inform the discussion. These studies were the first to empirically demonstrate the interplay between language and content assessments, validating researchers' and educators' intuitive beliefs that ELLs have divergent assessment needs. These studies also served to demonstrate that the specialized language of the classroom and of standardized assessments is not adequately measured by traditional language tests, thus clouding the picture of how ELLs are really doing in school.

## Historical Context

In the mid-1990s, when the impetus for standards-based education, with its goal of assuring equity in educational quality for all students, became a national priority, difficulties with the inclusion of ELLs in large-scale assessments became apparent. The problem of ELL inclusion was a perplexing one in many ways because of the complexities of language issues and the lack of standardized content tests normed for ELLs (see chapters 1 and 4 for discussion). In looking for a solution, educators turned to the use of test accommodations as a possible means for making test content in subject areas such as mathematics, science, and social studies more linguistically accessible. There was a precedent set for the use of accommodations in the efforts to assure the inclusion of students with disabilities in large-scale assessments, so in the absence of other viable approaches, the use of test accommodations with ELLs seemed promising. Thus, accommodations rapidly became the most widely used approach for trying to level the educational playing field so these students, who are involved in the dual enterprise of learning both a new language and new subject matter, can demonstrate what they know more effectively in testing situations. (See Bailey, chapter 1 for further discussion of issues related to test accommodations.)

Educators quickly recognized the problems inherent in the use of accommodations. Both the validity and reliability of standardized tests when administered with accommodations to ELLs were questioned. Butler and Stevens (1997) argued that even though the need for inclusion was both great and immediate, the lack of empirical evidence to support the use of accommodations with ELLs should give educators pause. They articulated a number of unresolved questions associated with the use of accommodations (e.g., Which populations of learners should be given accommodations? To what extent do accommodation strategies impact student performance?) and raised the fundamental question of the value and benefit of accommodations with ELLs. They stressed the need for "solid research . . . in which accommodations are systematically developed and tried out with different types of assessments" and recommended that "accommodated assessments" be examined for validity (p. 3).

An additional validity issue was the failure to apply accommodations systematically, according to specific guidelines. The National Research Council's study *Improving Schooling for Language-Minority Children* (August and Hakuta, 1997) called for research on accommodations, specifically requesting guidelines for their use. Clearly, research was needed to address the efficacy and value of the use of accommodations with ELLs, and further, a method was needed for making principled decisions about which accommodations to use, with whom, and when to use them.

Related to the concern about who should receive accommodations and when they should receive them was the general assumption by many decision makers that ELLs were a homogeneous group whose primary problem was English language proficiency. However, many researchers believe the use of accommodations is confounded when ELLs are treated without differentiation. While all ELLs are acquiring English as a second language and share the need to improve their academic language skills, they vary in English language proficiency levels and in a range of educationally relevant background variables such as length of time in the United States and years of formal schooling. LaCelle-Peterson and Rivera (1994) pointed out that diversity among ELLs needs to be recognized so that these students are not viewed as "a monolithic group with a single defining educational characteristic." They also argued that multiple characteristics relevant to all students should be considered when making educational decisions (pp. 59–60).

In responding to the concerns voiced by LaCelle-Peterson and Rivera (1994), Butler and Stevens (1997) presented a model for characterizing the differences among ELLs in which the student's sociocultural environment is represented by the elements of *home* (e.g., parental educational background), *school* (e.g., the quality and type of programs being implemented for ELLs), and *community* (e.g., socioeconomic status). Variables from each of these environments can help the process of articulating potential types of differences that can affect student performance. Indeed, the student's sociocultural environment is important because, as Butler and Stevens point out, "discontinuities between home, school, and the community frequently cause confusion and frustration, which can impact student performance in classroom activities and on assessments" (p. 10).

Among the variables discussed in Butler and Stevens's model, academic English proficiency is considered to be one of the most critical for making academic decisions about ELLs. Not only did Butler and Stevens see the need to create a valid measure of students' academic English proficiency that would determine if and how to provide accommodations, they also suggested a means for creating guidelines to assist educators in making valid accommodation decisions in a principled, systematic way (if indeed accommodations continued to be the approach of choice as a means of including ELLs in standardized assessments). The recognition of this need led to the design and implementation of several related studies (e.g., Aguirre-Muñoz, 2000; Bailey, 2000/5; Butler and Castellon-Wellington, 2000/5; Castellon-Wellington, 2000; Stevens et al., 2000), two of which are discussed in detail below. These studies provide empirical evidence of a distinct difference between the language skills measured on language assessments and the language used in standardized content assessments and highlight differences in ELL performance on both language assessments and standardized content tests.

The focus of the first study (Stevens et al., 2000) was on providing a comparative analysis of the language assessed by a traditional language assessment and the language that characterized a widely used standardized content assessment. In addition, the researchers examined the concurrent performance of ELLs on the same two tests. The researchers found the language of the two assessments to be very different in terms of breadth and difficulty, and that student performance on the tests varied depending on multiple factors, not all of which are language related.

The second study (Butler and Castellon-Wellington, 2000/5) carried out a similar analysis of ELLs' concurrent performance on a language assessment and a state-mandated standardized content assessment, but on a much larger scale. Using the same language assessment but a different content assessment than used in the first study described above, this study reported similar results in that the performance of ELLs on the content assessments varied even when their performance on the language assessments did not. Below we provide a summary of these two studies and their findings and then discuss how they paved the way for subsequent developments in research and test development and design.

## Study One: The Relationship between Language and Content Assessment

At one level, the overarching goal of this study (Stevens et al. 2000) was to better understand the relationship between language proficiency, as measured by traditional language assessments, and student performance on tests designed to measure knowledge and skills in specific content areas. At another level, the researchers hoped to gain a clearer view of the language that was being measured by language proficiency assessments widely used at the time as well as a better understanding of the type of language used in standardized content assessments. The researchers hypothesized that a mismatch existed between the type of language assessed on language tests and the language used on content tests.

To investigate these issues, Stevens et al. (2000) conducted a small-scale experimental study that took both qualitative and quantitative approaches to analyzing the relationship between the language on a language proficiency test and the language on a standardized content test. Implicit in this work was the notion that academic language is the conduit of the concepts being tested on standardized content assessments. The degree to which the most commonly used language proficiency tests reflect academic English is therefore important. Stevens et al. define academic English as the English used in the classroom or other academic contexts for the purpose of acquiring knowledge and operationalize it in terms of discourse, language functions, vocabulary, and syntax.

The data were collected from six seventh-grade social studies classrooms in three different schools in a Southern California school district. The students in the study spoke 10 languages besides English, with Spanish and Armenian speakers being the largest groups represented. In all, the sample consisted of 102 seventh-grade ELLs whose English proficiency was not high enough for them to function in mainstream English-only classrooms, and 19 English-only (EO) students who were in three of the classrooms that had a mix of ELL and EO students.

Two assessments were used in the study—the Language Assessment Scales (LAS) (Duncan and De Avila, 1990) and the Iowa Tests of Basic Skills (ITBS) Social Studies Test for Seventh Grade (Level

13), Form L (University of Iowa, 1993a). The LAS Reading Component, Form 3A was selected for analysis because it is a widely used test of language proficiency and was, at the time, used by the school district in this study for placement purposes. The ITBS was selected because it is one of the most widely used standardized test batteries in the United States for grades 1–8, and its content is representative of the test materials ELLs must be able to process linguistically.

The LAS Reading Component and the ITBS Social Studies Test were administered to the same students within approximately one month of each other. Two types of analyses were conducted. The first was a comparative analysis of the language of the two assessments. The second was data based, including descriptive statistics, reliability coefficients, correlational data, and item-response pattern analyses for the ITBS items. Since the goal of the study was to examine differential student performance on a language proficiency test to help determine sources of variability in scores on a content assessment, the item-response patterns of two subgroups of ELLs— the highest- and lowest-scoring ELLs on the content test—were also analyzed.

Comparisons of the language used on the tests showed a limited relationship between the language tested by the LAS and the language used on the ITBS. Thus, the LAS Reading Component does not adequately reflect the variety of language demands used on standardized content tests. The LAS is more limited in its range of grammatical constructions than the language of the ITBS. That is, the LAS items are less complex, containing fewer embedded clauses, temporal markers, and passive constructions. Moreover, the items on the LAS are relatively short and typically do not require processing pieces of discourse beyond two or more sentences. The ITBS Social Studies Test contains content-specific academic language reflective of the language that appears in textbooks (e.g., specialized content words such as *democracy* and *feudalism*), whereas the LAS contains more generic language, common to everyday contexts. Finally, because the ITBS includes a variety of item-response formats and prompts (e.g., sentence completion items, multiple choice questions, and multiple choice questions that require the processing of visuals), students are required to process a wider variety of language on the ITBS than on the LAS. The ITBS also contains *test language,* a special linguistic register of academic language that is marked by the use of formal grammatical structures in formulaic expressions, such as *which of these best describes,* whereas the LAS Reading Component does not.

Overall, the level of syntactic complexity, the variety of sentence structures, and the expanded vocabulary represented on the ITBS requires a more sophisticated use of language, one associated with academic discourse. Thus, the analysis of the language on the two tests confirms the hypothesis regarding the mismatch between the language assessed on the language proficiency test and the language used on the standardized achievement test. This mismatch speaks to the need for the development of language proficiency tests that more accurately reflect the demands of the classroom.

Another important finding of the study was that the ITBS reliability coefficients for ELLs were low. If reliability coefficients are high—and assuming validity has been established—test users can feel confident that a test is providing consistent information across administrations. In this study, the reliability coefficient (coefficient alpha) for ELLs was .864 on the LAS Reading Component but only .569 for the ITBS Social Studies Test. The published reliability for the ITBS spring 1992 norming sample is .87. Note, however, that only 0.9% of the seventh-grade norming sample was composed of limited English proficient (LEP) students (University of Iowa and Riverside Publishing, 1994). The small number of LEP students in the ITBS norming sample suggests that the ITBS is not intended for use with students whose English language skills are weak, and the lower reliability for the ITBS with the ELLs in this study confirmed the inappropriateness of using the test with these students without further norming studies. Reliability coefficients were not computed for the EOs in the study because of the small sample size.

In comparing overall performance, the EO students outperformed the ELL students as a group on both tests. However, the standard deviations and the minimum and maximum scores show considerable variability within the groups, especially on the LAS, with some students in each group obtaining perfect or near-perfect scores. The descriptive statistics in table 2.1 provide a snapshot of the performance of both the ELLs and the EOs on the two tests.

ELLs had a mean raw score of 37.82 (*SD* = 8.2) out of a possible 55 on the LAS. The minimum and maximum scores were 19 and 55, respectively. As shown in table 2.2 (which shows the LAS reading

**Table 2.1 Descriptive Statistics for ELL and
EO Performance on the LAS and ITBS**

|      | Test | *n* | No. of items | *M* | *SD* | Min | Max |
|------|------|-----|--------------|-----|------|-----|-----|
| ELLs | LAS  | 102 | 55 | 37.82 | 8.20 | 19 | 55 |
|      | ITBS | 102 | 44 | 12.85 | 4.98 | 0  | 28 |
| EOs  | LAS  | 18  | 55 | 47.72 | 6.33 | 30 | 54 |
|      | ITBS | 19  | 44 | 21.63 | 5.45 | 13 | 30 |

Source: *Stevens et al., 2000. Copyright 2000 by CRESST. Reprinted with permission.*

levels and their corresponding scores), the mean falls in the middle of the *limited reader* competency level.[1] The mean LAS score for EOs was 47.72 (*SD* = 6.33), which falls into the *competent reader* level, with minimum and maximum scores of 30 and 54 respectively. The range of LAS scores placed ELLs in *nonreader, limited reader,* and *competent reader* categories and EOs into the *limited* and *competent reader* categories.

On the ITBS, ELLs had a mean raw score of 12.85 (*SD* = 4.98) out of 44 possible, with minimum and maximum scores of 0 and 28 respectively. The EOs' mean score on the ITBS was 21.63 (*SD* = 5.45), with scores ranging from 13 to 30. The percentile rankings for the two groups were 16th and 50th respectively. Percentile rankings were calculated using the midyear conversions (University of Iowa, 1993b).

Table 2.3 provides the Pearson Product-Moment Correlations for ELL total LAS Reading and subscale scores with the ITBS total score.

With the exception of the LAS Reading for Information subsec-

**Table 2.2 LAS Reading Competency Levels**

| Reading level | Raw score range |
|---------------|-----------------|
| Nonreader | 0–32 |
| Limited Reader | 33–43 |
| Competent Reader | 44–55 |

Source: *Adapted from Stevens et al., 2000.*

**Table 2.3 Pearson Product-Moment Correlations and Significance Levels for ELL LAS Reading Scores (Total and Subsection) with ITBS Scores ($n = 98$)**

|      | Total LAS | Synonyms | Fluency | Antonyms | Mechanics | Reading for information |
|------|-----------|----------|---------|----------|-----------|-------------------------|
| ITBS | .4482     | .4030    | .3787   | .3717    | .2578     | .1839                   |
|      | (.001)    | (.001)   | (.001)  | (.001)   | (.01)     | (.07)                   |

Source: *Stevens et al., 2000. Copyright 2000 by CRESST. Reprinted with permission.*

tion, all of the correlations for LAS subsections and the total LAS are significant at the .01 level or better. However, the magnitude of the correlations is weak. For example, the $R^2$ for the strongest correlation, the total LAS with ITBS, is .20, which means that performance on the LAS accounts for 20% of the variance on ITBS scores. Thus, 80% of the variance is not explained by LAS Reading. The data indicate that the LAS may not be an adequate indicator of readiness either for standardized content assessments or for the assignment of accommodations since it does not help to explain variance in performance. This weak relationship is possibly due to the language the LAS assesses not being aligned with the language needed to perform well on tests such as the ITBS. Whether a higher correlation should be expected between a reading test and a content test such as a social studies test, which in fact may contain reading passages, is an unexplored question. The answer, in part, depends on the nature of the items on both tests.

As mentioned above, in order to better understand ELL performance on content assessments, further comparisons were made of within-group ELL performance. In separating the top third performing ELLs from the lower third, we found a statistically significant difference ($p < .001$) between the means for these two groups on the LAS and the ITBS. Further analysis revealed large differences in percentile ranking for these students on the ITBS, with the highest-scoring ELL group falling into the 34th percentile and above and the lowest falling into the 10th percentile and below. Although the differences in the scores for the two groups were found to be statistically significant, both groups scored in the *limited reader* category of the LAS, indicating that the LAS proficiency categories are too broad.

The item-response patterns of the highest- and lowest-scoring ELL groups mentioned above, as well as those of the EOs in the study, showed both important similarities and differences. Although the EOs still had higher ITBS scores than the top-performing ELLs, analyses revealed that overall ITBS performance and the response patterns of the two groups were similar (e.g., they generally selected the same distracters when their answers were incorrect), whereas the lowest-scoring ELLs demonstrated no clear patterns associated with the patterns of either of the other two groups. In fact, response patterns of the top ELLs suggest that these students were able to process the language of the test in much the same way as the EOs but lacked the content knowledge to select the correct response. Conversely, for the lowest-scoring ELLs, both language factors and lack of content knowledge appeared to play a role in their perform-ance, since they performed poorly on both tests and also tended to select completely different distracters than the top-performing ELLs and EOs.

These results demonstrated that aggregating all ELLs for re-search and intervention is potentially misleading and inappropriate due to the diversity within ELLs as a group. In this study, disaggre-gating ELLs according to their performance on the ITBS and per-forming item-response analyses revealed that suspected differences in the performance of the two ELL groups is real. Poor ELL per-formance on standardized content assessments is often attributed to language difficulties. However, the weak performance of even the highest-scoring ELLs in the study cannot be attributed to language difficulties alone; it may, in fact, be a result of limitations in oppor-tunity to learn (OTL) or other academic and/or sociocultural fac-tors. These findings should impact the intervention-selection pro-cess for these students. For example, for the highest-scoring ELLs in this study, providing test accommodations, an approach currently being used to address potential language problems on standardized assessments (see Abedi, Hofstetter, Lord, and Baker 2001; Castellon-Wellington, 2000), would not be helpful. It is evident that these stu-dents could already process the language of the assessment but simply did not have the necessary content knowledge to do well. Test scores for these students and others like them may actually re-flect true gaps in knowledge, in which case their performance on content assessments may, in fact, be valid indicators of their content knowledge.

Overall, what this research showed was that the LAS and tests like it do not adequately measure the language of the classroom or help to distinguish between different student proficiency levels well enough with the current classifications (e.g., *limited reader*). It also showed that ELL performance is more complex than many realize and requires more detailed investigation to explain differences in performance, not only between ELLs and EOs but also between subgroups of ELLs. A better understanding of within-group ELL performance may help to improve instruction and assessment for these students. We turn now to discussion of a second study that investigated concurrent performance of ELLs on a language proficiency test and a content assessment on a larger scale.

## Study Two: Concurrent Performance by ELLs in Grades 3 and 11 on Tests of Language Proficiency and Academic Achievement

A second, larger study (Butler and Castellon-Wellington, 2000/5) included students at two different grade levels (third and eleventh) and compared these students' performance on a standardized content assessment with concurrent performance by the same students on a measure of English language proficiency. Specifically, student performance on the content assessment was examined based on proficiency categories established by the language proficiency test. As in Stevens et al. (2000), the LAS was the measure of language proficiency used—although, in this instance, both the LAS Reading and Writing components were administered. Instead of the ITBS, the state-mandated Stanford Achievement Test Series, ninth edition (Harcourt Brace Educational Measurement, 1996)—henceforth in the chapter referred to as the Stanford 9—was the standardized content test used. The LAS was administered approximately one month after administration of the Stanford 9.

The data were collected by two Southern California school districts—an elementary school district and a high school district; both ELLs and EO students participated. A total of 778 third-grade students from nine elementary schools were tested. Of these students, 296 (38%) were categorized by the school district as EO, 77

(10%) as fluent English proficient (FEP), and 409 (52%) as LEP. At the high school level, 184 eleventh-grade students from three high schools were tested, of which 115 (63%) were categorized as EO, 30 (16%) as FEP, and 39 (21%) as LEP. All of the designations above were district classifications based on test scores obtained prior to this study.

The guiding research question in this study asked: What is the relationship between performance of ELLs on a standardized content test and performance by the same students on a test of English language proficiency? The study is significant because it compared concurrent performance on these two types of measures. The analyses conducted for the study included descriptive statistics, reliability, and correlational data.

Results on the LAS and the Stanford 9 showed, as expected, that at both third and eleventh grades, EOs scored higher than ELLs in general, with FEPs scoring higher than LEPs. However, the considerable range of scores within each group on both tests indicated unexplained variability. Indeed, some LEP scores were very high on both the LAS and the Stanford 9, suggesting that those students with high scores might fall into the district's redesignated FEP (RFEP) classification. Because the district had not yet carried out its redesignation procedure for the year at the time of the study, and due to the apparent potential for within-group ELL differences, the district redesignation criteria available (the language test scores and the Stanford 9 Reading score) were applied to the third-grade LEP group. The result was that 40 students who were classified as LEP by the district during the previous year were reclassified as RFEP for the purpose of further analyses. Because of the small sample size of LEP students at the eleventh-grade level, redesignation criteria were not applied to that group. Tables 2.4 and 2.5 provide the descriptive statistics for this study.

Disaggregating the RFEP students from the larger ELL group at the third grade revealed that these students outperformed the EO students on the language tests (see table 2.4) and on two of the Stanford 9 subtests: math and language (see table 2.5). That is, in each instance, the mean score for the RFEP students was higher than the mean score for the EOs. (Note, however, that due to the small number of RFEP students, the mean differences were not tested for statistical significance.)

The performance of these RFEP students suggests that when

**Table 2.4 Standard Score Descriptive Statistics for LAS Reading and Writing by Language Proficiency Category (Grades 3 and 11)**

|  | | Grade 3 | | | Grade 11 | | |
|---|---|---|---|---|---|---|---|
|  | LAS | n | M (SD) | Min-Max | n | M (SD) | Min-Max |
| EO | Reading | 292 | 92.6 (10.6) | 31–100 | 104 | 96.9 (4.7) | 71–100 |
|  | Writing | 280 | 79.0 (11.1) | 3–100 | 109 | 81.1 (11.0) | 60–100 |
| FEP | Reading | 77 | 90.2 (13.6) | 24–100 | 28 | 94.8 (6.0) | 80–100 |
|  | Writing | 75 | 76.4 (9.0) | 57–97 | 29 | 72.9 (9.1) | 60–87 |
| RFEP | Reading | 40 | 96.2 (3.4) | 84–100 | — | — | — |
|  | Writing | 40 | 85.3 (5.0) | 80–97 | — | — | — |
| LEP | Reading | 369 | 78.8 (15.2) | 36–100 | 36 | 85.6 (10.5) | 55–100 |
|  | Writing | 343 | 67.5 (12.0) | 13–97 | 36 | 66.8 (8.0) | 44–82 |

Note: *EO = English only, FEP = fluent English proficient, RFEP = redesignated fluent English proficient, LEP = limited English proficient*
Source: *Adapted from Butler and Castellon-Wellington, 2000/5.*

ELL student mean scores (table 2.4) are in the mid-90s on LAS Reading and mid-80s on LAS Writing, ELL student performance is similar to EO performance on content tests (table 2.5). That is, ELL student performance is average (50) or above in terms of norm group (normal curve equivalent [NCE]) scores. Although the size of the RFEP group was small ($n = 40$), the performance of these students indicates that they had acquired English sufficiently well to demonstrate their content knowledge through English. While this group was excluded from some analyses due to the small number of students, the mean differences in performance and the range of scores suggest that some students who are designated LEP upon entering school are making progress in both English and content knowledge. There is, of course, the possibility that some of these third-grade students were misplaced upon entering school and had a high degree of English proficiency to begin with.

In another related finding in the study, the performance of some third-grade EO students raises questions about the criteria ELLs are being held to in order to receive FEP or RFEP status. Of the 296 EO third graders, only 140 (47%) met the same redesignation criteria being used with ELLs. This finding gives the appearance that ELLs are being held to a standard that many EOs themselves can-

**Table 2.5 Normal Curve Equivalent Descriptive Statistics for Stanford 9 subtests by Language Proficiency Category (Grades 3 and 11)**

|  |  | Grade 3 | | | Grade 11 | | |
|---|---|---|---|---|---|---|---|
|  |  | *n* | *M (SD)* | *Min-Max* | *n* | *M (SD)* | *Min-Max* |
| Reading | EO | 294 | 55.9 (18.9) | 6.7–99.0 | 100 | 57.0 (18.6) | 6.7–99.0 |
|  | FEP | 68 | 48.4 (15.4) | 15.4–84.6 | 29 | 37.7 (17.3) | 1.0–66.3 |
|  | RFEP | 40 | 52.0 (7.3) | 42.5–67.7 | — | — | — |
|  | LEP | 352 | 29.1 (12.8) | 1.0–65.6 | 34 | 22.4 (10.7) | 1.0–42.5 |
| Math | EO | 296 | 58.9 (21.8) | 1.0–99.0 | 102 | 69.2 (22.4) | 15.4–99.0 |
|  | FEP | 73 | 51.4 (21.3) | 1.0–99.0 | 28 | 43.6 (19.9) | 10.4–86.9 |
|  | RFEP | 40 | 62.1 (14.5) | 32.3–93.3 | — | — | — |
|  | LEP | 368 | 40.3 (16.5) | 1.0–89.6 | 33 | 34.9 (13.7) | 13.1–60.4 |
| Language | EO | 294 | 54.3 (21.0) | 6.7–99.0 | 101 | 65.0 (20.2) | 1.0–99.0 |
|  | FEP | 70 | 48.7 (17.5) | 10.4–99.0 | 27 | 44.3 (16.9) | 1.0–74.7 |
|  | RFEP | 39 | 55.0 (10.6) | 41.3–82.7 | — | — | — |
|  | LEP | 360 | 22.7 (13.7) | 1.0–72.8 | 33 | 31.5 (10.1) | 10.4–45.7 |
| Science | EO | — | — | — | 102 | 65.5 (20.3) | 17.3–99.0 |
|  | FEP | — | — | — | 28 | 38.0 (17.8) | 13.1–75.8 |
|  | RFEP | — | — | — | — | — | — |
|  | LEP | — | — | — | 33 | 30.6 (10.9) | 1.0–56.4 |
| Social Science | EO | — | — | — | 101 | 72.9 (21.7) | 15.4–99.0 |
|  | FEP | — | — | — | 29 | 46.0 (21.3) | 6.7–86.9 |
|  | RFEP | — | — | — | — | — | — |
|  | LEP | — | — | — | 34 | 38.9 (14.8) | 10.4–70.9 |

Note: *EO = English only, FEP = fluent English proficient, RFEP = redesignated fluent English proficient, LEP = limited English proficient*

Source: *Adapted from Butler and Castellon-Wellington, 2000/5.*

not reach. In fact, the finding may indicate that a large percentage of EOs are also struggling with language, OTL, or both, or that the criteria against which ELLs are being judged are too demanding.

The reliability coefficients for the LAS were high for both grade levels, indicating the strong internal consistency of the test. The reliability coefficients (coefficient alpha) for LAS Reading by language proficiency category for the third grade are EO, .889 ($n = 292$); FEP, .916 ($n = 77$); and LEP, .876 ($n = 369$). The coefficients for the language proficiency categories for the eleventh grade are EO, .781 ($n =$

104) and FEP/LEP, .848 ($n$ = 64). Because of the small sample sizes for the eleventh-grade FEP and LEP groups, the two groups were combined to compute the reliability coefficient.

The reliability coefficients for LAS Writing are EO, .821 ($n$ = 280); FEP, .753 ($n$ = 75); and LEP, .828 ($n$ = 343). The RFEP group was not included in the calculations due to the restricted range for the group and the small sample size. Reliability coefficients are not provided for LAS Writing for the eleventh grade because one of the items on the writing test is an essay and is weighted differently from the other five items. The generally high reliability coefficients show that the LAS components are basically measuring the same construct across the proficiency groups. The state's item-level data for the Stanford 9 subtests were not available and thus the reliability coefficients could not be calculated.

In comparing the results of student performance based on the English language proficiency categories established by the LAS, clear performance differences emerged among the ELL groups. Tables 2.6 and 2.7 show student performance on the content assessment vis-à-vis the language test categorizations for the third grade. The same comparisons could not be made for the eleventh grade because of the small numbers of FEP and LEP students.

When comparing the student means for the Stanford 9 according to LAS proficiency categories: *competent, limited,* and *nonreader* or *nonwriter,* these data (tables 2.6 and 2.7) show that third-grade ELLs who meet the redesignation criteria (RFEP) and who qualify as competent readers and writers according to LAS scoring criteria score at the mean (NCE 50) or above on the Stanford 9 subtests. However, LEP students who are in the competent category but do not meet the redesignation criteria perform quite differently from those in the RFEP group. These students did not reach the national norm for average performance on the content test. In fact, neither LAS test discriminated well among students at the higher end of the LAS proficiency spectrum (see LAS scores for EO and FEP students in table 2.4). There was a ceiling effect with the LAS: most ELLs received a high score on the test, rendering the results inadequate for distinguishing differences at the upper range of English language ability. This finding is consistent with information provided in the *LAS Examiner's Manual* (Duncan and De Avila, 1988). It is possible that the LAS Reading and Writing criterion for the *compe-*

**Table 2.6 Stanford 9 Normal Curve Equivalent Means and Standard Deviations for Reading, Math, and Language by LAS Reading Level (Grade 3)**

| LAS Reading Level | Stanford 9 Reading | | Stanford 9 Math | | Stanford 9 Language | |
|---|---|---|---|---|---|---|
| | n | M (SD) | n | M (SD) | n | M (SD) |
| Competent Reader | | | | | | |
| EO | 256 | 58.5 (16.4) | 257 | 61.4 (20.6) | 255 | 56.8 (19.1) |
| FEP | 62 | 49.8 (15.1) | 65 | 53.8 (20.0) | 62 | 50.9 (17.2) |
| RFEP* | 40 | 52.0 (7.3) | 40 | 62.1 (14.5) | 39 | 56.5 (10.6) |
| LEP | 211 | 35.0 (10.4) | 217 | 46.5 (14.9) | 213 | 38.1 (12.9) |
| Limited Reader | | | | | | |
| EO | 18 | 26.1 (8.3) | 18 | 33.1 (11.0) | 18 | 26.0 (8.8) |
| FEP | 5 | 34.6 (11.2) | 7 | 27.4 (20.3) | 7 | 30.0 (5.7) |
| LEP | 92 | 21.8 (8.3) | 98 | 33.1 (13.8) | 95 | 25.0 (9.4) |
| Non-Reader | | | | | | |
| EO | 6 | 16.9 (7.4) | 7 | 27.4 (13.1) | 7 | 20.3 (8.9) |
| LEP | 35 | 12.5 (7.0) | 39 | 24.0 (11.8) | 38 | 20.8 (8.7) |

*RFEP students are only in the competent category by virtue of the redesignation criterion for LAS Reading.*
Source: *Butler and Castellon-Wellington, 2000/5. Copyright 2000 by CRESST. Reprinted with permission.*

*tent level* is not the appropriate language criterion for judging whether students have sufficient mastery of English to perform at average levels (NCE 50 or above). In fact, due to perceived shortcomings of the LAS for ELL mastery of English for placement decisions, the district redesignation criteria included the Stanford 9 Reading score to help ensure that students who did not have sufficiently strong English language skill would not be placed in mainstream classes without language support.

When correlating the performance between the LAS standard scores for reading and writing with the Stanford 9 subsection NCE by language proficiency category for grades 3 and 11, the magnitude of the correlations is generally moderate, with the squared coefficients indicating that one test accounts for relatively little of the variance in performance on the other. The Pearson Product-Moment Correlations are provided below in tables 2.8 and 2.9.

The RFEP category is not included in table 2.8 because three subtests used in the correlations—LAS Reading, LAS Writing, and

**Table 2.7 Stanford 9 Normal Curve Equivalent Means and Standard Deviations for Reading, Math, and Language by LAS Writing Level (Grade 3)**

| LAS Writing Level | Stanford 9 Reading | | Stanford 9 Math | | Stanford 9 Language | |
|---|---|---|---|---|---|---|
| | n | M (SD) | n | M (SD) | n | M (SD) |
| Competent Writer | | | | | | |
| EO | 146 | 62.2 (17.8) | 146 | 67.8 (19.3) | 145 | 63.2 (19.0) |
| FEP | 28 | 57.3 (13.7) | 29 | 61.0 (16.9) | 28 | 56.9 (15.4) |
| RFEP* | 40 | 52.0 (7.3) | 40 | 62.1 (14.5) | 39 | 56.5 (10.6) |
| LEP | 32 | 34.9 (9.1) | 34 | 47.9 (12.6) | 34 | 38.5 (12.4) |
| Limited Writer | | | | | | |
| EO | 122 | 47.9 (17.9) | 124 | 47.5 (18.8) | 123 | 43.8 (18.5) |
| FEP | 37 | 42.0 (13.5) | 41 | 43.0 (20.9) | 39 | 42.7 (17.2) |
| LEP | 244 | 30.3 (11.6) | 254 | 40.2 (15.1) | 247 | 32.8 (13.3) |
| Non-Writer | | | | | | |
| EO | 2 | 58.5 (16.5) | 2 | 37.4 (3.2) | 2 | 48.1 (7.2) |
| LEP | 37 | 14.1 (8.1) | 40 | 26.2 (13.2) | 40 | 23.6 (9.8) |

*RFEP students are in the competent category only by virtue of the redesignation criterion for LAS Writing.
Source: *Butler and Castellon-Wellington, 2000/5. Copyright 2000 by CRESST. Reprinted with permission.*

Stanford 9 Reading—were used for the redesignation of LEP students to the RFEP category. All of the correlations at the third grade are significant at the $p < .001$ level, and at $p < .01$ at the eleventh grade, with one exception (LAS Writing with Math). The higher correlation between the LAS Reading score and the Stanford 9 Reading score for LEP students at the third grade ($r = .72$), combined with the fact that the LEP means on the LAS Reading and Stanford 9 are well below the means of EO and RFEP students, may indicate that those LEP students did not have the language proficiency required to do well on either test.

Overall, this study suggests that there is a strong relationship between the English language proficiency of ELLs and their performance on a content assessment. However, the specifics of that relationship are not clear. The lack of discrimination within the current LAS *competent* range is a limitation not only in this study, where it clouds the comparison of language and content scores, but also for educators attempting to make decisions about accommodations

Table 2.8 Pearson Product Moment Correlations for LAS Standard Scores for
Reading and Writing with Stanford 9 Normal Curve Equivalents for Reading, Math,
and Language by Language Proficiency Category (Grade 3)

| | LAS | Stanford 9 Reading | | | Stanford 9 Math | | | Stanford 9 Language | | |
|---|---|---|---|---|---|---|---|---|---|---|
| | | n | r | p | n | r | p | n | r | p |
| EO | Reading | 280 | .67 | .001 | 282 | .53 | .001 | 280 | .59 | .001 |
| | Writing | 270 | .42 | .001 | 272 | .55 | .001 | 270 | .53 | .001 |
| FEP | Reading | 67 | .46 | .001 | 72 | .50 | .001 | 69 | .55 | .001 |
| | Writing | 65 | .51 | .001 | 70 | .48 | .001 | 67 | .44 | .001 |
| LEP | Reading | 338 | .72 | .001 | 354 | .53 | .001 | 346 | .56 | .001 |
| | Writing | 313 | .50 | .001 | 328 | .41 | .001 | 321 | .37 | .001 |

Source: *Butler and Castellon-Wellington, 2000/5. Copyright 2000 by CRESST. Reprinted with permission.*

and redesignation. Thus, the study points to the need for a test of language proficiency that assesses a broader range of student language ability than does the LAS. Without a test that adequately mirrors the language used on content assessments and that discriminates well at the upper range of the language proficiency continuum, it will remain difficult to tell whether students who are identified as competent by the LAS and other commonly used language assessments are, in fact, skilled enough in the language to handle the material on standardized tests.

Finally, it is important to note that, as reported in the first study described above, a possible factor in the performance of LEP students who are in the competent category is related to the students' classroom experiences. These students may be unable to achieve at the NCE level of 50 on the Stanford 9 not because of their language ability but rather because they have not had the opportunity to learn the content material covered on the test. LEP students are often not exposed to the same curriculum as mainstream students because their educational focus is usually on acquiring English in special programs, so regardless of improvement in language proficiency, they may not have had access to the content covered on tests such as the Stanford 9.

**Table 2.9 Pearson Product Moment Correlations for LAS Standard Scores for Reading and Writing with Stanford 9 Normal Curve Equivalents for Reading, Math, Language, Science, and Social Science by Language Proficiency Category (Grade 11)**

| | LAS | Stanford 9 Reading | | | Stanford 9 Math | | | Stanford 9 Language | | | Stanford 9 Science | | | Stanford 9 Social Science | | |
|---|---|---|---|---|---|---|---|---|---|---|---|---|---|---|---|---|
| | | n | r | p | n | r | p | n | r | p | n | r | p | n | r | p |
| EO | Reading | 90 | .55 | .001 | 92 | .42 | .001 | 91 | .58 | .001 | 92 | .38 | .001 | 91 | .46 | .000 |
| | Writing | 96 | .57 | .001 | 98 | .58 | .001 | 97 | .59 | .001 | 98 | .62 | .001 | 97 | .57 | .000 |
| FEP/LEP | Reading | 58 | .67 | .001 | 56 | .36 | .007 | 56 | .57 | .001 | 56 | .53 | .001 | 58 | .46 | .000 |
| | Writing | 61 | .44 | .001 | 59 | .25 | .055 | 58 | .56 | .001 | 59 | .45 | .001 | 61 | .41 | .001 |

*Source: Butler and Castellon-Wellington, 2000/5. Copyright 2000 by CRESST. Reprinted with permission.*

## Going Forward: Linking Research to Change

The two studies discussed above verified long-held beliefs that traditional language tests may not assess the full range of English necessary for students to handle the material on standardized content tests. In these studies, the LAS Reading Component was determined to be an inappropriate means of assessing readiness for taking standardized assessments in English, since the language it measures is not aligned to the language of standardized assessments as typified by the language of the ITBS. In addition, the LAS proficiency categories are too broad (e.g., in the first study discussed above, two groups of student scores were statistically different yet fell into the same proficiency level), and the LAS Reading Component has a ceiling effect that can result in some students testing out of programs before they have sufficient English ability to perform the full range of tasks needed for success in mainstream classrooms.

The studies reported in this chapter showed how the use of language proficiency tests that do not assess the full spectrum of school English can potentially lead to incorrect assumptions or decisions about ELLs. If students are expected to take standardized assessments when they are not ready linguistically, the resulting test scores will not be valid. We conclude, therefore, that appropriate language measures are needed to help determine the degree to which language demands interfere with content performance and to establish test-taker readiness.

One of the studies also verified that further research is needed to establish the reliability and validity of standardized achievement tests when used with ELLs. The reliability figures in the study were low for ELLs taking the ITBS, and the number of ELLs in norming data was inadequate. Unfortunately, no data were available for the Stanford 9. In order to ensure that the validity and reliability of content assessments is addressed with respect to ELLs, future norming studies should include larger numbers of ELLs.

Finally, these studies hint at problems in the use of accommodations in general and in the assignment of accommodations to ELLs in particular. The effective use of accommodations hinges, at least in part, on having appropriate measures of language proficiency available for gauging the type of accommodation that would be most beneficial to a specific ELL in taking a standardized test. If educators cannot rely on measures of language proficiency to help determine a student's relevant strengths and weaknesses in language ability, then it becomes difficult to assign an appropriate accommodation to meet that student's needs. Further, the use of accommodations should not be considered in isolation from other relevant educational variables. For example, if a student has not been exposed to the material on a standardized test, then no amount of language accommodation can, or indeed should, help that student perform better on the content knowledge and concepts assessed on the test.

In fact, these two studies revealed that differential performance of ELLs is not related only to language. Even though some ELLs scored at the *limited reader* level on the language test, analyses indicated other factors such as OTL may have played a role in these students' poor performance on the content assessments. These findings suggest that further investigation into the sources of variability in ELL performance is warranted.

Although these studies did not resolve the issues identified in this chapter, they have opened the door to further debate about assuring test validity for ELLs, including the appropriate use of accommodations with standardized achievement tests. Most important, they engendered greater emphasis on research and development in the area of K-12 language assessment. Now researchers are working toward a better understanding and characterization of the language of school with the goal of creating improved language and testing programs to meet the needs of this diverse group of students.

## Note

1. The LAS yields three competency levels for the Reading and Writing Components: *nonreader (writer), limited reader (writer),* and *competent reader (writer)*.

## References

Abedi, J., Hofstetter, C., Lord, C., and Baker, E. (2001). *NAEP math performance and test accommodations: Interactions with student language background* (CSE Tech. Rep. No. 536). Los Angeles: University of California, National Center for Research on Evaluation, Standards, and Student Testing.

Aguirre-Muñoz, A. (2000). *The impact of language background characteristics on complex performance assessments: Linguistic accommodation strategies for English language learners.* Unpublished doctoral dissertation. University of California, Los Angeles.

August, D., and Hakuta, K. (1997). *Improving schooling for language-minority children.* Washington, DC: National Academy Press.

Bailey, A. L. (2000/5). Language analysis of standardized achievement tests: Considerations in the assessment of English language learners. In *The validity of administering large-scale content assessments to English language learners: An investigation from three perspectives* (CSE Tech. Rep. No. 663). Los Angeles: University of California, National Center for Research on Evaluation, Standards, and Student Testing (CRESST).

Butler, F. A., and Castellon-Wellington, M. (2000/5). Students' concurrent performance on tests of English language proficiency and academic achievement. In *The validity of administering large-scale content assessments to English language learners: An investigation from three perspectives* (CSE Tech. Rep. No. 663). Los Angeles: University of California, National Center for Research on Evaluation, Standards, and Student Testing (CRESST).

Butler, F. A., and Stevens, R. (1997). *Accommodation strategies for English language learners on large-scale assessments: Student characteristics and other considerations* (CSE Tech. Rep. No. 448). Los Angeles: University of California, National Center for Research on Evaluation, Standards, and Student Testing (CRESST).

Castellon-Wellington, M. (2000). *The impact of preference for accommodations: The performance of English language learners on large-scale academic achievement tests* (CSE Tech. Rep. No. 524). Los Angeles: University of California, National Center for Research on Evaluation, Standards, and Student Testing (CRESST).

Duncan, S. E., and De Avila, E. A. (1988). *Language assessment scales (LAS) reading and writing examiner's manual: Forms 1a and b, Forms 3a and b.* Monterey, CA: CTB/McGraw-Hill.

Duncan, S. E., and De Avila, E. A. (1990). *Language assessment scales (LAS) reading component: Forms 1a, 2a, and 3a.* Monterey, CA: CTB/McGraw-Hill.

Harcourt Brace Educational Measurement. (1996). *Stanford achievement test series, ninth edition: Form T.* San Antonio, TX: Harcourt Brace.

LaCelle-Peterson, M., and Rivera, C. (1994). Is it real for all kids? A framework for equitable assessment policies for English language learners. *Harvard Educational Review, 64,* 55–75.

Stevens, R., Butler, F. A., and Castellon-Wellington, M. (2000). *Academic language and content assessment: Measuring the progress of ELLs* (CSE Tech. Rep. No. 552). Los Angeles: University of California, National

Center for Research on Evaluation, Standards, and Student Testing (CRESST).

University of Iowa. (1993a). *Iowa tests of basic skills complete battery, level 13: Form L.* Chicago: Riverside.

University of Iowa. (1993b). *Iowa tests of basic skills norms and score conversions: Form L, complete and core batteries.* Chicago: Riverside.

University of Iowa and the Riverside Publishing Company. (1994). *Integrated assessment program, technical summary I.* Chicago: Riverside.

# CHAPTER 3

# Policy Needs: What Federal and State Governments Need from Language Research

JAN MAYER

The enactment of the No Child Left Behind Act of 2001 (NCLB, 2001a) brought significant new accountability requirements to states regarding English learners (ELs).[1] This law was a catalyst for renewed dialogue among educators about how to appropriately address the linguistic and academic characteristics of this group as we focused on developing new standards, assessments and reporting systems. This chapter is organized by topics that first address accountability provisions for English learners in the NCLB Act Titles I and III (NCLB, 2001b, 2001c) and then continue with an explanation of how California implements the federal policy at the state level. The chapter begins with a historical summary of federal policies for English learners in order to highlight the significance of the changes brought forth by the NCLB Act. Subsequently, background information regarding the California English learner population is presented to provide a context for the issues considered in the development of the Title III accountability policies. The topics that follow focus on the NCLB Act accountability requirements for academic achievement, English language proficiency, and the corresponding annual targets and objectives. Throughout the chapter, research questions are presented that highlight information that would be beneficial to the development of thoughtful policy.

## Background Context

Since the initiation of the federal Elementary and Secondary Education Act (ESEA, 1965) in the 1960s, Title VII provided funding for English learners through competitive grants. Under each prior reauthorization of the law, there were no mandates for this group of students to be included significantly within large-scale accountability systems. During that time, English learner performance data were primarily reported through individual project evaluations and state performance reports that were submitted to the U.S. Department of Education, For federal reporting purposes, when data were disaggregated there were no specific "English learner" categories; instead, their results were combined with those of other students and reported as part of "all students at a school" or by ethnicity and socioeconomic status.

The NCLB Act ushered in a new era for English learners with Title III (NCLB, 2001c) and the creation of the Office of English Language Acquisition, Language Enhancement, and Academic Achievement for Limited English Proficient Students (OELA). In addition to changing the funding structure to a formula base rather than through competitive grants, Title III brought English learners fully into the educational reform effort by setting expectations for them to meet grade-level content standards as well as annual English language proficiency objectives.

Under the previous reauthorization of ESEA, the Improving America's School Act (IASA, 1994), states had already developed content standards to meet Title I requirements. The content standards specified the expectations of what students should know and be able to do, by grade level, in English language arts (ELA) and mathematics. These were the same standards for all groups of students, including English learners. One of the inadequacies of the IASA accountability system was that the achievement of English learners was not reported as a group. That meant that if most students at the school were performing at or above grade level, the overall achievement level could be skewed and the low performance of English learners was not apparent.

The NCLB Act required states to report and be held accountable for the achievement of English learners as a subgroup, with their progress being reported publicly and reviewed annually. In addition, the NCLB Act required the development of a new set of standards that was unique for English learners: English language proficiency (ELP) standards. Related state mandates included the development of an English language proficiency assessment aligned to the ELP and ELA standards and the implementation of a system to hold local educational agencies (LEAs) accountable for meeting annual performance targets. In 1997, legislation in California required the creation of English language development (ELD) standards and the implementation of a single ELD assessment. However, it wasn't until the NCLB Act was authorized in 2001 that all states and LEAs were held accountable for English learners as a distinct subgroup for both their academic achievement and progress in acquiring English. At the heart of the overlap of Title I and Title III lies the development of academic English.

## One State's Research Needs: The Case of English Learners in California

In the 2002–3 school year, the National Clearinghouse for English Language Acquisition (NCELA, 2004) reported that there were just over 5 million English learners enrolled in schools throughout the United States and territories. This number represents approximately 10% of the total kindergarten-twelfth grade enrollment and is a 45.4% increase over the 1997–98 school year. In 2002-3 (the year of the NCELA report), 1,559,542, or approximately 31%, of the students were enrolled in California schools. Other large EL-enrolling states included Texas (660,707), New York (302, 961), Florida (292,077), Illinois (169,414), and Arizona (149,354).

In California, a census of English learners is taken at each school every spring. The 2004 *Language Census* (California Department of Education, 2004) reports that California enrolled nearly 1.6 million English learners in kindergarten through grade 12. This figure represents one out of every four students. Nearly 70% of the English learners are in kindergarten through sixth grade, and over 30% are in the secondary schools. Although there are 56 languages spoken by a significant number of students, the Spanish speakers are the predominant group, comprising 85% of the English learner population in the state of California (see figures 3.1 and 3.2).

In 1998, the voters in California approved Proposition 227 (English Language in Public Schools Initiative Statute, 1998). This law requires English learners to be placed in settings where instruction is provided overwhelmingly in English unless there are approved parental waiver requests to have children placed in alternative (bilingual) settings. The structured English immersion settings vary with regard to how they are designed and implemented across classrooms, schools, and districts. For example, there are programs that

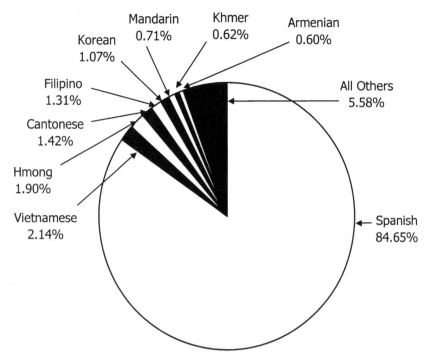

Figure 3.1. Distribution of predominant first languages among
California EL students, from Language Census Report
(April 1, 2004), California Department of Education.
http://data1.cde.ca.gov/dataquest

offer varying degrees of primary language assistance or instruction,
and others provide services only in English (American Institutes of
Research, 2004.)

Nearly 90% of the English learners are reported as enrolled in
structured English immersion or mainstream English settings, and
approximately 9%, or 137,902, students are enrolled in bilingual
programs (California Department of Education, 2004). The placement of students in alternative settings is an important consideration in policy discussions regarding assessment practices and the
components of accountability systems. Students enrolled in alternative programs have less exposure to English, especially in the initial phases of the program, and typically receive the majority of the
content-area instruction in their primary language. Nonetheless,
schools with significant primary language instruction are able to

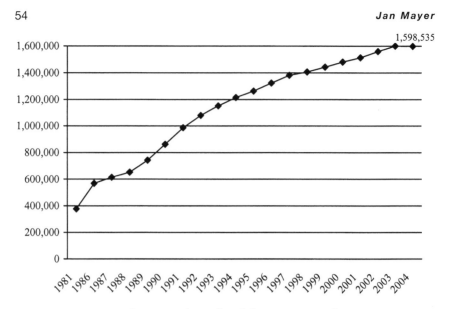

Figure 3.2. Growth in number of California EL students over time, from Language Census Report (April 1, 2004), California Department of Education. http://data1.cde.ca.gov/dataquest

demonstrate some gains on English performance measures, if not as great as those of their counterparts without such instruction (Jepsen and de Alth, 2005). Policy discussions would benefit from further research regarding the best uses of assessments in English and the primary language for students at different stages of language development enrolled in bilingual instructional settings

Policy development discussions would also benefit from research that would inform assessment practices for students who are not receiving primary language instruction due to state policy or who are from low-incidence language groups, who are not enrolled continuously in a single school setting, or have special needs that might impact their language facility. The following research questions follow from the impact of the law in these circumstances.

## Research Questions

- What elements contribute to a valid and reliable assessment when the students are limited in their English proficiency and receive instruction primarily in English?

- What accommodations, or variations, are appropriate for English learners at the earliest proficiency levels when they are enrolled in English-only settings? How long should the accommodations be permitted?
- How can mobile students (e.g., migrants and students enrolled in juvenile facilities or alternative school settings) be effectively included in an assessment and high-stakes accountability system?
- What primary language assessments and/or accommodations should be provided to students who are speakers of low-incidence languages?
- How can the results from primary language assessments be incorporated into accountability systems when they are not universal indicators (i.e., not every student takes this test)?

## The Dual Obligations of Serving English Learners

Federal and state statutes and court cases have established that there is a dual obligation for serving English learners in our schools: the Civil Rights Act of 1964, Title VI, Federal Equal Educational Opportunity Act of 1974, *Casteneda v. Pickard* (1981). In addition to providing appropriate programs for them to meet grade-level standards in the content areas, as is required for all students, there is an additional and unique component necessary for English learners: that is, to develop their English language proficiency. Schools must under these laws provide programs for English learners that meet both of these important requirements.

The dual obligations are reflected in the NCLB Act. States and LEAs are now held accountable specifically for both the academic and language progress of English learners. The academic progress of English learners is measured and reported under Title I, and Title III requires that the progress and attainment of English listening, speaking, reading, writing, and comprehension be reported. The following sections describe how the dual obligation for serving English learners is addressed in California's policies to meet federal accountability requirements.

## *Academic Achievement: Title I Accountability Requirements*

Title I requires states to adopt content standards in English language arts and mathematics and establish yearly growth targets known as adequate yearly progress (AYP) for both of these areas. Progress is defined as meeting an annual target for increasing the percentage of students scoring at the "proficient" level. California adopted an ambitious definition of "proficient"; therefore, a student must have strong academic English skills to score at this level. Tests aligned to the state's standards are used to determine whether students score at the far below basic, below basic, basic, proficient, or advanced levels. The state tests are closely aligned to state academic standards for each subject tested and include the California Standards Tests (CST, Educational Testing Services, 2003), the California High School Exit Examination (CAHSEE, Educational Testing Services, 2001), and the California Alternate Performance Assessment (CAPA), which is used with students who have significant cognitive disabilities and are unable to take the CSTs. The NCLB Act requires that 100% of the students score at the proficient level in English language arts and mathematics by the year 2014.

Annually, district- and school-level AYP data for all students must be reported. The AYP data must also be disaggregated and reported for numerically significant subgroups of students, including English learners. This requirement was the cause of concern for educators across the United States because English learners exit the "limited English proficient" (LEP) category when they become fluent in English and have a better chance of scoring at higher levels on state standards tests. Consequently, it is difficult if not impossible to document current LEP students who are "proficient" on the state standards, especially if the achievement measures are administered in English. Moreover, since the LEP subgroup is not static (e.g., new students are continually added and others are reclassified out of LEP status), it is difficult to track the progress of ELs over time and account for their academic progress. In recognition of the difficulty every state and LEA has in meeting Title I AYP for the LEP subgroup, the U.S. Department of Education issued guidance in February 2004 that allowed for adjustments at both ends of the ELP continuum: (1) the inclusion of fluent English proficient student scores for a limited amount of time; and (2) the exclusion of the scores of English learners during their first year attending a U.S. school. In California, the Title I LEP subgroup includes the scores of reclassified English learners until they score proficient on the English language arts portion of the California Standards Test three times over any number of subsequent years.

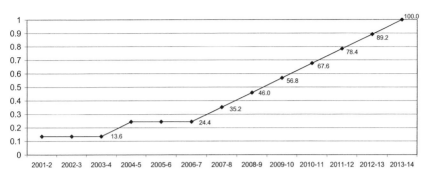

Figure 3.3. California's intermediate goals for English language arts for elementary schools, middle schools, elementary school districts, and middle school districts, from NCLB Accountability Workbook (January 31, 2003), California Department of Education. http://www.cde.ca.gov/nclb/sr/sa/documents/workbook082305.pdf

Figure 3.3 shows California's AYP targets for English language arts for the elementary and middle school grades (K-8). Similar projected trajectories are made for unified districts and the high school grades. All students, including each numerically significant subgroup, must meet the annual AYP targets. The AYP targets are not based on a growth model; instead, they define the percentage of students that must score at the proficient level each year. Each state adopted its own targets through the year 2014. The targets were not required to increase each year, which results in a "stair step" target structure over time. There is no comparability of the AYP measurements or targets across states.

## English Language Development: Title III Accountability Requirements

Title III of the NCLB Act requires states to develop three Annual Measurable Achievement Objectives (AMAOs) for English learners that relate to their development and attainment of English proficiency. The AMAOs are based on results from the state's annual English language proficiency assessment that must be aligned to the English language proficiency standards. Title III requires that the standards and assessment include all English learners (kindergarten through grade 12) and that each student be assessed in four skill areas: listening, speaking, reading, and writing. The required comprehension score is derived from the listening and reading components.

California adopted English language development standards in July 1999 (California State Board of Education, 1999) and began using the assessment aligned to the standards in 2001, the California English Language Development Test (CELDT, CTB/McGraw-Hill, 2004). The ELD standards are organized into four grade spans: kindergarten through grade 2, grades 3 through 5, grades 6 through 8, and grades 9 through 12. There are five proficiency levels: beginning, early intermediate, intermediate, early advanced, and advanced. The standard-setting procedures employed when developing the CELDT identified the cut scores for each of the five proficiency levels. Educators familiar with the progression of language acquisition for ELs from each grade span worked with technical experts to set the cut scores for each language proficiency level. Only the subskills of listening and speaking are addressed in kindergarten and first grade, but those skills along with reading and writing are included for grades 2 through 12.

The CELDT is initially given to all new English learners upon enrollment and annually in subsequent years until they are reclassified as fluent English proficient. When a student reaches the early advanced level overall, and no subskills are below the intermediate level, he or she may be considered for reclassification or redesignation to fluent English proficient status (RFEP). It should be noted that a student must also meet academic criteria and have positive feedback from parents and evaluations from school staff before reclassification may occur.

Currently, the CELDT does not fully comply with the NCLB Act requirements; to do so, reading and writing will need to be tested in kindergarten and first grade. Historically, since the 1970s when services for English learners in California were initiated, English language proficiency has been tested only for listening and speaking skills in kindergarten and first grade; the literacy components were added beginning with second grade. (See Bailey, chapter 1 for some of the issues and concerns with the literacy assessment of young EL students.) These policy decisions have implications for future research. Critical questions that need to be addressed include the following.

## Research Questions

- What elements contribute to a valid and reliable ELD assessment of literacy skills for young students? How does this differ from early literacy assessments such as are given to monolingual English-speaking students?
- What are the key strategies for developing the academic English skills needed for students to reach the proficient level on state content standards and assessments?

The operationalization of English language and literacy skills is evident in the three key Title III Annual Measurable Achievement Objectives.

## Annual Measurable Achievement Objective 1

The first AMAO focuses on annual gains in the percentage of children making sufficient progress in learning English. In order to establish AMAO 1, the metric for the annual growth target first needed to be established. To do so, a number of analyses were conducted on the first two years of data to determine the most reliable method for calculating annual growth in ELD as measured by the CELDT. It was not possible to use scale scores because the proficiency levels were not vertically equated across grade spans. Therefore, it was determined that changes in proficiency levels would be used to determine growth.

In California, there are three ways for students to demonstrate annual progress on the CELDT, depending upon their previous year's scores.

- Students at the beginning, early intermediate, and intermediate levels must gain one proficiency level per year until they reach the level where they are considered English proficient (early advanced overall, with no language subskill scores below Intermediate).
- Students at the early advanced level overall but with one or more subskills below intermediate must bring those subskills up to the intermediate level or higher.

- Once students reach the level considered "English proficient," the expectation is for them to maintain that level while they are working to meet academic content skills or other criteria required for reclassification. Students must continue to be tested with the CELDT annually until they are reclassified. Maintaining a proficient score can be justified as "progress" because the test becomes more difficult as students advance through the CELDT grade spans.

AMAO 1 TARGETS

The NCLB Act requires states to set annual increases in the percentage of students meeting the annual growth target. California adopted a rate of increase with smaller increments of growth at the beginning and larger increases in later years, to allow time for school personnel to increase their skills in helping students reach English language proficiency.

The Title III goal structure defines what percentage of students in an LEA makes the expected annual progress each year. The methodology for determining the starting point is similar to the Title I AYP requirements. In that method, schools are ranked, and the starting point is set at the percentage of students that meets the target in the school at the twentieth percentile of the state's total enrollment. For Title III, only LEP students with CELDT data were used. Also, Title III requires that LEAs be held accountable rather than schools, contrary to Title I growth determinations. Using the Title I method of selecting the starting point, 51% of students were making progress in learning English in 2003-4.

The Title III AMAOs require annual increases from 2003-4 to 2013–14. However, in Title III, LEAs are not expected to reach 100% proficient in 2013–14, as is required in Title I for academic performance. This makes sense because there are always new ELs entering the system; consequently, there is never a single point in time when all students will be proficient. The targets are shown on figure 3.4. Over the next few years, the AMAO reports and research about CELDT growth patterns could be helpful in identifying best practices for meeting the linguistic needs of students.

## Annual Measurable Achievement Objective 2

The second AMAO requires annual increases in the percentage of students attaining English language proficiency according to the

Proportion of Students Meeting Annual Growth Objective

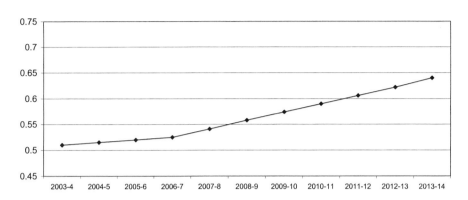

Figure 3.4. Annual Measurable Achievement Objective 1 targets, 2003-4 to 2013-14, from Information Guide, Preliminary 2004-05 Title III Accountability Data, California Department of Education. http://www.cde.ca.gov/sp/el/t3/documents/T304prelimguide.doc

state's English language assessment. AMAO 2 focuses on what percentage of students attains English language proficiency. Since this AMAO reflects the amount of time an individual child has been enrolled in a program, it allows the use of a cohort analysis. This system is reasonable because it allows for the analysis of longitudinal data. Targets can be set for students based on their English language proficiency levels when they enter California schools and their corresponding attainment of the English proficient level over time.

STUDENT COHORT

Unlike AMAO 1, the cohort for AMAO 2 does not include all students. Since this cohort measures the number of students who achieve English proficiency, it is unreasonable to expect all students to achieve English proficiency each year. Therefore, the cohort for AMAO 2 includes only those students who can reasonably be expected to reach English language proficiency at a given point in time. For example, a beginning-level student should not be expected to be proficient in English the following year. Students included in this cohort are those who have attended U.S. schools for four or more years, those who scored at the intermediate proficiency level the previous year, and those who scored at the English proficient level their second year who had been below the intermediate proficiency level the previous year. These targets allow for the growth of at least one level per year and expect continuous progress from students so that they do not remain in one level for an unreasonable amount of time. This timeline is consistent with literature in the field that indicates that it can take four or more years to acquire English proficiency (Collier, 1987; Cummins 1981; Hakuta, Butler, and Witt, 2000; Klesmer, 1994; Worswick, 2001).

The 2003 annual CELDT results showed that 33% of the state's English learners scored at the intermediate level. Forty-six percent of the students scoring at the intermediate level on the 2001 CELDT remained at that level in 2002. In 2003, 47% of the students who scored at the intermediate level made progress the following year. The inclusion of students scoring at the intermediate level on the previous year's test in the AMAO 2 cohort is intended to encourage school personnel to provide students with appropriate instruction so that they do not plateau at this level.

AMAO 2 TARGETS

The targets for AMAO 2 are parallel in structure to those adopted for AMAO 1. The twentieth percentile of the state's English learner enrollment with CELDT data determined the starting target, which was 30% of the cohort of students. As was done with the first AMAO, there are smaller gains targeted for the first three years. This is a rigorous target but should be achievable if LEAs provide more focused and effective instruction targeted to the needs of English learners. Figure 3.5 shows the target structure and the percentage of LEAs meeting the targets for AMAO 2.

Questions naturally follow from these two assessment objectives for EL students. These entail knowing more about assessment with young children and literacy development in EL students in particular. Moreover, to meet these targets, educators need to know more about what teaching and learning needs to occur for students to effectively progress each year.

## Research Questions

- How can literacy measures be appropriately included on language proficiency tests used for identifying English learners and measuring their progress in kindergarten and first grade?

Proportion of Students Achieving English Language Proficiency

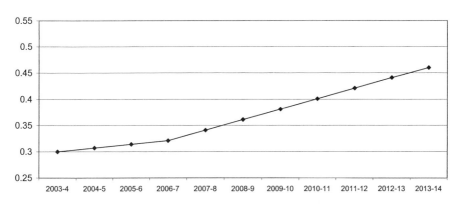

Figure 3.5. Annual Measurable Achievement Objective 2 targets,
2003-4 to 2013-14, from Information Guide, Preliminary 2004-05
Title III Accountability Data, California Department of Education.
http://www.cde.ca.gov/sp/el/t3/documents/T304prelimguide.doc

- How do early literacy tests designed for monolingual students
  differ from those that should be administered to English learners?
- What are the most effective strategies that can be used with students at each proficiency level to help them progress in their acquisition of English?
- In California, over one-third of the students are at the intermediate language proficiency level. What strategies help to move students beyond the intermediate level when they reach a plateau
  (e.g., they have scored at this level for more than one year)? Do
  these strategies differ by grade span?

## The Development of Academic Language:
## The Intersection of Title I and Title III

The ultimate goal for educating English learners is for them to become proficient in English and achieve at grade level; this also represents the intersection of Title I and Title III. For students to be
considered for reclassification, they must reach specified language
and academic criteria that demonstrate they can participate in
school on a par with their English-only peers. In other words, they
must possess academic English skills. In order to be fluent English
proficient in California, students must score at the early advanced

or advanced level overall, with no subskill scores below intermediate on the CELDT. (See also Bailey, chapter 1 for more information on the skills that are tested.) In California, this CELDT score is also known as the "English proficient" score. However, this criterion alone is not sufficient to reclassify students. They must also score at the basic to midbasic levels, at a minimum, on the CST for English language arts. Table 3.1 provides an overview of the component skills tested by the CST in English language arts and mathematics. Additionally, there must be parent consultation and a teacher evaluation regarding the student's readiness for reclassification.

On the 2004 CELDT, 279,295 of all English learners who took the annual test had scored at the English proficient level in 2003 and had not been reclassified as fluent English proficient. What are the possible reasons these students remained in the English learner category, scoring at the "English proficient" level and still not reclassified? Some of the students will be reclassified after they demonstrate readiness on the next cycle of the academic tests. Others may have become fluent in English, but still do not possess the academic English skills needed to score at the basic or higher levels on the CST. California has set high standards, and the linguistic demands needed to demonstrate proficiency are considerable. When faced with academic English, students encounter less frequently used vocabulary, complex syntax, abstract expressions, and are asked to interpret and produce complex oral and written language. They need to use the appropriate speech register and language appropriate for the function of the task at hand.

**Table 3.1 California Standards Test Components of ELA and Mathematics**

|  | Skills Tested | |
| --- | --- | --- |
| English Language Arts | | Mathematics |
| Literary response and analysis | | Number sense |
| Reading comprehension | | Algebra and functions |
| Word analysis, fluency and systemic vocabulary development | | Measurement and geometry Statistics, data analysis, probability |
| Writing strategies | | |
| Written and oral English language development conventions | | |

In order to thoroughly investigate the relationship of language proficiency scores and academic performance on state tests, there is a need for a longitudinal database with individual student identifiers to track actual progress and match scores across various tests. Until that time, it is not possible to fully investigate important basic questions in this area on a statewide level.

## Annual Measurable Achievement Objective 3

Many consider the third AMAO to represent the "academic English" objective, as it reports the percentage of English learners scoring at the state's proficient level on state assessments for English language arts and mathematics. The targets for this objective are the same as the Title I AYP targets established for all students, discussed above. The calculations for AYP of the English learner subgroup include (RFEP) students who have not scored proficient or above on the CST for English language arts three times.

Under Title I, if the English learners compose a numerically significant subgroup, they are included as part of the school-level accountability system. However, there are settings in which English learners are enrolled throughout schools within a district in small or scattered numbers. Under these circumstances, the academic achievement levels of English learners would not be reported under Title I. Title III provides a safeguard to ensure that the performance of English learners does not fall through the accountability cracks. AMAO 3 requires that the academic performance reflected in AYP for all English learners be aggregated and reported at the local educational agency level, which is usually a school district.

## Research Questions

- If a student is "fluent" in English (i.e., English proficient) but not scoring proficient on academic measures (e.g., CST), what specific instructional strategies and interventions are the most effective?
- What linguistic structures and functions need to be taught for various grades levels and content areas?

## From Research to Policy and Back Again

The NCLB Act Title III made significant changes to the ESEA regarding educational policies for English learners. For the first time, states were required to develop integrated accountability systems, including English language proficiency standards, assessments, and annual objectives for student performance. Similarly, reporting of the academic achievement of English learners as a distinct subgroup was required under Titles I and III. The targets for student progress in academics and English language are known as Annual Measurable Achievement Objectives. The English language proficiency objectives, AMAOs 1 and 2, are calculated based on data from the CELDT. AMAO 3 is based on AYP data from the CST, the CAPA, and the CAHSEE. The percentage of students that must meet the AMAOs increases each year through 2014.

The legal framework that governs the education of English learners in California is comprised of a complex set of state and federal statutes and court cases. This chapter includes a discussion of the legal framework because it provides the context for understanding how educational services are organized for English learners within the state and informs the development of accountability policies.

The professional literature and available empirical data informed the development of the Title III accountability policy. However, a variety of topics surfaced that would benefit from further research. Many of the current research needs fall under the umbrella of identifying the best strategies for assessing students under varying conditions. Other topics are focused on identifying effective instructional practices to further the academic and linguistic proficiency of English learners.

## Note

1. "English learner," a term used by the State of California, refers to limited English proficient students in federal statute.

## References

American Institutes of Research. (2004). *Effects of the implementation of proposition 227 on the education of English learners, K-12.* Washington, DC: Author.

California Department of Education. (2004). *Language census report.* Retrieved January 2005, from cde.ca.gov/ds/sd/lc/elprct.asp

California State Board of Education. (1999). *English language development standards for California public schools: Kindergarten through grade twelve.* Sacramento: California Department of Education.

*Casteneda v. Pickard.* (1981). 5th Circuit Court of Appeals, Texas, Document 648F.2d989.

Civil Rights Act. (1964). Document PL88-352, 88th Congress, July 2.

Collier, V. P. (1987). Age and rate of acquisition of second language for academic purposes. *TESOL Quarterly, 21,* 617–641.

CTB/McGraw-Hill. (2004). *California English language development test: Form D.* Monterey, CA: Author.

Cummins, J. (1981) Age on arrival and immigrant second language learning in Canada: A reassessment. *Applied Linguistics, 1,* 132–149.

Educational Testing Services. (2001). *California high school exit examination (CAHSEE).* Princeton, NJ: Author.

Educational Testing Services. (2003). *California standards test (CST).* Princeton, NJ: Author.

Elementary and Secondary School Act. (1965). Public Law 89-10, April 11.

English Language in Public Schools Initiative Statute. (1998). California Proposition 227.

Equal Educational Opportunities Act. (1964). Title VI.

Equal Educational Opportunities Act. (1974). Title 20, Chapter 39. Document 20USC, Sec. 1703.

Hakuta, K., Butler, Y. G., and Witt, D. (2000). *How long does it take English learners to attain proficiency?* (Policy Report 2000-1). Santa Barbara UC Linguistic Minority Research Institute.

Improving America's Schools Act. (1994). Public Law 103-382, October 20.

Jepsen, C., and de Alth, S. (2005). *English learners in California schools.* San Francisco: Public Policy Institute of California.

Klesmer, H. (1994). Assessment and teacher perceptions of ESL student achievement. *English Quarterly, 26*(3), 8–11.

National Clearinghouse for English Language Acquisition. (2004). Retrieved January 2005, from www.Ncela.gwu.edu/policy/states/reports/statedata/2002LEP/ *GrowingLEP0203pdf.*

No Child Left Behind. (2001a). Conference Report to Accompany H.R., 1, Rep. No. 107-334, House of Representatives, 107th Congress, 1st Session, December 13.

No Child Left Behind. (2001b). Title I: Improving the academic achievement of the disadvantaged. 107th Congress, 1st Session, December 13. (Printed version Washington, DC: George Washington University, National Clearinghouse for Bilingual Education.)

No Child Left Behind. (2001c). Title III: Language instruction for limited English proficient and immigrant students. 107th Congress, 1st Session, December 13. (Printed version Washington, DC: George Washington University, National Clearinghouse for Bilingual Education.)

Worswick, C. (2001). *School performance of the children of immigrants in Canada, 1994–8* (No. 178). Ottawa: Statistics Canada.

# CHAPTER 4

# A Conceptual Framework of Academic English Language for Broad Application to Education

ALISON L. BAILEY AND FRANCES A. BUTLER

In this chapter we describe a conceptual framework that antici-pated the needs laid out by Mayer in chapter 3 for the development of academic English language (AEL) tests, related curricula, and professional development materials (Bailey and Butler, 2002/3). The work that has gone into this framework addresses the needs of the states as the No Child Left Behind Act (2001) has come into ef-fect. The framework we have developed is evidence-based in that we are documenting the information needed to operationalize the AEL construct. The most immediate goal of this work is to characterize AEL for test development purposes so that test specifications and prototype tasks can be created to reflect language usage in aca-demic settings.

The initial evidence of the impact of language demands in aca-demic settings was present in studies of differential student perfor-mance where native-speaking or English-only (EO) students tended as a group to outperform English language learners (ELLs) (Abedi and Lord, 2001; Abedi, Lord, Hofstetter, and Baker, 2000; August and Hakuta, 1997; Butler, Stevens, and Castellon, chapter 2; Mac-Swan and Rolstad, in press). Researchers have inferred from this finding that lack of fluency in the English language is a barrier to student demonstration of content-area knowledge. Our plan has been to go beyond this inference and follow new lines of inquiry that will allow us to more directly specify the AEL demands critical to school performance that must underlie the development of for-mal test specifications and AEL tasks as well as the creation of classroom-based assessments and instructional strategies. (See also Davidson, Kim, Lee, Li, and López, chapter 6 and Heritage, Silva, and Pierce, chapter 7.)

The strength of an evidence-based approach to defining the AEL construct is that it provides a mechanism for capturing not just the linguistic features of language—vocabulary, syntax, and discourse and the characteristics of language use within and across content areas—but also the linguistic demands created and/or assumed by a broader array of stakeholders. That is, the wider educational community provides evidence of academic language in national content standards (e.g., National Science Education Standards, NRC, 1996), state content standards as well as standards-based tests (e.g., the California Standards Test, Educational Testing Services, 2003), and standardized achievement tests (e.g., California Achievement Test-6; CTB/McGraw-Hill, 2003; the Iowa Tests of Basic Skills, University of Iowa and Riverside Publishing, 1993). To facilitate this effort, classroom language demands must be systematically identified and prioritized according to specific criteria. In determining the basis of evidence for the language demands, we will continue to concentrate on what would count as evidence of AEL in the classroom. We are interested in capturing the language students actually encounter in school through input such as teacher oral language and textbooks and other print materials.

In sum, our current bases of evidence for specifying language demands (explicated further later in this chapter) are the following:

1. Empirical studies of ELL/EO student performance and language demands of content and ELD assessments
2. The language demands assumed in national content standards[1]
3. The language demands assumed in state content standards
4. The language demands assumed in English as a second language (ESL) standards
5. Teacher expectations for language comprehension and production
6. Classroom exposure to AEL, including teacher talk and textbooks

## Impact of Content Areas and Grade Levels

Achieving operational descriptions of AEL will require research in a range of academic contexts and will necessitate attention to at least two dimensions of potential variation: content-specific subject matter and grade level (Butler and Stevens, 2001). The first dimension of this work will cut across content areas (science, social studies, math, and language arts) to investigate a common core of AEL present in all subjects as well as to identify proficiency in AEL uniquely required in individual content areas. Figure 4.1 shows the hypothesized relationships between common core AEL and content area-specific AEL.

The second dimension will cut across grade levels (elementary through high school) to determine what AEL is developmentally appropriate for the specific grade levels and grade-level clusters. In the same manner we hypothesize a common core of AEL across content areas, we hypothesize a common core of AEL across grade clusters as well as grade or grade-cluster-specific AEL. Both types of information are necessary to provide an evidentiary basis for the AEL demands that must be assessed to determine ELL readiness for participation in the mainstream curriculum and for taking content tests in English.

The types of evidence laid out previously will allow for a comprehensive characterization of AEL across content areas and grade levels and thereby provide a strong evidential base for the develop-

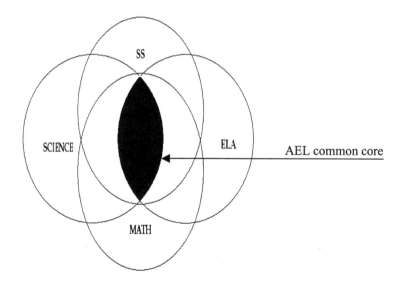

Figure 4.1. Hypothesized relationships between common core AEL and content area-specific AEL in the domains of math, science, social studies (SS), and English language arts (ELA), from Bailey and Butler, 2002/3. Copyright 2003 by CRESST. Reprinted with permission.

ment of specifications for AEL proficiency tasks and curricula. Throughout this chapter we illustrate design decisions and chosen approaches with examples from fifth-grade science content, classroom language, texts, standards,and so on, where possible.

## Evidentiary Basis for Operationalizing Academic English Language Proficiency

To move from the existing descriptions of the AEL construct presented by Bailey in chapter 1 to the development of tasks and test items that measure its proficiency, we need to adopt a framework that documents the sources of information that will feed into the operationalization of the construct. The recent National Research Council (NRC, 2002) call for evidentiary bases to educational research in general provides one of the main motivators (along with the need to reflect the many different contexts within which AEL arises) to assemble a wide array of data from a variety of sources to operationalize the AEL construct; thus we integrated within one model (1) content assessment language demands; (2) national standards of professional organizations (e.g., NRC); (3) state content standards (California, Florida, New York, and Texas); (4) ESL standards; (5) teacher expectations of language comprehension and production across grades; and (6) analyses of classroom language and textbooks. As mentioned above, in each case possible, we have focused on the science content area and the fifth grade (or clusters including fifth grade) to provide in-depth examples. However, the following framework we describe can be applied to all grade levels or grade clusters, to the four major content areas (language arts, math, science, and social studies), and to all four modalities of language (listening, speaking, reading, and writing). Figure 4.2 schematizes the different types of evidence we have been able to identify for the purpose of operationalizing proficiency in AEL. Each of the sources feeds into the AEL construct definition. The construct itself can serve as the basis for generating new assessments as well as new curriculum and teacher professional development materials. Each of these three applications is, of course, related to the others, as captured by figure 4.2. To be most effective, assessment and curricular development should ideally go hand in hand, and both, perhaps most critically, will rely on teacher understanding of the nature and

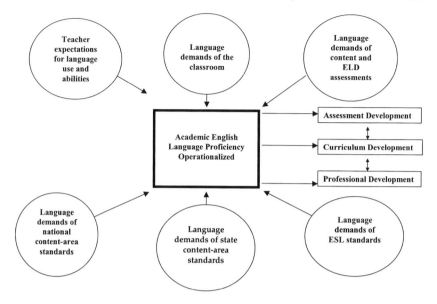

Figure 4.2. Evidentiary bases for the operationalization of AEL
proficiency, adapted from Bailey and Butler, 2004.

development of AEL. We turn now to examine each of the six evidentiary sources of the AEL construct.

## ELL/EO Student Performance and Language Demands of Content and ELD Tests

Research on the assessment of ELL students to date has focused
primarily on the validity of content assessments and the role of accommodations to provide a valid and reliable measure of ELL
school performance. As mentioned earlier, numerous studies of differential student performance have found that native speaking or
EO students tend as a group to outperform ELLs (Abedi and Lord,
2001; Abedi, Lord, et al., 2000; August and Hakuta, 1997; Butler et
al., chapter 2; MacSwan and Rolstad, in press). Abedi, Leon, and
Mirocha (2000), for example, found that ELL student performance
suffers in those content-area subtests that are thought to have greater
language complexity than others. These findings suggest that student language proficiency impacts performance on standardized
content assessments according to the nature of the English lan-

guage demands of the content area assessed. While this finding is not surprising and has already been widely assumed, Abedi, Leon, et al. provide statistical evidence, across multiple school districts and across multiple states, of weaker ELL performance in contrast with much higher EO performance in general and in content areas that have greater language demands (e.g., language arts).

Furthermore, Butler et al., chapter 2 report on a pivotal study that examined student performance on language proficiency assessments and concurrent performance on content assessments. This study provides baseline data for identifying a threshold of language ability needed to determine whether ELLs' content assessment performance is considered a valid measure of their content knowledge. Butler et al. show evidence of some ELL students classified as fluent English proficient (FEP) and redesignated fluent English proficient (RFEP) performing on a par with EO students (50 normal curve equivalent [NCE] or above) on the content assessment subtests, suggesting that for those students, performance on the content test reflected their content knowledge. Other ELL students, however, those designated as limited English proficient (LEP), while scoring in the competent range on the language assessment, did not score on a par with EO students on the content assessment subtests. These results suggest that further differentiation of language performance in the upper proficiency range on ELD assessments is imperative to determine if these particular students are struggling with language, content, or both.

The research to date shows clear relationships between language proficiency and performance on content tests for ELLs. However, these findings are strongly tempered by a number of major concerns and considerations. While language is likely a dominant factor for ELLs, student English language proficiency does not explain all the variation found in content performance. Additional background factors play a role in predicting student performance, namely parent educational level and family income level. Opportunities to learn and display knowledge of both content and academic language are also potentially important predictors of student performance. These factors are not, to our knowledge, included in the extant data sets supplied by school districts, nor are they factors that are easily measured and quantified. While previous research has been useful in answering some of the questions about assessment validity, serious limitations have curtailed the ability to draw useful conclusions about the assessment of ELL students. These limitations are laid out more specifically in Bailey, Butler, and Abedi (2000/5), as:

*The lack of uniformity in defining ELL students.* Terms such as ELL, FEP, LEP, RFEP, and bilingual are used in the national dialogue about students who are acquiring English as a second language. Unfortunately, these terms are often operationalized differently across school sites within a district, across districts, and across states, causing difficulties with respect to data interpretation. For example, some districts and states have redesignation criteria that are based on different measures or different cut scores. Furthermore, students are not redesignated at the same time during the school year across districts and states. Therefore, student designations may not be accurate at the time research data are compiled or collected.

*The lack of comprehensive data sets.* Often existing data files do not include important data elements such as student ethnicity, parent education, and family income because the data were not collected for research purposes. In addition, item-level data are often not available.

*Limitations regarding the aggregation of small numbers of ELL students across districts.* While we are interested in ELL/EO comparisons at the national level, the variability in student background variables and the designation criteria across districts do not allow us to combine data sets in order to make large-scale comparisons. This issue is even more critical when studying assessment issues by subgroups of ELLs.

*The limitations of language assessments.* A major weakness in the study of ELL assessment is the lack of a standard instrument that can be used to assess English language proficiency in a manner that is parallel to the way language is used on the content assessments.

This last limitation brings us to the crux of the purpose of developing AEL proficiency assessments. The number and degree of difficulty of lexical, syntactic, and discourse demands students encounter on content-area tests has already been documented (Bailey, 2000/5; Butler et al., chapter 2). However, there is a mismatch between these language demands and the lesser demands found in ELD tests (Butler et al., chapter 2). The content of many existing language proficiency tests is not adequate to measure the level of language proficiency necessary for taking standardized achievement tests and for full participation in the mainstream classroom.

A test expressly developed to test knowledge of the kind of English language skills (i.e., AEL) needed for school success would seem a more logical approach in the fair assessment of ELL students (Bailey and Butler, 2004).[2]

When we began our work on this framework for AEL applications, we envisaged tests of AEL proficiency that could serve as an intermediate step between English language tests for ELLs that primarily focus on social uses of language and the content-area assessments that contain the language of academic settings (Bailey and Butler, 2002/3). At that time we saw the potential of AEL tests to fill the assessment "gap" between the language demands of the existing ELD tests and the language demands we had identified on content tests. However, since that time, one effect of Title III of the NCLB Act has been to lead states to begin to replace their former ELD tests with assessments of AEL (see Bailey, chapter 1 for a review of tests and Mayer, chapter 3 for discussion of Title III impact).

In response to these large-scale changes, we would caution that we do not now neglect the need to know how well students are also acquiring social uses of English alongside both general and content-specific academic English. One way to have test developers, and educators more broadly, still pay attention to both social and academic uses of language is to adopt a modular approach to ELD test development. For instance, at each grade level or cluster of grades, a test of ELD could be comprised of a grade-appropriate social component or module, a general academic language module, and various discipline or content-specific modules that capture the specialized language of the life sciences, chemistry, history, and so on.

## Language Demands of National Content Standards

National standards for the different content areas have been created by national organizations such as the National Research Council and the National Science Teachers Association. We focused our analysis on the National Science Education Standards published by the NRC (1996). These science standards comprise six chapters of standards for science teaching, professional development, assessment, content, education programs, and systems. The chapter that focuses on science content was examined for the language that students are expected to comprehend and use in science classrooms.

These national standards for science content are organized around what students are expected to know. There are eight standards presented in grade clusters—K-4, 5–8, and 9–12—with the exception of the standards for *unifying concepts and processes,* which cut across all grades in acknowledgment that this knowledge continues to develop over time. We focus on the 5–8 cluster in order to characterize the national science standards in some depth.

The 5–8 content standards include seven additional categories: *science as inquiry, physical science, life science, earth and space science, science and technology, science in personal and social perspectives,* and *history and nature of science.* We examined the implicit and explicit assumptions about the prerequisite language necessary for students to meet the standards (Butler, Bailey, and Borrego, 2002). Specifically, we identified the linguistic behaviors required of students by the standards. These language descriptors provide some measure of what students are expected to do in service of cognitive operations, for example, processing information in a specific manner or for a specific purpose. Thus, the fundamental abilities and concepts that underlie the *science as inquiry* category have students *focus; clarify* questions; *inquire; design* an investigation; *make* observations; *organize* and *collect* data; *take* measurements; *use* appropriate methods (e.g., math) and tools (e.g., computers); *interpret, summarize,* and *describe* data; *report* on inquiries by *writing, drawing,* and *graphing; communicate* scientific explanations; *describe* and *explain* findings; *identify* cause and effect; and *critique* and *consider* alternative explanations. The additional six categories document the content material (facts, scientific processes, etc.) that students are expected to know rather than characterize in linguistic terms how students will demonstrate knowledge.

## Language Demands of State Content Standards

The implicit and explicit statement of the prerequisite language made in the content standards of four states with large proportions of ELL students (California, Florida, New York, and Texas) provides further specificity about desired language proficiency at the different grade levels or clusters. As mentioned earlier, the language of standards reveals assumptions about what students must be able to do with language in the different content areas at the different grade levels. For example, an analysis of state content standards revealed that state science standards share common language functions and descriptors (Butler et al., 2002). Examination of the manner in which the standards for the four states refer to the language students will need at the elementary level revealed that students must be able to *analyze, compare, describe, observe,* and *record* scientific information. At the middle school level, students in all four states were required to *compare, explain, identify,* and *recognize.* At the high school level, the four states share just three language-related descriptors of desired student language use: *describe, explain,* and *recognize.*

These verbs provide a greater or lesser degree of explicitness in terms of what language is expected from students. That is, beyond the use of the verbs themselves, in order to compare science concepts and objects, students will likely need to know related vocabulary (e.g., other verbs such as *contrast*), already know rules for creating comparative adjectives (e.g., *bigger, wider*), be able to use syntax that sets up parallel constructions to make a comparison (e.g., phrasing such as *The green one is better than the yellow one . . . because the green one is clean and the yellow one is dirty*), and understand the purpose of comparison discourse in the academic setting (e.g., functions to explain science concepts, justify selections, argue a point of view, etc.).

Looking across the four states at one grade level (sixth),[3] we find that the language used in both California and Florida state standards is confined to what students should *know* or *understand.* The standards reflect the content students need to master, but there is no reference for how students should be able to demonstrate knowledge or the type of language students should be able to use to do this. New York and Texas, on the other hand, organize the standards by the science content students need to know as well as by how students need to demonstrate the knowledge with sample tasks. Indeed, both of the latter states provide a greater variety of descriptors in terms of language use than the former two states. For example, New York addresses the language associated with Earth science at the sixth grade by requiring students to be able to *explain* seasonal changes on Earth. Students must be able to create an Earth model and *describe* the arrangement, interaction, and movement of the Earth, moon, and sun. Also, students need to *plan* and *conduct* an investigation of the sky to *describe* the movement of celestial bodies. Students need to *explain* how the air, water, and land interact, evolve, and change, and *describe* volcano and earthquake patterns, the rock cycle, and weather and climate changes. This is evident when students *graph* temperature changes and *make* a record of earthquakes and volcanoes and *interpret* the patterns. The New York State standards provide sample tasks for teachers to use to judge whether a skill is evident in a student. For example, students are asked to construct an explanation based on their observations of a melting ice cube using sketches and a written description of what happens. These efforts by New York State can serve as just one useful resource to inform the development of specific AEL proficiency prototype tasks (see also Falk, 2005 for discussion of a standards-based approach).

## Language Demands of K-12 ESL Standards

ESL standards are also examined for assumptions about requisite language abilities for students to be considered advanced English language learners. At present we have examined the Teachers of English to Speakers of Other Languages (TESOL, 1997) standards, which represent a national set of standards to which many state ELD standards are aligned (e.g., New York). At the time of the writing of this volume, the TESOL organization is set to adopt the new WIDA standards as a replacement to the existing K-12 ESL standards (WIDA Consortium, 2005). Future work will need to look at the individual state ESL/ELD standards to determine the alignment between the TESOL/WIDA standards and those of other (i.e., non-WIDA) states. Currently, the TESOL standards are clustered in three grade groups. For the purposes of this chapter, we have collapsed across clusters because most of the language descriptors cut across all three grade clusters. The standards make a distinction between language identified by the TESOL standards for social and personal interaction (goal 1) and standards for classroom interaction for academic purposes (goal 2). There is some overlap, with a number of descriptors (35) that relay the kind of language necessary for each of the goals. These include *ask, clarify, express, imitate, listen, negotiate, participate, request,* and *respond,* which are required across all three grade clusters as well.

In both the social and academic contexts, students are expected to know a wide array of additional language functions: however, these are far more extensive in the academic standards (64 language-related descriptors in the academic language standards and 30 in the social language standards). Verbs unique to the academic language standards that cut across the three grade clusters include *ana-*

*lyze, contrast, define, elaborate, hypothesize,* and *justify.* Verbs unique to the social language standards that cut across the three grade clusters include *communicate, describe, elicit, engage, restate, recite,* and *talk.*

An important caveat here is that any effort to align an AEL assessment to national standards, individual state content standards, or ESL standards is undermined by the absence of data to support the choice of language repertoire, content coverage, and levels of difficulty that they adopt. For example, the TESOL standards identify *describe* as the kind of language needed to meet social language standards but not the academic language standards. However, *description* was seen to be used for academic purposes in observations of science classrooms (Bailey, Butler, LaFramenta, and Ong, 2001/4; Bailey, Butler, Stevens, and Lord, chapter 5). There are concerns about the validity of the standards on which the AEL conceptual framework is partially based. The underlying assumption is that the standards have all been systematically developed and validated and are all, therefore, of high quality in terms of completeness, reflection of the construct, and so on. The reality is that no matter how well intentioned the developers, the development of the standards, ELD and content area, was often a political process that yielded a compromise document. Furthermore, the ELD standards, if not based completely on ELA standards, come or are coming (not all states have ELD standards yet) from a domain (i.e., AEL) that is still evolving. The ELD standards, thus, should periodically be reevaluated as the construct becomes better understood.

One potentially powerful outcome of the linkage between state ELD standards and content standards and the alignment of ELD standards to ELD tests mandated by Title III of the NCLB Act (2001c) could be the acceptance of standards as working documents that are systematically updated and validated as matter of practice. McKay (2000) has specifically called for further theoretical and empirical work around the construction of standards in the ESL arena. Schleppegrell (2002), following suit, has made a critical analysis of the California ELD standards, showing discrepancies within them. Standards may be a reflection of ideals for school reform by a particular group of educators rather than a source of evidence for what and how students are being taught. Thus, we caution against taking standards at face value; rather, we recommend using them as a helpful starting point for identifying the kinds of language found in academic settings.

## Language Expectations of Teachers

Very little study of the linguistic expectations of mainstream teachers has been made, and even less is known about the language expected of ELL students as they are reclassified and enter mainstream (fluent English proficient) classrooms. (See, as an example of work in this area, the National Languages and Literacy Institute of Australia [NLLIA] ESL Bandscales [McKay, Hudson, and Sapuppo, 1994], in which ESL learners' language development is mapped in the context of mainstream learning in K–12.) However, it is conceivable that teachers have definite expectations for the linguistic sophistication of their students. Hicks (1994) points out that students are expected to respond to teacher interactions with context—appropriate uses of language, and that this expectation is part of the system of formalized schooling. Wong Fillmore and Snow (2000) argue that general education teachers, like all language users, tend not to make language expectations explicit to their interlocutors. However, in the case of students learning English, such explicit expectations for their language sophistication and use are exactly what they need to know. This is an issue to which we return later in this chapter.

Elsewhere there are suggestions that teachers do signal to students when they should and should not interact in the classroom and that these signals are related to grade-level expectations (e.g., Hadley, Wilcox, and Rice, 1994). A survey by Solomon and Rhodes (1995) reports vocabulary choice, parts of speech, and functions of language in the classroom setting as the most commonly articulated notions of AEL by ESL teachers. For further discussion of these few studies of teacher expectations and understandings of AEL, see Bailey, chapter 1. Certainly, given that there are so few studies in the area, we strongly suggest further study of teacher expectations of mainstream and ELL students across the grade levels. Such studies will help determine the language demands ELL students face in the opinions of the teachers who currently teach them or who eventually will.

## Language Demands of the Classroom

By describing the language embedded in oral and written classroom discourse, particularly characterizing the AEL of mainstream content-area classes that can serve as a baseline for AEL expectations, it will be possible to create a framework for English language assessment that is aligned with the language of classroom instruction and curricula materials (see also Scarcella, 2003). Available work comes primarily from the area of atypical language development, where researchers have found it difficult to articulate norms for language development in school-age children. This difficulty is due perhaps to the individualistic nature of language development after the early school years (i.e., the range of particularistic AEL contexts to which children are exposed by their choices of content classes in later grades, Nippold, 1995).

In the past, few studies examined the language of actual lessons over an extended period of time in order to carefully document and conceptualize academic language as it actually occurs (Solomon and Rhodes, 1995). Recently, researchers have begun to make sample selections of language in the classroom in both the oral and print domains as reviewed by Bailey, chapter 1. For example, Schleppe-grell (2001, 2004) contrasts such linguistic features as lexical density and clausal structures requiring nominalization and sentence embedding in spoken discourse and a textbook selection. By illustration, she finds the textbook language to be much more lexically dense and likely to use nominalization strategies (e.g., *the devastation of the Civil War*) rather than showing the pronominalization strategies more commonly found in oral discourse (e.g., *It was a devastating war*).

In chapter 5 Bailey et al. (see also Bailey et al., 2001/4) describe in some detail observations of fourth- and fifth-grade mainstream science classrooms, developing a matrix to illustrate teacher and student talk as they intersect different contexts of instruction (science concepts, vocabulary, application instruction). This information is complemented by linguistic and discourse analyses of fifth-grade math, science, and social studies textbooks. We suggest that such research initiatives be extended across all grade levels and content areas in the future in order to provide the specificity necessary for construct definition purposes.

## Evaluation of the Six Evidentiary Bases

The six bases from which we draw evidence of AEL will not and should not be given equal weight in the operationalization of AEL due to variation in the quality of information that they may yield. Specifically, given the need for validation of content and ESL standards, and the impressionistic nature of teacher expectations, the expert panel (personal communication, July 22, 2002) made the recommendation that CRESST focus on textbook analysis and analysis of classroom discourse in extant data sets as they become available. It was argued that this type of data will yield more consistent and higher-quality information than standards and expectations data. Current work under way on the language implicit in content standards will continue to inform our AEL operational construct efforts (Bailey and Butler, 2005). However, because of the issues stated above, the main focus will be on textbook and teacher language data. Further systematic examination of textbook language features and teacher language will provide a fuller picture of the language demands across both content areas and grade levels. Textbook analysis continues, with the investigation of language functions first examined in our classroom observation research, coupled with the analytic approach of Schleppegrell (2001, 2004) and others, to reveal the range of clausal complexity, lexical density, proportion of specialized academic words, and so on by content area and grade. In addition, differences in linguistic demands and features across genres (e.g., expository, evaluative, directive) have been noted. Our findings with regard to fifth-grade science textbooks generated by these types of analyses (reported in Bailey et al., chapter 5) can feed into AEL test specification efforts. These attempts to capture the linguistic characteristics of a range of genres go further than existing ELD assessments, which have tended to narrowly focus on narrative skills in their attempts to sample extended discourse skills.

## Broad Application of the AEL Construct Framework to Education

In the next sections, we focus on the application of the AEL construct in the areas of assessment development, curriculum development, and teacher professional development. Though the main focus will be assessment development, the other areas are included for completeness and to begin to outline a comprehensive treatment of AEL proficiency in educational arenas.

### Assessment Development

The *Standards for Educational and Psychological Testing,* published by the American Educational Research Association (AERA), the

American Psychological Association (APA), and the National Council on Measurement in Education (NCME) (1999), provides a comprehensive set of guidelines for test development and use and forms the basis of recent efforts by a number of agencies and organizations providing standards for assessment practice in K-12 education and the testing of individuals of diverse linguistic backgrounds more specifically. The CRESST *Standards for Educational Accountability Systems* (Baker, Linn, Herman, and Koretz, 2002) takes the joint AERA, APA, and NCME standards as a given and offers 22 guidelines for good testing practices, including 1that pertains directly to assessment practices with ELL students and 4 others that offer general guidance for sound assessment practices. Standard 12 focuses on issues of test validity with ELL populations who may differ from the general student population, on whom tests are typically normed (e.g., Davidson, 1994). AEL assessments and tasks will need extensive norming with students who are representative of the ELL students who will be expected to take the tests or accomplish the tasks. Validity in the test development process is crucial in this circumstance so that fair and equitable decisions can be made about the educational programming provided to ELL students. Baker, Linn, and Herman (2002) have argued that it is the responsibility of the states to request validity studies and data from the commercial test developers with whom they contract.

CRESST standards 4, 7, 9, and 11 are also pertinent to AEL assessment development and use because they (1) provide direction on issues of inclusion of all students (as now required by the NCLB Act [2001b]); (2) suggest the use of multiple tests, especially important with ELLs, in order to measure progress across a range of different contexts that may only occur in different testing contexts; (3) point out validity issues regarding the multiple purposes to which tests are often put, such as placement, progress, and diagnostic purposes; and (4) require that the technical quality of assessments be high. This is especially pertinent now that federal sanctions may be made against schools that do not demonstrate adequate yearly progress in ELD for ELL students as well as content-area knowledge for all students.

The Council of the Great City Schools and the National Clearinghouse for English Language Acquisition (2002) have recently offered a new set of standards expressly for the assessment of ELLs. The *Assessment Standards for English Language Learners* contains seven standards. We briefly review five that appear most relevant for AEL assessment, some with greater or lesser degrees of overlap with the CRESST assessment standards. Standard 1, like CRESST standard 4, makes inclusion of ELL students in content assessment a priority. Standard 2 calls for assessments that will allow students to demonstrate their language proficiency and academic achievement. Standard 4 raises the issue of norming all assessments used with ELL students, although it is not clear to us at this stage of inquiry on whom AEL assessments should be normed—redesignated ELL students or English-only students. The problem with norming assessments on redesignated ELL students is that the redesignation criteria are made through the use of the kinds of ELD assessments we have judged inadequate for the task of determining student proficiency in the language of academic settings. Standard 5, like CRESST standard 7, calls for multiple measures to be used so that decisions are not made on the basis of one test type. Finally, standard 6 advocates individual longitudinal data collection on ELL students. Indeed, this is a requirement now laid out in NCLB Title III (2001c) so that states will track progress at the student level. This seems particularly pertinent given the complexities of attempting to draw meaningful inferences from data aggregated at the school or district level due to high rates of ELL student mobility.

When done well, test development is a complex process that begins with determining what construct or constructs and associated skills are to be assessed. The process generally begins with a needs analysis that helps set the parameters for how the test(s) is to be used. A framework document is then developed to characterize the construct being tested. The framework draws from the research literature in the relevant fields and identifies gaps that may require additional research to help solidify the content base for next steps. The construct articulated in the framework must then be operationalized for actual test development. That is, the content in the framework document must be synthesized and translated into a working format/paradigm (facilitated by the creation of matrices) that will lead to test specifications, which in turn will guide task development.[4] The documentation of this process provides the validity foundation for the test(s) being produced (Bachman, 1990; Davidson and Lynch, 2002).[5]

The needs analysis for the current effort has identified shortcomings of widely used ELD tests (discussed in Bailey, chapter 1 and Butler et al., chapter 2). Performance on those tests does not provide a sufficiently broad indication of whether students have the English language skills necessary for success in the school setting; thus, there is a need at both the conceptual and practical level to move beyond the assessment of general/social language use exclusively to the assessment of AEL as well. Within school systems, a range of decisions must be made about ELL language ability, from intake decisions (whether students should receive ELD services or go directly to the mainstream classroom) to diagnostic evaluation to monitoring progress to redesignation decisions and readiness screening for content assessments. While this range of decision types is too broad for a single instrument, a framework such as the one we outline here that articulates an AEL construct can serve as a base for the development of multiple instruments for different purposes and can also provide the content base for curriculum development and teacher training. Each individual application would set parameters for specific needs.

At this time, we hypothesize that in this context, the student's ability to understand and use English across the four modalities and across content areas will be important. We envision a grade-cluster approach (K-2, 3-5, 6-8, 9-12) that will capture the developmental nature of AEL. Further, we anticipate combining modalities (reading/writing, listening/speaking, etc.) to capture the integrative nature of the modalities in the school setting (Gibbons, 1998). In addition, we acknowledge the interrelationship of language and cognition in the academic contexts being examined. While our focus is specifically on language, language is used for a purpose—often to achieve a function, to explain, to interpret, and the like—and thus is interwoven with cognition such that it is nearly impossible to exclude one from consideration of the other. For us the challenge is to create prototype AEL tasks that respect the interwoven nature of language and cognition but that have as their goal the assessment of language ability.

Our intent is an AEL framework that will provide guidance for moving from the conceptual to the ideal to the practical. We recognize that while operational constraints, both financial and logistical, are inherent in every testing situation, it is the ethical obligation of those who do test development and test administration to be principled in accommodating operational constraints. At a minimum, there must be a clear link between test tasks and the constructs being assessed. There must be adequate sampling of the skills being tested to allow for reasonable inferences about student ability. Administration and scoring must be carried out systematically by trained personnel. The unique needs of ELL students must be addressed in terms of test accessibility concerns, such as test presentation format, administration and response conditions, cultural interferences, and so on (see Kopriva, 2000 for further discussion). All of these factors influence the validity of inferences drawn from assessments (e.g., Messick, 1989).

Our immediate goal for operationalizing the AEL construct is to provide example specifications, task prototypes, and guidelines for teachers, agencies, and organizations needing to develop AEL assessments.[6] Our working characterization of AEL can be used as a point of departure for educators to develop their own test specifications, tasks, and related educational materials. Specifically, the example test specifications we provide will include the components shown in text box 4.1, which reflect earlier specification work by Butler, Weigle, Kahn, and Sato (1996). (See also Davidson and Lynch, 2002; Popham, 1978; and Turner, 1997, for important discussions on the development and use of test specifications.)

---

### Text Box 4.1

**Test Specification Components for Task Development**

1. General description—indicates behavior or skill to be tested.
2. Prompt attributes—detail what will be given to test taker, including directions.
3. Response attributes—describe in detail what test taker will do.
4. Sample item—explicit format and content patterns for item or tasks that will be produced from the specs.
5. Specification supplement—additional information including rating/scoring procedure, time allotment, etc.

---

Text box 4.2 provides an example of how components of the evidentiary framework we described above can be used to provide information to feed into test specifications. We can use results of the data analysis conducted on the textbooks to (1) inform the writing of test specifications (i.e., determine what characteristics of language demands need to be exemplified in test items); and (2) provide guidelines for evaluating and refining the language of the prototype AEL tasks themselves. Specifically, we will be able to align tasks to the data generated in the textbook analyses by conducting the same analysis on newly created AEL tasks. These tasks can be edited until language features and properties similar to the textbooks are obtained.

---

### Text Box 4.2

Example of Using an Analysis of Textbook Language Demands to Feed into Test Specifications

    The preponderance of fifth-grade science textbook selections analyzed across a variety of types and genres (e.g., expository reading passage, directives for lab activities, assessment) have a mean sentence length of between 10 and 18 words, and about 40% of these sentences required the processing of complex syntax (e.g., embedded clauses). Thus, fifth-grade prototype AEL tasks will need to reflect these linguistic features. Fifth-grade ELL students comprehending this type of language can be rated as advanced/proficient. Items reflecting the language of each grade (or grade cluster) will enable us to determine at what grade-level equivalent a student is comprehending language.

---

Text box 4.3 provides an example of test specification components applied to the creation of a draft prototype AEL task for the fifth grade using science as the situated context. This task is designed to measure student ability to comprehend an oral description (input), infer meaning from linking different parts of the description (a cognitive operation), and subsequently produce an explanation of what has been heard (output). This example also illustrates how information procured in the textbook analysis should inform the character of the linguistic features (e.g., sentence length and complexity) of the oral language prompt. The brief description of events that comprises the oral prompt has the science classroom as its theme but does not require knowledge of specific science content or concepts. However, comprehension of the task does assume the general (basic) knowledge that gravity will cause the glass bottle to drop to the floor if it falls off the table and that glass is a brittle matter that can shatter on contact with a hard surface. The series of comprehension checks can be used to indicate whether or not a student has initially understood the description. The student's performance on these comprehension questions must be taken into account when interpreting the student's performance on the explanation question. These checks will help assure a valid score of ability in explanatory language use by ruling out lack of comprehension as a source of interference. Moreover, examples and trial items before the presentation of the test item can be used to demonstrate to students that fully elaborated explanations (as exemplified in text box 4.3 by example response 3) are expected in order for a student to obtain a maximum score on such a task.

---

### Text Box 4.3

Example of Test Specification Components Applied to a Draft Prototype AEL Task

Domain, Oral Language: Comprehension of *Description* (Input) and Production of *Explanation* (Output)

*Situated context:* science lesson

*General description:* The task will test the test taker's ability to *listen to and comprehend* the language of description and in turn *produce* the language of explanation.

*Prompt attributes:* The test administrator will read aloud to the test taker a short passage with specified attributes that give sentence length and complexity, breadth and depth of vocabulary, etc., as determined by textbook and classroom discourse analysis (see also text box 4.2). The passage and explanation test question will be crafted to elicit the language of elaborated explanation. The task will have an academic theme or focus, but all information to provide an accurate response to the prompt will be included such that no specific content-area knowledge outside the prompt will be required.

*Response attributes:* The test taker will respond orally and will produce the necessary language to achieve the goals of the task, which include (1) demonstrating understanding of the language of description via responses to a series of comprehension questions; (2) using cognitive processes to infer relevant information from the descriptive passage; and (3) producing a fully elaborated explanation in response to the explanation question (see scoring guidelines under specification supplement below).

*Sample item/task read aloud by test administrator:* "I am going to read you a short passage and then ask you some questions about it."

A teacher specifically told a group of students to carefully place their experiments in a safe location in the classroom. One student placed his glass bottles very close to the edge of his desk. When the teacher turned around she was angered by what she encountered.

Who told the students to place their experiments in a safe location? (comprehension question)

Where did one student place his experiment? (comprehension question)

Who was angered? (comprehension question)

Explain as much as you can why the teacher was angry. (explanation question)

*Specification supplement (scoring guidelines):* (1) Test taker will need to accurately answer comprehension questions about the description heard (scored correct/incorrect regardless of language sophistication and fluency); (2) test taker will need to infer that the teacher in the prompt was angry because she saw that the student put his experiment in the wrong place; and (3) test taker will need to use the language of explanation (vocabulary, syntax, and discourse) to demonstrate that understanding to the tester.

*Rubric for scoring explanations:* Level 1: Response is characterized by an incomplete and/or incorrect answer.

Example response 1a: "The teacher was angry."

Example response 1b: "The teacher was angry because the student put the bottle on his desk."

Level 2: Response is characterized by a generally correct answer but the test taker has failed to elaborate how the inference (the bottle is in a dangerous position and could fall easily) was drawn.

Example response 2a: "He didn't follow directions."

Example response 2b: "The teacher was angry because the student did not follow directions."

(Note that in casual conversation, the explanations in responses 2a and 2b might be considered adequate. This highlights the difference between social uses of language and academic uses of language that hold speakers accountable for their claims, requiring them to verbally construct an argument citing evidence or logical conclusions to back up such claims. Moreover, these responses may be acceptable in many classrooms. Teachers may not require students to elaborate on their explanations in a way that overtly demonstrates to the teacher the necessary inferencing processes or steps in logical thinking.)

Level 3: Response is characterized by use of appropriate language to demonstrate a fully elaborated explanation. The test taker is able to infer that the teacher in the prompt was angry because the student put his experiment in the wrong place. The test taker demonstrates the use of the language of explanation to demonstrate that understanding (e.g., use of conditional tense for hypothetical events).

Example response 3: "The teacher was angry because the student did not follow directions. He put his bottle very close to the edge of the desk, which is a dangerous place because the bottle could fall and break."

*Source:* Bailey, A. L., and Butler, F. A. (2002/3). *An evidentiary framework for operationalizing academic language for broad application to K-12 education: A design document* (CSE Tech. Rep. No. 611). Los Angeles: University of California, National Center for Research on Evaluation, Standards, and Student Testing (CRESST).

---

We consider this a good draft prototype because it is both authentic and parsimonious. We believe it is authentic because it is reflective of the kinds of language students encounter and that we observed in fifth-grade classrooms described in Bailey et al., chapter 5. Among a number of speech functions, including comparison and explanation, students heard teachers provide descriptions of scientific terminology and describe scientific tasks and task-related materials. In turn, students were asked to give their own explanations of scientific concepts. Evidence of the need for familiarity with these particular language functions is further garnered from preliminary analyses of fifth-grade science textbooks. The inference that students must draw in this prototype AEL task is a cognitive operation that is frequently required in school (cf. observations of classrooms; the national, state, and ESL standards; and textbooks and standardized tests). Inference requires the student to do something with language—namely, make new meaning from already given meanings (see text box 4.3 for further details). The draft prototype task is parsimonious because it capitalizes on two modalities of language required of students in the classroom while serving to capture both input and output dimensions of language (see Bailey et al., 2001/4, figure 1). Specifically, the draft prototype task requires both listening comprehension—that is, the input from the teacher— and oral language production—that is, the output from the student.

In addition to the specifications for task development, in operational settings, specifications would also be produced for test assemblers. The test assembly guidelines would indicate the types and number of items needed to test specific skills and would include as well the ordering and formatting information for actually producing forms of the test.

Since assessments provide different kinds of educationally useful information, be that screening, formative, or summative (Gottlieb, 2001, 2003), different types of AEL assessments will be necessary to fulfill all the tasks to which assessments are generally put. An important guideline is therefore to first direct test developers to identify the specific purposes of the assessments they want to create (e.g., a screening measure for initial placement, monitoring individual student progress, creating diagnostic tools to inform instruction). Thereafter, test developers can move to create the types of tasks that are appropriate for the specific purposes of a given assessment.

## Curriculum Development

We offer here a brief and incomplete review of the few curricular initiatives that have explicitly addressed AEL. One relatively well-known curriculum is the Cognitive Academic Language Learning Approach (CALLA) devised by Chamot and O'Malley (1994) (see also Chamot, 2005 for an update on the approach). This comprehensive approach to integrating academic language throughout the different content areas provides teachers with a handbook of instructional strategies for explicitly teaching the nonspecialized academic language encountered across content areas as well as a number of self- and peer assessments for students and diagnostic assessments for teachers to use. In another initiative, a project aimed at high school and college students, Academic Language: Assessment and Development of Individual Needs (ALADIN), explicitly trains students how to process and learn from the language of college lectures and other academic presentation formats encountered in the college experience (Kuehn, 2000). Elsewhere, Kinsella (1997) has developed materials for classroom teachers, particularly in the area of teaching general academic vocabulary.

Although many methods and approaches for teaching ESL were originally designed for instructing adults, some have been adapted for use with K-12 students and intersect with general instructional pedagogy (e.g., Echevarria and Graves, 1998). Content-based language teaching/learning models currently used with ELLs offer teachers the opportunity to help students develop and enhance their second-language skills within meaningful academic contexts. Schools typically choose from a variety of language programs (e.g., ESL pull-out classes, bilingual classes, sheltered content/structured immersion, adjunct classes) that are designed to teach language skills concurrently with academic content (e.g., Snow and Brinton, 1997). All of these content-based models offer possibilities for combined emphases on academic language and content, with the goal being to support the development of both. Increasingly, general education teachers are facing the task of teaching ELL students within mainstream classroom environments with little or no help from existing curricular materials (Richard-Amato and Snow, 2005), although see Heritage et al., chapter 7 for an instructional approach that integrates academic language and content instruction applicable to all students. An approach to monitoring the quality of classroom instruction comes with the Sheltered Instruction Observation Protocol (SIOP) developed by Echevarria, Vogt, and Short (2000). This approach is less a curriculum, per se, than it is a way in which teachers can self-reflect on their own language input to ELL students. This can impact not only instruction but also teacher professional development.

Because all K-12 students must acquire academic language to some degree to be successful in the U.S. educational system, perhaps a second-language approach to teaching AEL would benefit native speakers and ELLs alike. Kuehn (2000) arrived at the same conclusion with high school seniors and college students needing to acquire AEL for the purposes of learning in higher-education settings. Students who are proficient in English are expected to acquire academic language as they move from grade to grade without necessarily receiving direct instruction specifically in AEL skills, and they do so presumably with varying degrees of success. ELLs, on the other hand, often receive direct instruction in language, though not necessarily in AEL, through the specially designed programs discussed previously. An implication of thinking about AEL as a second language is that mainstream teachers could benefit from professional development in proven pedagogical approaches for teaching ESL in an attempt to assure that all students learn AEL.

Teacher professional development in the area of AEL is the strand to which we now turn.

## *Teacher Professional Development*

The application of AEL to teacher professional development obviously overlaps with both AEL assessment and curricula development. Teachers need to know about the AEL construct to be in a better position to both assess and teach ELL students, and as we have speculated, perhaps all students. As Wong Fillmore and Snow (2000) point out, graduate courses that teach an understanding of language development have been sorely missed in teacher education programs to date. All teachers, not only ESL teachers, need to have a basic understanding and knowledge of linguistic features and processes. Without this background, teachers will not be able to adequately assess ELD nor target their teaching practices to student language needs. An example of work in the area of professional development and AEL includes Wellington (1994) who, while not referring to teachers of ELL students, nevertheless calls for a conscious awareness of language used by teachers in the science classroom in such a way that they can build up student understanding of words from simple names or labels to more challenging abstract concepts.

## Concluding Remarks

The results of the work proposed in this framework chapter should contribute to educational practices in the assessment and instruction of ELL students in multiple ways, among them the following goals (see also recommendations made by Bailey et al., 2000/5):

1. The identification of an empirically based ELL assessment validity threshold for defining the academic language proficiency of ELLs
2. The establishment of a much-needed set of principled procedures for implementing accommodations as an outgrowth of an established validity threshold for academic language proficiency
3. Impetus for teachers and those who teach teachers to extend the AEL construct to curriculum and professional development efforts

## Identification of an ELL Validity Threshold

An important outcome of the development and implementation of an AEL assessment will be the identification and recommendation of a threshold level of proficiency that would indicate when ELL performance on a standardized content test would be valid from a linguistic standpoint. The existing language tests do not appear to provide adequate specificity about student language at the upper range of proficiency (e.g., Butler et al., chapter 2) and thus are not likely candidates for establishing such a threshold. However, the notion of identifying a threshold of language proficiency is viable with an AEL test that will provide a clear indication that the language complexity of the content assessment is not a barrier to student performance. In order to establish a validity/language proficiency threshold, we propose the development of standards for defining proficient academic language ability in ELL students. One stumbling block to both research and policy with ELLs is the lack of uniformity in how school districts and states operationally define these students through their designations, such as LEP, FEP, RFEP, and bilingual. The lack of uniformity is due in large part to the different approaches states take to making their designations. An AEL test that allows for clear, objectively defined parameters for ranges of linguistic performance would help remove this stumbling block and make articulation of ELL performance uniform. These efforts would specify academic language proficiency characteristics aligned with the type of language used on content assessments and standards documents as well as that found in teacher expectations and classroom talk and print exposure. The threshold should be drafted based on extensive study of the academic language requirements for successful school performance and will require participation of language experts as well as policy makers.

## Formation of Principled Procedures for Implementation of Test Accommodations

While we have not focused specifically on test accommodations in this chapter due to the emphasis we wanted to place on AEL, there have been important research efforts directed at determining the effects of accommodation on test performance. One line of research in this area has been the simplification of the language of test items (e.g., modifying the language to enable students to more readily understand the content being tested). There is evidence that some ELL students benefit from a simplified form of content assessment, whereas others may not (e.g., Abedi, Courtney, and Leon, 2001; Rivera and Stansfield, 2001). One explanation for why there has been no unambiguous finding that simplification leads to better test results for ELL students is the criticism that language is not always easy to process if simplified (e.g., Wong Fillmore and Snow, 2000). Fragmenting extended discourse into shorter chunks can lead to difficulties when temporal and causal conjunctive adverbs (e.g., *however, moreover*) are removed from text.

Following Butler and Stevens (1997) and August and Hakuta (1997), where we see our initiative to measure AEL having an impact on the area of accommodations with ELL students is in the creation of a set of sorely needed procedures for implementing those accommodations. This would be an outgrowth of an established (i.e., validated) threshold for academic language proficiency. For example, if an AEL assessment determines that a student is having problems with AEL at the vocabulary level (i.e., has not reached a threshold for academic vocabulary, yet to be determined), then providing a dictionary as a form of test accommodation is meaningful. However, if a student's performance on an AEL assessment reveals challenges with extended discourse features of English, then no amount of thumbing through a dictionary is going to make the testing situation equitable or the student's score valid. While this example is perhaps overly simplistic, it is illustrative of the types of guidelines for the principled implementation of test accommodations called for by Haladyna and Downing (2004) and that can come from the assessment of AEL proficiency.

## Impetus for Extension to Curriculum and Professional Development

As the title of this chapter suggests and as we have outlined in brief above, we also see the framework as applicable to the development of instructional materials and for teachers' own learning. While the major focus of this volume and our own implementation of the framework for operationalizing AEL are on assessment, the detailed characterization of the language demands students encounter in the classroom has implications and immediate utility for these additional educational arenas. Detailed profiles of the types of lexical, grammatical, and discourse features that make up the language of classrooms, texts, and tests can serve not only as specifications for assessments but also as specifications for the content of curricula designed to explicitly teach AEL. Professional development programs can make use of the evidentiary bases of AEL to prepare teachers across all subject areas for the language demands of school. We encourage those with expertise in these areas to extend the framework and the research that comes from it for these purposes. Indeed, the objective of developing the framework is for all three educational arenas (instruction, assessment, and professional development) to be integrated in this manner so that the language constructs underlying what we teach, assess, and learn to teach and assess are well aligned.

Mayer, in chapter 3, detailed the scope and ramifications of the federal mandate for the annual assessment of English language proficiency. The current chapter, we hope, has identified the sources of information that should go into a comprehensive definition of the language demands students encounter in school so we can best monitor the growth in that proficiency. The next chapter shows how the framework we have described here has provided guidance for conducting relevant research of the AEL construct.

## Notes

1. The standards have assumptions about language expectations that we have to infer from the text.
2. By *school success* we mean access to curriculum materials, understanding teacher talk, participation in class with teacher and peers, and ability to handle content assessments—standardized and teacher diagnostic assessments and measures of progress and the like.
3. This was the grade closest to our chosen example grade (fifth) for which we were able to make suitable comparisons, given that the grade clusters used by the four states cut across the elementary and middle school levels in some instances.
4. Following Davidson and Lynch (2002), we use *task* to mean both individual *items*, such as a multiple-choice item, and constructed-response *tasks*, such as producing a writing sample.
5. See Butler et al., 1996; Butler, Weigle, and Sato, 1993; Kahn, Butler, Weigle, and Sato, 1995; and Weigle, Kahn, Butler, and Sato, 1994, for the description of a process for the California Department of Educa-

tion that led to specifications and prototype tasks anchored to the Adult English-as-a-Second-Language Model Standards for California.

6. *Prototype tasks* are defined here as tasks that have been tried out and revised and ultimately determined to produce ratable samples of student language (productive skills) or indications of student comprehension (receptive skills) and can serve as models for task writers.

## References

Abedi, J., Courtney, M., and Leon, S. (2001). *Language accommodations for large-scale assessment in science* (Final Deliverable to OERI, Contract No. R305B960002). Los Angeles: University of California, National Center for Research on Evaluation, Standards, and Student Testing (CRESST).

Abedi, J., Leon, S., and Mirocha, J. (2000/5). Examining ELL and non-ELL student performance differences and their relationship to background factors: Continued analyses of extant data. In *The validity of administering large-scale content assessments to English language learners: An investigation from three perspectives* (CSE Tech. Rep. No. 663). Los Angeles: University of California, National Center for Research on Evaluation, Standards, and Student Testing (CRESST).

Abedi, J., and Lord, C. (2001). The language factor in mathematics tests. *Applied Measurement in Education, 14*(3), 219–234.

Abedi, J., Lord, C., Hofstetter, C., and Baker, E. (2000). Impact of accommodation strategies on English language learners' test performance. *Educational Measurement: Issues and Practice, 19*(3), 16–26.

American Educational Research Association, American Psychological Association, and National Council on Measurement in Education. (1999). *Standards for educational and psychological testing.* Washington, DC: American Educational Research Association.

August, D., and Hakuta, K. (Eds.). (1997). *Improving schooling for language-minority children: A research agenda* (Committee on Developing a Research Agenda on the Education of Limited-English-Proficient and Bilingual Students, Board on Children, Youth, and Families, Commission on Behavioral and Social Sciences and Education, National Research Council, Institute of Medicine). Washington, DC: National Academy Press.

Bachman, L. F. (1990). *Fundamental considerations in language testing.* Oxford: Oxford University Press.

Bailey, A. L. (2000/5). Language analysis of standardized achievement tests: Considerations in the assessment of English language learners. In *The validity of administering large-scale content assessments to En-*

*glish language learners: An investigation from three perspectives* (CSE Tech. Rep. No. 663). Los Angeles: University of California, National Center for Research on Evaluation, Standards, and Student Testing (CRESST).

Bailey, A. L., and Butler, F. A. (2002/3). *An evidentiary framework for operationalizing academic language for broad application to K-12 education: A design document* (CSE Tech. Rep. No. 611). Los Angeles: University of California, National Center for Research on Evaluation, Standards, and Student Testing (CRESST).

Bailey, A. L., and Butler, F. A. (2004). Ethical considerations in the assessment of the language and content knowledge of English language learners, K-12. *Language Assessment Quarterly, 1*(2-3), 177–193.

Bailey, A. L., and Butler, F. A. (2005, April). *ELD standards linkage and test alignment under Title III.* Paper presented at the American Educational Research Association Annual Conference, Montreal, Canada.

Bailey, A. L., Butler, F. A. , and Abedi, J. (2000/5). General discussion and recommendations. In *The validity of administering large-scale content assessments to English language learners: An investigation from three perspectives* (CSE Tech. Rep. No. 663). Los Angeles: University of California, National Center for Research on Evaluation, Standards, and Student Testing (CRESST).

Bailey, A. L., Butler, F. A., LaFramenta, C., and Ong, C. (2001/4). *Towards the characterization of academic language in upper elementary science classrooms.* (CSE Tech. Rep. No. 621). Los Angeles: University of California, National Center for Research on Evaluation, Standards, and Student Testing (CRESST).

Baker, E., Linn, R. L., and Herman, J. (2002, Spring). No child left behind [Special issue]. *CRESST Line.* Los Angeles: University of California, National Center for Research on Evaluation, Standards, and Student Testing (CRESST).

Baker, E., Linn, R. L., Herman, J., and Koretz, D. (2002, Winter). *Standards for educational accountability systems* (Policy Brief No. 5). Los Angeles: University of California, National Center for Research on Evaluation, Standards, and Student Testing (CRESST).

Butler, F. A., Bailey, A. L., and Borrego, M. (2002, December). *Standards-based language assessment: A growing global challenge.* Paper presented at the Language Testing Research Conference, Hong Kong.

Butler, F. A., and Stevens, R. (1997). *Accommodation strategies for English language learners on large-scale assessments: Student characteristics and other considerations* (CSE Tech. Rep. 448). Los Angeles: University of California, National Center for Research on Evaluation, Standards, and Student Testing (CRESST).

Butler, F. A., and Stevens, R. (2001). Standardized assessment of the content knowledge of English language learners, K-12: Current trends and old dilemmas. *Language Testing, 18*(4), 409–427.

Butler, F. A., Weigle, S. C., Kahn, A. B., and Sato, E. Y. (1996). *California Department of Education adult English-as-a-second-language assessment project: Test development plan with specifications for placement instruments anchored to the model standards.* Los Angeles: University of California, Center for the Study of Evaluation (CSE).

Butler, F. A., Weigle, S. C., and Sato, E. Y. (1993). *California Department of Education adult English-as-a-second-language assessment project* (Final Rep., Year 1). Los Angeles: University of California, Center for the Study of Evaluation (CSE).

Chamot, A. U. (2005). The Cognitive Academic Language Learning Approach (CALLA): An update. In P. Richard-Amato and M. A. Snow (Eds.), *Academic success for English language learners* (pp. 87–102). White Plains, NY: Longman.

Chamot, A. U., and O'Malley, J. M. (1994). *The CALLA handbook: Implementing the cognitive academic language learning approach.* Reading, MA: Addison-Wesley.

Council of the Great City Schools and National Clearinghouse for English Language Acquisition and Language Instruction Educational Programs. (2002, March). *Assessment standards for English language learners* (Draft Executive Summary). Washington, DC.

CTB/McGraw-Hill. (2003). *TerraNova: The second edition (CAT-6).* Monterey, CA: Author.

Davidson, F. (1994). Norms appropriacy of achievement tests: Spanish-speaking children and English children's norms. *Language Testing, 11*(1), 83–95.

Davidson, F., and Lynch, B. (2002). *Testcraft: A teacher's guide to writing and using language test specifications.* New Haven, CT: Yale University Press.

Echevarria, J., and Graves, A. (1998). *Sheltered content instruction: Teaching English-language learners with diverse abilities.* Needham Heights, MA: Allyn and Bacon.

Echevarria, J., Vogt, M., and Short, D. J. (2000). *Making content comprehensible for English language learners: The SIOP model.* Needham Heights, MA: Allyn and Bacon.

Educational Testing Services. (2003). *California standards test (CST).* Princeton, NJ: Author.

Falk, B. (2005). Possibilities and problems of a standards-based approach: The good, the bad, and the ugly. In P. Richard-Amato and M. A. Snow (Eds.), *Academic success for English language learners* (pp.342–362). White Plains, NY: Longman.

Gibbons, P. (1998). Classroom talk and the learning of new registers in a second language. *Language and Education, 12*(2), 99–118.

Gottlieb, M. (2001). Four "A"s needed for successful standards-based assessment and accountability. *NABE News, 24*(6), 8–12.

Gottlieb, M. (2003). *Large-scale assessment of English language learners: Addressing educational accountability in K-12 settings* (TESOL Professional Papers #6). Alexandria, VA: Teachers of English to Speakers of Other Languages (TESOL).

Hadley, P. A., Wilcox, K. A., and Rice, M. L. (1994). Talking at school: Teacher expectations in preschool and kindergarten. *Early Childhood Research Quarterly, 9,* 111–129.

Haladyna, T. M., and Downing, S. M. (2004). Construct-irrelevant variance in high-stakes testing. *Educational Measurement: Issues and Practice, 23,* 17–27.

Hicks, D. (1994). Individual and social meanings in the classroom: Narrative discourse as a boundary phenomenon. *Journal of Narrative and Life History, 4*(3), 215–240.

Kahn, A. B., Butler, F. A., Weigle, S. C., and Sato, E. Y. (1995). *California Department of Education adult English-as-a-second-language assessment project* (Final Rep., Year 3). Los Angeles: University of California, Center for the Study of Evaluation (CSE).

Kinsella, K. (1997). Moving from comprehensible input to "learning to learn" in content-based instruction. In M. A. Snow and D. M. Brinton (Eds.), *The content-based classroom: Perspectives on integrating language and content* (pp. 46–68). White Plains, NY: Longman.

Kopriva, R. (2000). *Ensuring accuracy in testing for English language learners.* Washington, DC: Council of Chief State School Officers.

Kuehn, P. (2000). *Academic language assessment and development of individual needs. (A.L.A.D.I.N.): Book one.* Boston: Pearson Custom.

MacSwan, J., and Rolstad, K. (in press). Linguistic diversity, schooling, and social class: Rethinking our conception of language proficiency in language minority education. In C. Paulston and G. Tucker (Eds.), *Essential readings in sociolinguistics.* Oxford: Blackwell.

McKay, P. (2000). On ESL standards for school-age learners. *Language Testing, 17*(2), 185–214.

McKay, P., Hudson, C., and Sapuppo, M. (1994). The NLLIA ESL bandscales. In P. McKay (Ed.), *ESL development: Language and literacy in schools.* Canberra: National Languages and Literacy Institute of Australia.

Messick, S. (1989). Validity. In R. L. Linn (Ed.), *Educational measurement* (3rd ed., pp. 13–103). New York: Macmillan.

National Research Council. (1996). *National science education standards.* Washington, DC: National Academy Press.

National Research Council. (2002). *Scientific research in education (*Committee on Scientific Principles for Education Research, R. Shavelson and

L. Towne, Eds., Center for Education, Division of Behavioral and Social Sciences and Education). Washington, DC: National Academy Press.

Nippold, M. A. (1995). Language norms in school-age children and adolescents: An introduction. *Language, Speech, and Hearing Services in Schools, 26,* 307–308.

No Child Left Behind. (2001a). Conference Report to Accompany H.R., 1, Rep. No. 107-334, House of Representatives, 107th Congress, 1st Session, December 13.

No Child Left Behind. (2001b). Title I: Improving the academic achievement of the disadvantaged. 107th Congress, 1st Session, December 13. (Printed version Washington, DC: George Washington University, National Clearinghouse for Bilingual Education.)

No Child Left Behind. (2001c). Title III: Language instruction for limited English proficient and immigrant students. 107th Congress, 1st Session, December 13. (Printed version Washington, DC: George Washington University, National Clearinghouse for Bilingual Education.)

Popham, W. J. (1978). *Criterion referenced measurement*. Englewood Cliffs, NJ: Prentice-Hall.

Richard-Amato, P., and Snow, M. A. (2005). Instructional strategies for K-12 mainstream teachers. In P. Richard-Amato and M. A. Snow M.A. (Eds.), *Academic success for English language learners* (pp. 197–223). White Plains, NY: Longman.

Rivera, C., and Stansfield, C. W. (2001, April). *The effects of linguistic simplification of science test items on performance of limited English proficient and monolingual English-speaking students.* Paper presented at the annual meeting of the American Educational Research Association, Seattle, WA.

Scarcella, R. (2003). *Academic English: A conceptual framework* (Tech. Rep. No. 2003-1). Santa Barbara: UC Linguistic Minority Research Institute.

Schleppegrell, M. (2001). Linguistic features of the language of schooling. *Linguistics and Education, 12*(4), 431–459.

Schleppegrell, M. (2002, May). *Grammatical and discourse features of the target genres in California's English language development (ELD) standards.* Paper presented at the UC LMRI Annual Conference, University of California, Berkley.

Schleppegrell, M. (2004). *The language of schooling: A functional linguistics perspective.* Mahwah, NJ: Lawrence Erlbaum.

Snow, M. A., and Brinton, D. M. (Eds.). (1997). *The content-based classroom: Perspectives on integrating language and content.* White Plains, NY: Longman.

Solomon, J., and Rhodes, N. (1995). *Conceptualizing academic language* (Research Rep. No. 15). Santa Cruz: University of California, National Center for Research on Cultural Diversity and Second Language Learning.

Teachers of English to Speakers of Other Languages (TESOL). (1997). *ESL standards for pre-K-12 students.* Alexandria, VA: Author.

Turner, J. (1997). Creating content-based language tests: Guidelines for teachers. In M. A. Snow and D. M. Brinton (Eds.), *The content-based classroom: Perspectives on integrating language and content* (pp. 187–200). White Plains, NY: Longman.

University of Iowa. (1993). *Iowa tests of basic skills-complete battery, level 13: Form L.* Chicago: Riverside.

Weigle, S. C., Kahn, A. B., Butler, F. A., and Sato, E. Y. (1994). *California Department of Education adult English-as-a-second-language assessment project* (Final Rep., Year 2). Los Angeles: University of California, Center for the Study of Evaluation (CSE).

Wellington, J. (1994). Language in science education. In J. Wellington (Ed.), *Secondary science* (pp. 168–188). Chatham, UK: Mackays of Chatham.

WIDA Consortium. (2005). Retrieved January 31, 2005, from http://www.wida.us.

Wong Fillmore, L., and Snow, C. (2000). *What teachers need to know about language.* ERIC Clearinghouse on Languages and Linguistics. Retrieved August 1, 2000, from http://www.cal.org/ericll.

# CHAPTER 5

# *Further Specifying the Language Demands of School*

ALISON L. BAILEY, FRANCES A. BUTLER,
ROBIN STEVENS, AND CAROL LORD

Information about exposure to academic English in the classroom context can provide the linguistic and discourse data necessary for the creation of language demand specifications. The details of the language to which students are exposed in oral interaction and in print during science lessons, mathematics problem solving, and social studies activities can be used in conjunction with the other factors (e.g., state content standards) we have identified already in chapter 4 (figure 4.2) as critical in the operationalization of the AEL construct.

The nature of the academic language that students encounter in K-12 classrooms can be articulated in terms of four broad language domains: oral academic language exposure, written academic language exposure, oral academic language production, and written academic language production. Academic language exposure and production can be characterized as input (from teachers) and output (from students), respectively. Academic language exposure experienced by students includes teacher talk and exposure to classroom print materials such as textbooks and worksheets. Academic language production by students includes student talk and print materials produced by students such as essays and completed worksheets.

A detailed documentation of the academic language used in mainstream content-area classes can serve as a baseline for the development and refinement of assessments of academic language proficiency and curricula materials. The two studies described in this chapter provide such baseline data. The first study was an exploratory research project that employed qualitative methods to characterize the oral academic language used by teachers and students in fourth- and fifth-grade mainstream science classrooms.[1]

The second study provides detailed analyses of textbook language in three subject areas—mathematics, science, and social studies—at the fifth-grade level. The study yields descriptions of vocabulary, grammar, and the organization of textbook discourse as well as comparisons across these three subject areas. Together the two studies attempt to further our understanding of what students are required to do with language in mainstream classrooms. The findings allow us to begin to fill in the gaps that surround the academic English language (AEL) proficiency construct.

While there have been numerous attempts to promote content-based English as a second language (ESL) instruction (e.g., Coelho, 1982; Kinsella, 1997; Richard-Amato and Snow, 1992; 2005; Snow, 2001; Snow and Brinton, 1997), the dearth in content-based language tests has been recognized in the field of ESL study (Turner, 1997). The need to define, operationalize, and document academic language in order to create such assessments remains. Describing oral and written classroom language has implications for both educational research and practice. The information from the research efforts described in this chapter could have broad applications by providing empirical evidence about the nature of the language all students must understand and use in and across subjects. Not only test developers but teacher trainers, curriculum developers in subject areas, and textbook writers all benefit from this information. While our main focus in this chapter is on implications for AEL test development, we also note instances when our research findings may impact curriculum and teacher professional development, where appropriate.

The work described in this chapter focused on the upper elementary grades for a number of reasons. First, by empirically documenting language demands within just one or two adjacent grades, we can provide more in-depth descriptions of the language used rather than surface-level findings that demand further research before researchers can have confidence in the results. Additionally, concentrating the initial efforts at one level allowed for the creation and refinement of instrumentation before expanding efforts to other grade levels.

Second, upper elementary grades were selected for these studies because beginning in the fourth grade, instruction focuses less on literacy skills embedded in social language and more on negotiating academic content. Instead of learning to read, upper elementary students are reading to learn (National Research Council, 1998). In the upper elementary grades, the content areas become more specialized, and the classroom discourse becomes more linguistically complex and cognitively demanding.

Third, the focus on a key transitional grade such as the fifth grade (commonly the last grade in elementary school) is helpful because it sets the target criteria by which teachers and students can judge the end point of students' developmental progress throughout the elementary grades. The target in this instance is the use of language by fifth-grade mainstream content-area classes, and progress can be operationalized as how well students are acquiring and, from an instructional perspective, being equipped with the necessary academic language to meet the demands expected of students as they graduate the elementary level. Other key transition grades that would be equally well served by such a concentration of language research effort are, of course, the last grades of middle school or junior high, as students prepare to move on to high school, and the last grade of high school, as they encounter the language demands of increasingly discipline-specific classes (e.g., chemistry, psychology).

## Characteristics of Oral Academic Language in the Science Classroom

For the first research study, the emphasis was on oral language in the classroom. Teacher and student oral language was observed during science content instruction over a period of several weeks across several different science lessons taught by a number of different teachers. This type of observation data allows for a broad descriptive representation of language use and vocabulary choice rather than fine-grained structural analyses that require transcription of verbatim speech. The primary research questions of this study included (1) How does teacher language function in the classroom? and (2) How do teachers support academic vocabulary growth? The inductive approach taken toward the data led to the development of a matrix of teacher-produced academic language within three instructional contexts: concept instruction, vocabulary instruction, and process/application instruction.

We deliberately focused on mainstream science lessons to help determine the language demands that English language learners

(ELLs) will eventually face once they have been redesignated for instruction in mainstream classes. A guiding assumption of the work reported here is that equitable inclusion of ELLs in the classroom and in the assessment process for accountability begins with equitable exposure to and learning of the language of the classroom and of standardized content assessments. While ELLs may have well-developed proficiency in everyday talk in their first language and very often in English—their second language—these students may not have had the opportunity to gain proficiency in the language of the classroom (Gibbons and Lascar, 1998).

There has been increasing interest within the field of science education in the role of language in science instruction and learning (e.g., Fradd and Lee, 1999; Halliday and Martin, 1993; Keys, 1999; Rivard and Straw, 2000). This interest appears to comprise at least two strands. One pertains to issues of equity—namely, the opportunity to learn or access science curricula and the fairness of current assessment procedures used with cultural and linguistic minority students that mirrors the very motivation of this research in spirit (e.g., Lee, 2001). The second strand, to which this research may also contribute in part, focuses on the nature of classroom discourse and how it can inform educators about the conundrum of why student scientific understanding does not necessarily change and mature as a result of being taught science concepts (e.g., Lemke, 1990). Specifically, it was hoped that this research would illuminate how science concepts are presented to students linguistically—revealing the assumptions teachers may make about students' linguistic capabilities to handle science concepts as well as how students may incorporate the language of science and the academic environment into their own scientific reasoning.

To capture the use of academic language in mainstream science lessons, teacher oral language used in the classroom (henceforth *teacher talk*), and to a lesser degree student talk, was observed during content instruction and then analyzed. Evidence of academic language use in a variety of functional contexts within science lessons was the focus of the data analyses in this study.

The term *academic language* has meant different things to different researchers (see Cummins, 2000 for a recent review) as well as different things to different teachers (Solomon and Rhodes, 1995). This empirical study of classroom language expanded prior operationalizations of AEL (namely, lexical, syntactic, and discourse/

rhetorical [Bailey, 2000/5]) to include greater emphasis on the functions of language in the classroom. This view of AEL corresponds to that of many of the teachers reported in Solomon and Rhodes. These teachers identified academic language in terms of the language needed by students to effectively participate in classroom activities. According to Chamot and O'Malley (1994), academic language functions (e.g., being able to *explain, describe, contrast*) are "the tasks that language users must be able to perform in the content areas" (p. 40). They are the range of communicative intents for which a teacher or student may use language in the classroom. This feature of analysis, and one of the central foci of the work reported here, draws on the speech act theories of Austin (1962) and Searle (1970), which suggest that each communicative attempt serves a functional purpose or role. The communicative intent of the interaction serves as the unit of analysis. That is, each intent was categorized discretely by language function (e.g., *explanation, description*) rather than structural/formal boundaries.

ELL students who are reasonably proficient speakers of everyday English but who have not had as extensive an exposure to complex syntax, idioms, and depth of vocabulary (e.g., antonyms, synonyms) as most native speakers of English of the same age may find lessons more challenging because their language proficiency levels do not match the demands of the academic language of the classroom. ELL students may easily understand an interrogative sentence such as *Where do you think the fins on a whale are?* because it is the sort of language that they may encounter in everyday speech or in widely read materials such as newspapers and magazines. However, the same request for information may be conveyed in very different language in a classroom setting. For example, *What is your best estimate of where the fins are located on a whale?* This version of the question includes not only the unfamiliar use of *best* (to mean *most accurate*) and the formal *are located* for *are,* but also an embedded wh-question in the second clause: . . . *where the fins are located on a whale?*

The acquisition of academic language is critical for effectively negotiating the content and interaction of the classroom, and teachers have a range of instructional approaches available to help them support student acquisition of academic language. A brief review of pedagogical approaches helps to provide a framework for characterizing the practices observed in the science lessons and the academic language associated with these practices. Constructivists view learning as an active endeavor that involves mental manipulation and revision of existing schema. According to this view, children learn best through active interaction with others and their environment. These interactions lead them to continually assimilate or interpret new information, fitting this information into existing structures or schema (Piaget and Inhelder, 1969). In extending this view to the teaching of academic language, teachers would build on existing schema, in this case less formal language skills, to help students expand their language skills to the academic domain (e.g., Gibbons, 1998).

Piaget (1967/1972) theorized that as children develop cognitively, more language is necessary to support thought structures or schema. As students progress through school and continue to construct and refine their knowledge of the world, they are forced to elaborate their language use in the academic domain. Students are often required to access three kinds of knowledge—social arbitrary, physical, and logico-mathematical—to demonstrate their understanding of a given concept. For example, in a science classroom, a teacher may ask students to compare two objects. To do this, students must incorporate social arbitrary knowledge (e.g., use of a term such as *centimeters*), physical knowledge (e.g., descriptions of the objects), and finally logico-mathematical knowledge (comparison of the objects' various features). Vygotsky (1962) viewed language as an important tool that mediates understanding. Through language children construct their understanding of reality. In addition, Vygotsky (1978) believed that children learn best through the help of experts who present challenges within a child's zone of proximal development (ZPD), the distance between the child's actual developmental level (what can currently be accomplished independently) and the level of potential development that can be achieved with adult guidance. In the classroom, for example, teachers often scaffold activities for students to help them complete tasks through discussion, use of open-ended questions, problem solving, or modeling. (For a recent example of constructionist influence on science instruction, see Polman and Pea, 2001.)

Common components within many constructivist-influenced curricula that were evident in the teaching observed in this study are discussion and active student participation within activities, incorporation of students' prior knowledge, collaborative work, and joint problem solving. Initially, teachers and students discuss what students already know or wish to know about a thematic subject and may even create semantic maps or charts to remind students of their learning journey. Teachers may also explicitly teach metacognitive or metalinguistic strategies to help students independently construct knowledge later. Examples of constructivist curricula and practice include cooperative learning, inquiry- or project-based learning (i.e., learning through authentic activities), and performance-based assessments.

Direct instruction also promotes active student involvement within learning. In contrast to constructivist teaching, which encourages students to participate in shaping the content and concentration of the lesson, in direct instruction the teacher explicitly teaches students skills in the desired content area (e.g., Gersten and Carnine, 1986; Rosenshine, 1986; Rosenshine and Stevens, 1986). Several direct instruction curricula, such as the Direct Instruction Model of the University of Oregon (trade name DISTAR) in the reading/language arts, math, and social studies domains (Adams and Engleman, 1996) promote highly regimented and teacher-scripted approaches to learning. Common components of direct instruction curricula that were observed in this study include choral response and repetition of information by students, a rapid pace of instruction, systematic and scripted lessons, and explicit and immediate student correction.

In many mainstream classrooms today, teachers use a variety of instructional strategies within an individual lesson in order to convey knowledge, introduce vocabulary, and create mental models for their students. Most teachers use both explicit and implicit approaches by incorporating both constructivist and more directive or behavioral strategies. Effective teachers appear to be better attuned to the type of instruction and level of challenge that individual students require (McDonald, Pressley, and Hampston, 1998). They are also better able to coordinate different techniques and to incorporate minilessons or serendipitous events into ongoing instruction.

Many educators and theorists promote teaching strategies that incorporate multiple modalities or multiple intelligences (Gardner, 1993). For instance, students may be guided to construct knowledge via a kinesthetic route through their involvement in physical games and hands-on activities. Teachers may incorporate visual aides such as graphs or diagrams into instruction, use technology to "concretize" concepts, or display artifacts for independent student exploration within the classroom. Indeed, because students have a range of learning styles, teachers need multiple instructional strategies to help them acquire academic language proficiency.

Effective instruction requires teachers to combine their pedagogical beliefs and content knowledge with effective instructional discourse. As Wong Fillmore and Snow (2000) write, "Teachers need to understand how to design the classroom language environment so as to optimize language and literacy learning and to avoid linguistic obstacles to content area learning" (p. 8). In presenting material, a teacher must not only have a solid grasp of conceptual information but must also be able to use effective communicative strategies. In addition, teacher awareness of student home-language patterns and communication styles is essential (Wong Fillmore and Snow, 2000). Culture and culturally influenced discourse patterns (e.g., Delpit, 1995; Heath, 1983; Philips, 1972) can hinder communication between teachers and students and may increase the risk of misinterpretation or miscomprehension. For some students, academic discourse patterns present greater challenges in understanding content material. Teacher communicative strategies, therefore, are key to students' active construction of new information or knowledge.

There is a tradition of research exploring the social and cultural dynamics found within classroom discourse (e.g., Cazden, 1980, 1988, 2001; Erickson, 1987; Gee, 1996; Gutiérrez, 1995; Philips, 1972). Using ethnographic methods, researchers have investigated the social organization of classrooms and its influence upon discourse patterns. The current study of classroom language, however, concentrates primarily on the language functions and academic vocabulary that teachers and students use within the classroom.

The techniques and approaches for teaching ESL also provide insight into academic language instruction for all students, including native English speakers. Justification for this stems from the articulation of *academic English as a second language* for many students. In this view, academic language is thought to be learned primarily in a formal, structured context rather than in the informal environment of a student's home. However, we know that the closer a student's home language matches the language used in school, the less likely the schism between academic uses of language and everyday uses of language. Students who are proficient in English are expected to acquire academic language as they move from grade to grade without necessarily receiving direct instruction specifically in academic language skills, and they do so with, presumably, varying degrees of success. ELLs, on the other hand, often receive direct instruction in language, though not necessarily in academic language, through specially designed programs, discussed above. Within this context, a question pursued here is: Do mainstream teachers currently support the acquisition of academic language in some of the ways ESL teachers support the acquisition of ESL? An implication of this inquiry (e.g., as noted by Kaufman, 1997) is that mainstream teachers could benefit from professional development in proven pedagogical approaches for teaching ESL in an attempt to assure that all students learn requisite English language skills.

Furthermore, many K-12 content-area teachers now experience the pressures of teaching ELLs without the benefit of training in ESL methodology. Although methods and approaches for teaching ESL were originally designed for instructing adults, some have been adapted for use with K-12 students and intersect with general instructional pedagogy. (See Echevarria and Graves, 1998 for examples of adaptation.)

## Study Methods

### *Participant Schools*

The data collection methodology for this study included a series of observations of fourth-, fourth/fifth- combined, and fifth-grade classrooms within four Southern California public school districts and a publicly funded school not affiliated with a school district. The five schools included in this study represent economically and ethnically diverse populations within the Los Angeles County area. Anywhere between 25% and 71% of a school's student population was eligible for free or reduced-price lunch, an indication of the income status of the students' families. Enrollment by ethnicity also varied among the schools. Although most of the observed classrooms had Caucasian students as the majority ethnic group, Latino students represented a significant proportion of the student population in four out of five schools and were the majority in two of the five schools. In addition, African American students were significantly represented in one school.

In total, 10 classes were observed across the grade levels. Ten teachers and one technology instructor were observed. While the choice of classes was general education science, in reality, the English language skills of the students could not be assumed to be uniform across the 10 classrooms. Indeed, the proportions of students still considered to be acquiring English by their teachers in these general education classes differed considerably, ranging from a few students to more than half of the students in one class; all of these ELL students had been designated by the district as sufficiently proficient in English to be included in a mainstream classroom.

## Instrumentation

In order to document teacher talk, the Academic Language Exposure Checklist (ALEC), an observation checklist for classroom language use, was developed a priori based on the literature dealing with functional approaches to language use (Austin, 1962; Searle, 1970) and existing instruments. (For a similar instrument designed for teacher use in the classroom, see Chamot, 2005; Chamot and O'Malley, 1994). The ALEC has four main sections. The first, *Classroom Activities,* contains four questions on classroom activities observed, materials used, and interlocutors addressed. The second, *Teacher's Language Use in Instruction,* consists of four questions involving oral language functions and academic vocabulary. The third, *Student Oral Language,* involves five questions on oral language functions, academic vocabulary, and student lack of understanding. The fourth, *English Only (EO) versus English Language Learners (ELLs) Practices,* consists of two questions on teacher and ELL/EO language use.

## Procedures

Prior to observations, teachers were notified that the focus of the study would be on the academic language encountered by students during regular science classes. Study participants were asked not to make any special preparations so that—as much as possible—a typical science lesson could be observed. Each classroom was observed twice during regular science periods, except for one class that was observed three times. The observations ranged from 40–70 minutes, with an average of 55 minutes. There were at least two and sometimes three observers during the 21 observations to help maximize the breadth and depth of the observation field notes. It was hoped that by having multiple observers, the information transferred to the checklists from the field notes would be a more complete and accurate portrayal of the language used in the classroom interactions. If teachers were available after class, they were asked if the specialized academic vocabulary used during lessons had been introduced to the students previously. This allowed observers to differentiate when teachers were introducing new vocabulary from when they were reviewing vocabulary.

The language of the students was primarily noted in terms of student responses and interactions with the teacher in a whole-class setting. To form a more complete picture of academic language used within science classrooms, observers collected artifacts that were used during classroom visits. The print items collected consisted of textbooks, teacher-created worksheets, published materials, and website activities. In addition, before each class began, researchers made note of the language used on bulletin boards, posters, and other print media in the classroom.

A number of steps were necessary for data reduction after classroom observations and observer checklists were completed. The data were entered into the format for NUD*IST 4.0 (1996-2000). NUD*IST 4.0 allowed for the examination of teacher and student language across observations using the same categories preassigned on the ALEC. The task of coding teacher talk was divided among the research team, with one team member responsible for the initial coding of a specific part of the ALEC. Given the exploratory nature of this research, coding decisions were then discussed by the entire team to reach consensus. A research analyst blind to the initial coding decision-making process was then trained to independently code 16% of the data in terms of communicative intent, context of instruction and, where relevant, subtype for vocabulary and process/application instructional contexts. Reliability was calculated as the percentage of agreements divided by agreements and disagreements. Agreement on coding communicative intents was 95%, agreement for coding contexts of instruction was 93%, and agreement for subtypes within vocabulary and process/application instruction was 90%.

Because this study was exploratory, the sample size was relatively small. While the generalizability of the findings is thus limited, a major intent of the study was to develop a methodology for future research of this nature applied beyond science classrooms and the upper elementary grades.

## Science Lesson Content

The science topics covered were relatively similar across grades. Science content that combined the fourth- and fifth-grade Science Content Standards for California Public Schools for physical, life, and earth science topics were taught. There were, however, two exceptions: one fourth/fifth-grade class and one fifth-grade class included units on ocean life such as whales that did not appear in the state standards at these grade levels. These standards are desired by the state but are offered as guidance and are not obligatory (California State Board of Education, 1998). Classrooms were also similar in terms of participant structures. However, more experiments were conducted by the students themselves in fifth-grade classrooms. The fourth/fifth-grade and fifth-grade classes also appeared to include more variety in terms of activities (e.g., discussion of videos, creation of crossword puzzles, use of magnifying glasses and microscopes).

### Teacher Talk Observed during Science Lessons

Figure 5.1 provides a visual representation of the categories used for the analysis of teacher talk observed during science lessons.

This matrix illustrates the intersection of instructional contexts (the relationship of a given utterance within the larger classroom dialogue) and teacher communicative intents (the purpose of a given utterance). Three categories of instructional contexts appear on the horizontal axis: (1) science instruction; (2) academic vocabulary exposure or instruction; and (3) process/application instruction. On the vertical axis, three categories of communicative intents appear: (1) oral language functions; (2) repair strategies; and (3) classroom management. The shaded cells indicate the relative frequency of instances in which a specific communicative intent (explanation, description, etc.) was observed across classroom visits. The shading of the cells represents only a rough indication of the occurrences of oral language functions, repair strategies, and classroom management discourse across the contexts of instruction. There was no a priori criterion (i.e., no external reference point) by which to judge

| | Context of Instruction | | | | | | | | |
| --- | --- | --- | --- | --- | --- | --- | --- | --- | --- |
| | Science Instruction | Academic Vocabulary Exposure or Instruction | | | | Process/Application Instruction | | | |
| | Concept Instruction | Introduces term using definition | Introduces term using synonym | Introduces term using example | Introduces term using repetition | Presents and ensures students understand task | Presents instructions/ techniques to accomplish task | Presents materials needed to accomplish task | Presents a strategy to help students accomplish task |
| **Oral Language Functions** | | | | | | | | | |
| **Explanation** | | | | | | | | | |
| **Description** | | | | | | | | | |
| **Comparison** | | | | | | | | | |
| **Assessment** | | | | | | | | | |
| **Repair Strategies** | | | | | | | | | |
| **Clarification** | | | | | | | | | |
| **Paraphrasing** | | | | | N/A[a] | | | | |
| **Classroom Management** | | | | | | | | | |
| **Directing Instruction** | | | | | | | | | |
| **Directing Behavior** | | | | | | | | | |

Note. Darkly shaded cells occurred most frequently across observations (> 10 instances). Lightly shaded cells occurred less frequently. The unshaded cells indicate that no interaction for those categories was observed. This does not mean that the specific communicative types would not occur in instruction.

[a] This cell cannot be filled because a paraphrase by definition cannot be a verbatim repeat of a previous utterance, but rather must modify it in some way.

Figure 5.1. Matrix of individual instances of teacher talk observed during fourth- and fifth-grade science lessons, from Bailey et al., (2001/4). Copyright 2004 by CRESST. Reprinted with permission.

whether the frequency of instances of any given type of communicative intent was high or low and therefore representative of other science classes at the same grade levels.

Within *context of instruction,* teaching practices—the methods teachers use to impart information to students—are defined as (1) science instruction; (2) academic vocabulary exposure or instruction; and (3) process/application instruction. A combination of deductive and inductive approaches was used to formulate these categories. In addition, these approaches capture the variety of instructional contexts observed in fourth- and fifth-grade science classrooms. Science instruction entails the teaching of content material that includes, but is not limited to, scientific theories, concepts, and facts. Academic vocabulary exposure and instruction includes both nonspecialized and specialized academic vocabulary that may be explicitly or implicitly introduced by the teacher. Finally, process/application instruction involves the multiple teaching practices teachers use to assist students in classroom activities.

Within *communicative intent,* a combination of deductive and inductive approaches to the data analyses enabled the identification of the following salient teacher communicative intents: four oral language functions, two repair strategies, and two classroom management categories. The four oral language functions identified are: (1) *explanation,* defined as "to make clear or easy to understand by giving information, to give reasons for"; (2) *description,* defined as "to say or write what something is like, to provide a verbal picture"; (3) *comparison,* defined as "to examine or look for differences and/or similarities between two or more things" (adapted from the Cambridge International Dictionary of English, 2001); and (4) *assessment,* which for the purposes of this study is defined as a language function that denotes the informal evaluation of students' comprehension and knowledge during the course of a lesson and not formal testing. The critical distinction made in the operational definitions for this study between an explanation (e.g., *Plants require sunlight and water for development*) and a description (e.g., *A sunflower has bright yellow petals and a long green stem*) is that an explanation addresses a scientific process whereas a description provides a characterization of a scientific object or phenomenon. These are the functions for which teachers put their language to use in the science classrooms observed in this study. While other functions of language are possible in a classroom context (e.g., summation of what students learn in a lesson), they were not observed in these classrooms.

Repair strategies are those utterances used by a speaker when communication breaks down. They differ from the language functions because their intent is to recommunicate the original information to make it accessible to the listener. They are interactive in nature in that they usually require some indication on the part of the listener that the communication failed. Teachers, then, will use a repair strategy when they sense that their original utterances failed to adequately transmit the intended information to students. These repairs may be self-initiated on the part of the teacher (e.g., the teacher realizes that students do not understand something by their silence) or they may be other-initiated (e.g., students signal to the teacher that they do not understand) (Schegloff, 2000; Schegloff, Jefferson, and Sacks, 1977). Repair strategies here exclude those instances in which teachers reformulate their own ungrammatical sentences. However, in other regards, a broad approach to repairs is taken compared with other applied linguistics research that has confined repair analysis to adjacent or relatively closely occurring utterances (Schegloff, 2000). This is done in order to best capture teachers' attempts to repair their communicative acts either by clarifying (e.g., teachers can clarify by repeating, elaborating, or providing more specificity) or by paraphrasing their previous utterances and/or printed texts used during a lesson or even across lessons.

The two repair strategies identified in the data are (1) *clarification,* defined as "to make clear or easier to understand by giving more details or a simpler explanation"; and (2) *paraphrasing,* defined as "to repeat something written or spoken using different words, often in a simpler and shorter form that makes the original meaning clearer" (Cambridge International Dictionary of English, 2001). These repair strategies were used by the teachers in conjunction with any or all of the language functions, presumably to ensure that students understood the information being presented. Although elaboration is a form of clarification that may occur in the classroom context, teachers were primarily observed clarifying by repeating themselves or providing more specificity (e.g., distinguishing among concepts) in terms of the science concepts, academic vocabulary, or activities they were teaching.

In the literature, paraphrasing has been identified as a form of conversation repair (e.g., Abunahleh et al., 1982). However, in some instances, paraphrasing has a pedagogical purpose that differs from clarification. Although it sometimes appears similar to clarification in that it supports the repair of communication problems across instructional contexts and can itself be a form of clarification, it can also function to avoid repair in some instances. By first using language familiar to students and then paraphrasing what was said using academic language, some teachers were able to avoid having to repair their explanations and descriptions because they guided and scaffolded students' meaning making from the outset of the interaction. In this latter sense, paraphrasing may not be useful simply for the avoidance of problems—rather, it may be used as a proactive teaching tool taught to teachers for ESL/EFL instructional purposes.

The two classroom management categories are (1) *directing instruction;* and (2) *directing behavior.* Both were identified inductively from the data. Directing instruction refers to occasions when teachers give students explicit instructions during classroom activities (e.g., "Write your name on the top of the paper"). Directing behavior refers to occasions when teachers give students instructions regarding how they should behave in the classroom (e.g., "You should be sitting quietly during the movie"). Directing instruction was observed in academic vocabulary instruction and process/application instruction; directing behavior was observed only in process/application instruction.

To facilitate fourth- and fifth-grade science instruction, teachers used the oral language functions of explanation, description, comparison, and assessment and the repair strategies of clarification and paraphrasing. Explanation and comparison were most frequently recorded on the ALEC and were observed in 8 of the 10 classrooms. Assessment and paraphrasing were observed in three classrooms, description in two, and clarification in just one.

During science lessons, teachers exposed students to academic language within a range of instructional contexts. It was possible to characterize the primary instructional contexts as science instruction, academic vocabulary exposure or instruction, and process/application instruction. In each of these three contexts, teachers used all four language functions and both repair strategies. Regardless of context, the students were predominantly exposed to the language of explanation and description. Use of the classroom management categories by teachers was almost entirely confined to process/application instruction, rarely surfacing in the context of academic vocabulary instruction and not at all in the context of science instruction. In sum, students were required to attend to multiple functions across all instructional contexts during science lessons. Below we provide greater detail and examples of these main findings.

## The Context of Science Instruction—Developing Basic Conceptual Understanding

Instruction fell into just four functional categories—*explanation, description, comparison,* and *assessment*—though additional categories such as synthesis and summation might be expected in the science classroom.

EXPLANATION

Explanation was most frequently used to (1) demonstrate scientific relationships; (2) make scientific concepts understandable; and (3) give reasons for scientific theories and experiments.

(1) Teachers explained the scientific relationships of the stars and the sky, predators and prey, and plants and insects, among others. In example 1, the teacher explains how certain fish might have mutualistic relationships.[2]

EXAMPLE 1 (FOURTH GRADE)

*Teacher:* Does it have a mutualistic relationship? The clown fish will actually protect the sea anemone. That's a mutualistic relationship.

(2) Teachers also used the language function of explanation to make scientific concepts understandable. Some of the scientific phenomena that teachers explained were territorial fish, hybrid plants, plant reproduction, and photosynthesis. In example 2, the teacher explains the function of roots in a plant.

EXAMPLE 2 (FOURTH/FIFTH GRADE)

*Teacher:* The roots of the plants. Its job is to deliver water. Running up the stem, it only goes one way. It always goes up.

(3) Explanation was used to give the scientific reasons for theories and experiments. In a different fourth/fifth-grade classroom, the teacher introduced the scientific process of "crossing." He explained to the students that a scientist might take two of the same type of flowers but of different colors and then cross them. This process would produce the same flower but of a third color. The students then interacted in a lab to practice "crossing" paper flowers. After the lab was completed, the teacher introduced the concept of controlled pollination and then explained the reason why scientists cross flowers and plants, as illustrated in example 3.

EXAMPLE 3 (FOURTH/FIFTH GRADE)

*Teacher:*   What you did was you controlled the pollination. You crossed your flower with someone else's flower. Scientists do this to produce new types of flowers and fruits.

DESCRIPTION

Teachers used description to give students a mental picture of a scientific concept. Teachers described food chains, sand erosion, and plant growth, among other things.

One fourth/fifth-grade teacher described the process of photosynthesis. She told the students that a plant makes its own food by taking light from the sun. In example 4, she describes how a plant absorbs light through its leaves.

EXAMPLE 4 (FOURTH/FIFTH GRADE)

*Teacher:*   It moves. The plant has leaves like a dish, a satellite dish, to get light.

Although this example could be categorized as a comparison, it has a distinct feature that makes it a description. In this case, the teacher likened the leaves of a plant to a satellite dish to help the students see in their minds how the flat and long leaves move toward the sun to absorb as much light as possible. The teacher was not trying to compare the mechanical aspects of the satellite dish with a plant, but rather was attempting to paint a detailed, visual picture for her students.

COMPARISON

Comparison was used in fourth- and fifth-grade science instruction to compare (1) a new scientific theory, concept, or fact to another theory, concept, or fact that is familiar to the students; and (2) the similarities and differences among two or more scientific theories, concepts, or facts.

(1) Teachers introduced new scientific theories, concepts, or facts by comparing them to other theories, concepts, or facts that were already familiar to the students. This technique is aligned with the constructivist notion of activating student background knowledge. In one classroom, a teacher described the differences in the seasons of the Northern and Southern hemispheres. First, he asked the students what the weather was like in Southern California in

the summer. The students replied that it was sunny and hot. Then he asked an English language learner from the Southern Hemisphere what the weather was like in July in her country. She said the weather was cold because it was winter. Finally, to ensure that the comparison had taught the students that seasons are opposite in the Northern and Southern hemispheres, he asked a comparative question, as seen in example 5.

EXAMPLE 5 (FOURTH/FIFTH GRADE)

*Teacher:*     When it is summer here, what is the weather in Perth, Australia?

*Student:*     Opposite season. Winter.

In this example, the language function of comparison serves multiple purposes. The teacher was able to activate student prior knowledge, introduce a new scientific fact, and assess whether the concept was learned by using a series of comparative questions.

(2) Teachers frequently compared two or more scientific theories, concepts, or facts, presumably to ensure that students understood their differences and similarities. This helped students learn how to categorize multiple scientific concepts, for example. Teachers compared the solar system to the digestive system, gray whales to orcas, and omnivores to herbivores and carnivores. One teacher discussed the function of each individual part of a flower with his class. He demonstrated that a plant needs the stigma of the flower to reproduce. The function of the stigma, then, is to attract pollen. In example 6, the teacher illustrates how a stigma attracts pollen by comparing it to a magnet.

EXAMPLE 6 (FOURTH/FIFTH GRADE)

*Teacher:*     This right here would be yellow white, called the *stigma,* a sticky part. (*Teacher uses a diagram shown on an overhead projector.*) What does your brain say would be the reason for [the] sticky part? Think about a *magnet (gestures, with hands coming together).*

*Student:*     Something gets stuck.

*Teacher:*     Yes, something gets stuck. . . . [A] flower has a *mechanism,* if very colorful "bzzz" (*makes the sound of a bumblebee*) *attracted* for [*sic*] *pollen.*

After the teacher was certain that the students understood how the stigma of a flower functioned like a magnet, the teacher compared the stigma to a previous science unit on whale reproduction.

EXAMPLE 7 (FOURTH/FIFTH GRADE)

*Teacher:*  Flowers have *mechanisms* of *attraction* like whales have *echolocation.*

In examples 6 and 7, comparison allowed the teacher to demonstrate the interconnectedness of three seemingly different scientific concepts: magnetism, plant reproduction, and whale communication.

ASSESSMENT

Assessment was used as an informal method of determining (1) student prior knowledge; and (2) whether students had learned previously taught scientific concepts.

(1) Many teachers initiated their lessons by asking the students what they already knew about a scientific concept. Assessment was used in this case to determine the students' prior knowledge of a specific science topic. In example #8, the teacher is very explicit about assessing prior knowledge.

EXAMPLE 8 (FOURTH/FIFTH GRADE)

*Teacher:*  Can you tell me what you already know?

In the majority of classes, however, the teachers assessed prior knowledge without alerting the students that they were doing so, as in example 9.

EXAMPLE 9 (FIFTH GRADE)

*Teacher:*      How does sand get to the beaches?

*Student 1:*   From the waves.

*Student 2:*   From the beaches.

(2) When teachers began their lessons, they often assessed whether students had learned previously taught science material. Teachers assessed knowledge regarding whether stars are planets, how sand arrives on beaches, how rocks are formed, and more. In example 10, the teacher explicitly states that she is assessing a concept that she had previously taught.

EXAMPLE 10 (FOURTH/FIFTH GRADE)

*Teacher:*  What did we learn in our last unit on water properties? What does the ocean water have besides salt that makes it different?

Because the teacher had already taught a unit on water properties, she expected the students to be able to answer her questions.

In this example, she also used assessment to connect the new science lesson on ocean movement to the previous lesson on water properties.

Of the repair strategies, very little clarification was observed around conceptual instruction. For whatever reasons, students did not seem to signal the need for clarification of science concepts. There were, however, isolated cases of paraphrasing used for (1) clarification of requests; and (2) repair avoidance (see also Bailey, in press for further discussion of academic language uses of paraphrasing).

(1) The teacher of a fifth-grade lesson on whale behaviors tries to elicit student responses to her question about why whales breach. When she does not get the correct answer, she urges the students in example 11 to describe the motion of the whale to her. A student explicitly signals nonunderstanding, and the teacher responds by rephrasing her request to repair the communication.

EXAMPLE 11 (FIFTH GRADE)
*Teacher:*   Describe it, though.
*Student:*   I don't understand.
*Teacher:*   Make me see what it is.

(2) In example 12, taken from a fourth-grade classroom, the teacher explains that the sun and the earth work together.

EXAMPLE 12 (FOURTH GRADE)
*Teacher:*   The sun and the earth work together. They have a relationship.

No student response is elicited in this instance; instead, the teacher goes on to rephrase her explanation of the solar system, possibly first introducing the more accessible phrasing (*work together*) to avoid the need to repair the meaning of *relationship*.

## *The Context of Academic Vocabulary Instruction—Developing Nonspecialized and Specialized Academic Vocabulary*

A range of nonspecialized and specialized academic vocabulary was observed during science lessons. Frequently, teachers used academic vocabulary without any apparent support. However, when teachers did highlight academic vocabulary, the supports of definitions, synonyms, examples, and repetition were used. Overt instruction occurred for specialized more often than for nonspecialized vocabulary and frequently took the form of examples in the process of providing description, explanation, and comparison of science concepts. The use of definitions repeatedly required teachers to clarify, and the use of synonyms often required teachers to paraphrase whole sentences. In addition, some terms were found to have precise scientific meanings as well as nonacademic discourse usage (the word *cross* in *cross-pollination* is an example of a scientific use versus a nonacademic use, as in the phrase *to cross the street*). Although these cases were not always overtly contrasted for students in the study reported here, the nonacademic meaning of a word, perhaps more familiar to students, could be referred to as the teacher introduces the less familiar meaning of the word used in the academic context. Indeed, Gibbons (1998) notes that students' familiarity with everyday language should be seen as a conduit for developing "the unfamiliar registers of school" (p. 99) and when a teacher introduces a more scientific term for a word used by a student to talk about an observation or phenomenon, the two co-construct concepts to allow the student to acquire the specific scientific terminology.

## *The Context of Process/Application Instruction—Engaging Students in Classroom Learning Activities*

Most teachers incorporated both constructivist and direct instruction practices in their teaching. Strategies such as K-W-L charts,[3] choral response, and collaborative work were observed. Frequently, students shifted tasks at least once during the lesson (e.g., lecture to group work, video to discussion). Many of the tasks had an interactive component, whether it was a game to illustrate a scientific concept or the collaborative use of microscopes in a lab.

Although levels of student participation were not systematically measured during observation, there appeared to be large differences in the style and amount of student response elicited by teachers. In some classrooms, students felt free to call out questions or answers, while in other classrooms students were required to raise their hand or wait to be called upon for a response. In addition, some lessons appeared to promote more discussion and student interest than others, perhaps due to subject matter, relevancy to students, or teacher/student style of interaction.

There was evidence of all language functions, repair strategies, and classroom management categories occurring with at least one of the four process/application categories. Of the process/application categories, teacher instructions/techniques to accomplish a task were most frequently observed, whereas talking about the materials needed to accomplish these same tasks was the least observed. Although certain strategies (e.g., K-W-L) were used to guide classes through lessons, efforts to present outlines for and summations of lessons rarely occurred. In addition, review of prior lessons was typically done in an incidental manner as part of the ongoing instruction.

## Summary of Classroom Observations

The work reported here is a descriptive study of functional academic language use in fourth- and fifth-grade science classrooms. Although the effort was exploratory, the results are fundamental to refining a conceptual framework for future analyses of academic language. Indeed, an ideal future matrix of observed talk in science classrooms would expand figure 5.1 by including, where relevant, additional communicative intents and the unique linguistic features (discourse, syntax, and vocabulary) necessary to carry out the intents. While the need remains to more fully describe and characterize the language of the science classroom (and other content-area classrooms as well), this study documented teacher behavior primarily at a functional level and may suggest a direction for proposing effective communicative strategies for teaching/reinforcing academic language. Some teachers were observed using multiple language functions to solidify concepts and then finally assess student understanding.

While no conclusive recommendations are possible at this time, the functional approach to academic language taken here has provided an initial means for characterizing teacher language, and to a lesser extent student language, in one specific content area. To provide a more complete picture, future studies utilizing audio and video recordings would allow for detailed transcript analysis of verbatim speech. This methodology would yield data amenable to complementary formal linguistic description. These types of analyses would then allow for an extension of knowledge about academic language use in classrooms, thereby promoting an understanding of both the purposes of language use (functional approach) and the forms the language takes (formal linguistic approach) within and across content areas. These efforts would ideally benefit both EO and ELL students.

## The Language Demands of Textbooks

To operationalize the language used in academic texts, the second study reported here provides descriptions of the language used in selected representative fifth-grade mathematics, science, and social studies textbooks.[4] The evidence-based framework discussed by Bailey and Butler, chapter 4 is applied at one grade level to supplement the classroom discourse research detailed above. These data expand on previous exploratory analyses of fifth-grade and eighth-grade mathematics and science textbooks, which provided preliminary empirical data on the language used in the two subject areas (Butler, Lord, Stevens, Borrego, and Bailey, 2004). This pilot work also played a crucial role in shaping our conceptual understanding and in refining our research design. Specifically, we have been able to capitalize on the methodologies that were developed for the characterization of textbook language. Other research efforts in the language of content areas such as science and mathematics (e.g., Dale and Cuevas, 1992; Lemke, 1990; Pimm, 1987, 1995) and academic uses of language more generally (e.g., Cazden, 2001; Chamot and O'Malley, 1994; Reppen, 2001; Scarcella, 2003; Schleppegrell, 2001; Short, 1993), provided guidance in the choice of the different language analyses.

The modality of reading was selected because it is a focal point of the NCLB legislation for all students and presents an especially critical burden for English learners, who must also be tested annually. All students are expected to read at grade level and must have the ability to do so in order to access and demonstrate knowledge on standardized assessments. In addition, reading provides increasingly complex linguistic input to students from grade to grade since the reliance on reading comprehension in instruction and assessment across subject matter increases with grade level (RAND, 2002).

Two questions guided the research:

1. What are the linguistic characteristics of mathematics word problems and multiparagraph texts in science and social studies at the fifth-grade level?
2. How do the identified characteristics of texts in different subject areas compare to one another?

Descriptions of the lexical, grammatical, and organizational features of the textbook selections allowed us to create profiles of what is typical in texts for each subject area (in terms of the features analyzed). The profiles can be used as part of the foundation for developing the AEL construct for educational applications. Characterization of texts across a range of subject areas provides information on content-specific language demands, while characterization of texts by grade level provides data on developmental demands. Information from the results is being used in test specification development for English language reading tasks appropriate for fifth grade (Bailey, Stevens, Butler and Huang, 2005). In addition, the profiles may also be useful as a means of facilitating changes in curriculum, materials, and teacher professional development.

## Method

To characterize the mathematics word problems and the science and social studies extended texts, we began by generating descriptive data for each text selection used in the study. Then, to more fully describe the texts, we looked specifically at the areas of vocabulary, grammar, and discourse.[5]

### *Descriptive Analysis*

Measures of sentence length provide basic descriptive data and have long been associated with reading difficulty (Zakaluk and Samuels, 1988). Longer sentences tend to pose greater challenges for students. These challenges are found to be even greater for students whose home language is not English (Abedi, Lord, and Plummer, 1997). For this reason sentence length is an important factor in creating subject-area text profiles. Other basic descriptive data compiled in the study include number of words, sentences, and paragraphs in the selections; mean sentence length calculated by topic and subject area; and mean number of sentences per paragraph. These descriptive data provided a means for evaluating similarities and differences in the nature of texts used in subject areas at the fifth grade.

### *Lexical Analysis*

For vocabulary, features believed consequential in defining academic vocabulary and for describing the acquisition and use of vocabulary in academic settings were identified in all text selections in mathematics, science, and social studies (see table 5.1 for examples of lexical coding). First, lexical diversity, a measure that reflects the variety of vocabulary in a given text, was calculated by dividing the number of different words (word types) by the total number of words (tokens) in that text. This lexical diversity ratio is important in characterizing texts because it helps establish the range of vocabulary students must be able to understand. The smaller the type/token ratio. the less diverse the vocabulary in a particular selection—that is, the use of word types is repetitious (e.g., Phillips, 1973). To calculate lexical diversity, we used the type/token approach utilized in studies of language development (e.g., Pan, 1994; Templin, 1957). For such an analysis to be comparable across subjects and across topics within subjects, we standardized the total number of tokens (overall number of words) by using the first 450 words per set of mathematics word problems and the first 450 words per text selection in science and social studies. Prior research has shown that use of greater than 200 tokens yields more stable ratio calculations (Richards, 1987). Using the FREQ (frequency count) function of the CLAN (Computer Language Analysis) programs of the Child Language Data Exchange System (CHILDES) (MacWhinney, 1995; MacWhinney and Snow, 1990), the number of different word types within this 450 was tallied, and the ratio of the number of types to the 450 tokens was interpreted to provide an indication of lexical diversity in the textbook selections.

Vocabulary that can be identified as part of the academic English lexicon by its usage in academic contexts includes both the specialized word usage within academic disciplines (e.g., *thermal, multiplication*) and the general academic vocabulary not exclusive to any one discipline (e.g., *synthesize, report*) (Chung and Nation, 2003; Nation, 2001; Nation and Coxhead, 2001). (See chapter 1 for further discussion of operationalizing the academic vocabulary construct.)

To help specify and define what constitutes an academic word and what does not beyond these contextual aspects (specialized versus nonspecialized uses), we also investigated discrete features of words in the text selections that included (1) vocabulary that appears on low-frequency word lists for the fifth-grade level (e.g., Zeno, Ivens, Millard, and Duvvuri, 1995);[6] (2) vocabulary that contains three or more syllables; and (3) vocabulary that is morphologically derived from root lexical forms. A synthesis of analyses is reported

**Table 5.1 Examples of Lexical Features Identified in Fifth-Grade Text Selections**

| Feature | Examples* |
| --- | --- |
| General academic vocabulary | *Resulted, contained, suppose* |
| Specialized academic vocabulary | *Denominator, anther, merchant* |
| Non-academic vocabulary | *Many, water, people* |
| Low-frequency words | *Mode, adaptive, declare* |
| 3-or-more-syllable words | *Milliliters, physical, profitable* |
| Morphologically derived words | *Savings, geometric, production* |
| Clause connectors | *If, when, after* |
| Nominalizations | *Enlargement, heaviness, strengthened* |

*Examples are not necessarily mutually exclusive across feature categories and are given one each from the mathematics, science, and social studies texts, respectively.*

whereby we examine the degree of overlap between vocabulary meeting the low frequency, three or more syllable, derived, and academic vocabulary criteria. Were the overlaps significant with any one (or more) of the features, it might be possible to use that feature(s) to identify academic vocabulary in future research and test development efforts to streamline the identification process.

Analysis of two additional lexical-level features was also included: frequency and variety of clause connectors and frequency of nominalizations. Specifically, the identification of adverbial clause connectors (often called adverbial subordinators) was an important part of the lexical analyses because they frequently signal meaning relationships between clauses. Since research suggests that students may not interpret these words correctly, resulting in possible misunderstanding of the meaning relationships they encode (see for discussion Celce-Murcia and Larsen-Freeman, 1983; Halliday and Hasan, 1976), the frequency of their occurrence should be reflected in the text profiles and taken into consideration in the test development stage. Nominalizations were included because they can increase semantic complexity (Martin, 1991) and provide additional descriptive information about lexical usage in academic texts.

## Grammatical Analysis

For grammar, we looked at the following features: percentages of sentence types used (i.e., simple, compound, complex, and compound-complex), numbers of dependent and coordinate clauses (including

**Table 5.2 Examples of Grammatical Features Identified in Fifth-Grade Text Selections**

| Feature | Examples* |
|---|---|
| Simple sentence | *The ice on the river melts quickly under the warm sun.* |
| Compound sentence | *Some deserts are very hot in the daytime, but temperatures can drop below freezing at night.* |
| Complex sentence | *Although human beings don't notice the noises of nature, a lot of animals react to the sounds around them.* |
| Compound-complex sentence | *Washington soon realized that the Nation was not functioning well, so he became an advocate in the movement leading to the Constitutional Convention.* |
| Passive verb form | *Water is absorbed by the ground and becomes groundwater.* |
| Prepositional phrase | *Our planet looks like a beautiful big blue marble from a distance.* |
| Noun phrase | *Water inside the tube.* |
| Participial modifier | *The number surviving was very small.* |

*\* Examples are not necessarily mutually exclusive across feature categories. Examples were constructed to represent the grammatical features typically found in text selections.*

percentages of total clauses), occurrences of passive-voice verb forms, prepositional phrases, length of noun phrases, and participial modifiers (see table 5.2 for examples of grammatical coding). Since clause types have been found to be a factor in student test performance, with higher frequency of dependent clauses associated with greater processing difficulty, range and frequency of sentence types, which reflect clause usage, are important considerations in text selection for assessment purposes (see Lord, 2002). Passive-voice verb forms, prepositional phrases, long noun phrases, and participial modifiers contribute to length and/or semantic complexity in texts, often increasing the processing load for the reader (Abedi et al., 1997). They are also identified with academic prose (see Schleppegrell, 2001, 2004) and are therefore important features to note.

## Organization of Discourse

For discourse, we looked at the organizational features of the selections in the study—the language functions and devices writers used to express ideas and present factual information. In addition to language functions, which are a key component of the language that students must use to interpret and derive meaning from texts (Butler, Lord, et al., 2004), writers often use different types of writing devices to provide additional detail, to exemplify a point, or to ensure reader comprehension, while they use other techniques to provide instructional guidance to students (e.g., by referring them to graphics or prior lessons). Therefore, in order to capture a broad spectrum of the features that exist in the textbooks, we analyzed both functions and additional features used by writers to convey ideas. Analyses concentrated on three levels of textual organization: rhetorical mode, dominant text features, and supporting text features (examples of coding of organizational structures are provided in the results below).

## Synthesis Procedures and Text Selection Rationale

The answer to the second research question required synthesis of the descriptive, lexical, grammatical, and discourse data into "profiles" of language for each subject area. The emphasis was on differences across topics and subjects rather than across individual textbooks from which selections were made. Description of variation is provided quantitatively with calculations of standard deviations and minimum and maximum values, as well as qualitatively with examples of specific lexical items encountered in the different analyses. The subject-area profiles were then compared, allowing commonalities and differences to be systematically compiled. Using analysis of variance (ANOVA) procedures and confidence interval calculations, we were able to determine which of the differences across the three subjects in terms of key descriptive, lexical, and grammatical features are statistically significant.

An important first step was to determine which texts would be selected for analysis in the three subject areas—mathematics, science, and social studies. We needed to determine which types of texts students encounter most frequently within and across subject areas; thus we needed texts that are both representative of *typical* texts and of sufficient length to provide material for test development.

The word problem was established as the unit of analysis for mathematics for two main reasons: (1) word problems provide a greater range of language use than other text types in mathematics textbooks; and (2) characterizing the language demands of word problems in textbooks would also best inform assessment development efforts; that is, the language of word problems mirrors the language that students commonly encounter on mathematics assessments that rely on word problems in addition to straight computation. Although the linguistic profile of mathematics word problems may not parallel that of math instructional prose, the linguistic features of word problems are important considerations for the language of mathematics assessments. Some of the word problems in the textbooks included graphics and required their use to solve the problem. For our research, we chose word problems without graphics and with a minimum of two sentences, one of which was a declarative statement that provided the setup for solving the mathematics problem.

Based on previous research (Butler, Lord, et al., 2004), multiparagraph texts were identified as the most frequently occurring type of text in science and social studies textbooks and were, therefore, chosen for analysis in this research. The text selection process began with identification of topics in the California subject-matter standards for fifth grade in each subject area. Three textbooks from different publishers were selected from the list of California-approved textbooks for each subject area as the sources from which to select the samples. Three were chosen in order to reduce bias (e.g., different textbooks might have different writing styles) that could result from analyzing textbook samples from only one publisher.[7] We then compared the topics in the subject-matter standards with the textbook topics to identify the closest matches possible in content (e.g., *matter, storms*). Since textbooks varied in their treatment of topics, we further narrowed our focus to topics that occurred in all three textbooks with similar subtopics, vocabulary, and concepts in order to ensure adequate and comparable topic coverage. For each of the three subject areas we chose four topics; we then chose three selections (one from each publisher) for each topic for a total of 12 text selections per subject. In total, 36 text selections were identified for analysis (see table 5.3 for the topics selected across subjects).

The fifth-grade textbooks we used in this study averaged 567 pages. To give a concrete sense of the amount of data that we analyzed in each textbook, we calculated the total number of textbook pages selected for analysis and divided the number by the total number of pages in the textbook. On average, the volume of data that we have analyzed constitutes around 3% of each of the nine textbooks. In absolute terms, this totals 154 pages of text analyzed.

**Table 5.3 Topics Selected for Each Subject**
**(n = 3 Selections per Topic)**

| Mathematics | Science | Social Studies |
|---|---|---|
| Decimals | Matter | Declaration of Independence |
| Fractions | Plants | Industrial Revolution |
| Multiplication | Storms | Pilgrims |
| Ratio | Water cycle | Slavery |

Note: *Total number of selections = 36.*
Source: *Butler et al., 2004. Copyright 2004 by CRESST. Reprinted with permission.*

In typical fifth-grade textbook layout we found this includes an average of one illustration per page. There is little variation in the average proportion of text pages selected across subject areas, ranging from 2.6% of the text in social studies textbooks to 3% of the text in science to 3.4% in mathematics.

In mathematics, we selected a number of word problems for each topic, carefully balancing the number of word problems and the total number of words selected from each textbook. In science and social studies, one multiparagraph passage per topic was selected per textbook. The passages all begin at a natural starting point for the topic, often signaled by a header in the textbook, and end at a natural breakpoint. We attempted to select texts that were of sufficient and similar length for linguistic analyses across the three subjects, though there is some variation in length due in part to differences in presentation across textbooks and in part to subject matter differences (e.g., the depth of topic coverage or the variety of subtopics presented within a topic). The social studies selections, for example, tend to be longer than the science selections. We felt it was more important to ensure a coherent piece of text by including the beginning and end of each selection rather than stopping abruptly in the middle of a selection to achieve uniform word length across subject areas and textbooks. Once all the selections were identified for a subject area, they were entered into electronic format for data analysis. To standardize comparisons across subject areas, we converted raw data into percentage, ratio, or rate data (i.e., number of instances of a feature per 100 sentences).

Visuals, graphics, and primary-source excerpts were not included at this stage of the study, with the exception of some social studies selections that included one- or two-sentence excerpts or quotes from primary sources that were an integral part of the selection.

## Reliability

Accuracy checks were conducted on the analyses that were non-subjective (e.g., word counts), while reliability was conducted for those analyses that required the judgment of raters based on specific criteria (e.g., subcategories of academic vocabulary, organizational features, including rhetorical mode, dominant text features, and supporting text features). We established a goal of 95% or higher for the accuracy checks and 85% or higher interrater reliability. Initial counts were established by the automated CLAN programs (MacWhinney, 1995; MacWhinney and Snow, 1990); we then verified the counts manually.

## Hallmarks of Academic English Language in Math, Science, and Social Studies Texts

Table 5.4 provides a cross-subject-area profile that lists the main linguistic features investigated in this study down the left-hand side and the values and ranges for each feature that typify the subject area text selections on the right-hand side. Each section of the table contains data drawn from the different analyses performed in the study (e.g., descriptive features, grammatical features). Commonalties in linguistic features across subject areas are candidates for assessments of general academic language (domain-general language), whereas differences in linguistic features are candidates for developing subject-area (domain-specific) assessments or subject-specific test modules to add on to a general academic language test.

## Descriptive Features

Across subjects, we found that the mean number of sentences ranges from 3.13 sentences per mathematics word problem to 4.18 sentences per science paragraph. At the sentence level, mean sentence length is slightly shorter in mathematics (11) than in science (13) and social studies (14). Social studies has a slightly wider range of sentence lengths (3–43 words) than in mathematics (1–39) and sci-

**Table 5.4 Linguistic Profiles of Fifth-Grade Mathematics, Science, and Social Studies Text Selections[a]**

| Linguistic Features | Math | Science | Social Studies |
|---|---|---|---|
| Mean no. of sentences per word problem or paragraph (range) | 3 (2–7) | 4 (1–8) | 4 (1–9) |
| Mean no. of words per sentence (range) | 11 (1–39) | 13 (1–37) | 14 (3–43) |
| Lexical diversity ratio | .43 | .41 | .49 |
| Percentage of all categories of academic vocabulary words[b] | 10% (14%) | 21% (27%) | 24% (24%) |
|     General academic words only | 3% (5%) | 6% (11%) | 3% (7%) |
|     Specialized academic words only | 4% (7%) | 14% (14%) | 9% (11%) |
|     Measurement words only | 3% (2%) | 1% (1%) | <1% |
|     Proper nouns only (specialized) | <1% | <1% | 7% (5%) |
|     Colloquialisms only | <1% | <1% | <1% |
| Vocabulary features | | | |
|     Low-frequency words | 8% (12%) | 8% (12%) | 8% (12%) |
|     3-or-more-syllable words | 6% (9%) | 10% (15%) | 12% (16%) |
|     Derived words | 2% (4%) | 6% (11%) | 8% (12%) |
| No. of unique clause connectors | 11 | 7 | 21 |
| Avg. percentage of nominalizations per selection | <1% | 2% (3%) | 2% (3%) |
| Avg. percentage of each sentence type per selection | | | |
|     Simple sentences | 81% | 61% | 63% |
|     Complex sentences | 17% | 36% | 33% |
|     Other sentence types | 2% | 3% | 4% |
| Avg. percentage of dependent clauses per selection | 6% | 29% | 28% |
| Mean no. of passive voice verb forms per sentence | .04 | .24 | .16 |
| Mean no. of prepositional phrases per sentence | 1 | 1 | 1 |
| Mean no. of words per prepositional phrase (range) | 4 (2–14) | 4 (2–17) | 4 (2–20) |
| Mean no. of noun phrases per sentence | .03 | .16 | .17 |
| Mean no. of words per noun phrase (range) | 2 (1–16) | 3 (1–23) | 3 (1–19) |
| Mean no. of participial modifiers per sentence | .03 | .17 | .17 |

*continued*

**Table 5.4** *continued*

| Linguistic Features | Math | Science | Social Studies |
|---|---|---|---|
| Dominant organizational features | | | |
| Classification | 0% | 17% | 0% |
| Description | 50% | 100% | 100% |
| Explanation | 0% | 42% | 33% |
| Scenario | 100% | 0% | 0% |
| Sequencing | 0% | 17% | 25% |
| Supporting organizational features[c] | | | |
| Comparison | 67% | 83% | 50% |
| Definition | 0% | 83% | 75% |
| Enumeration | 92% | 100% | 100% |
| Exemplification | 0% | 75% | 83% |
| Labeling | 0% | 100% | 100% |
| Paraphrase | 17% | 58% | 67% |
| Provide instruction or guidance | 25% | 25% | 0% |
| Quotation | 0% | 0% | 92% |
| Reference to text or visual | 0% | 83% | 58% |
| Sequencing | 75% | 42% | 58% |

[a]*Numbers in this table have been rounded to the nearest whole number for percentages and the nearest one hundredth for decimals.*
[b]*Percentages shown are token (type).*
[c]*The five most frequently occurring supporting features in each subject area are listed here.*
Source: *Butler et al., 2004. Copyright 2004 by CRESST. Reprinted with permission.*

ence (1–37). In the future the basic quantitative information that the descriptive analyses provided will allow us to select texts for test development that meet highly specific minimum, maximum, and central tendency criteria for sentence length and paragraph length. These basic descriptive criteria differed between mathematics selections and science and social studies selections, though not between the latter two.

## *Lexical Features*

Based on examination of type/token ratios, we found that social studies (.49) is slightly more lexically diverse than either mathematics (.43) or science (.41). However, the diversity ratios across subjects appear to be relatively low judged against the oral language ratios in the literature and given the assumption that one purpose of the textbooks is to introduce new grade-appropriate lexical items to students. Comparing academic vocabulary usage across subjects, we found that mathematics word problems contain fewer academic words than science and social studies passages overall, whereas science and social studies have comparable percentages of academic vocabulary. In examining the percentages of academic words by subcategories, we observed that all subjects contain more specialized academic vocabulary than any other subcategory. However, the proportions of other subcategories of academic words vary slightly from subject to subject. Mathematics contains a larger percentage of measurement words than science and social studies. On the other hand, science has the largest proportion of general academic vocabulary across subjects. Although social studies does not have as many general academic vocabulary words, it contains the highest percentage of specialized proper nouns.

In terms of low-frequency vocabulary, the percentages of total word types and tokens are similar across subjects. Low-frequency words play a relatively minor role in total word counts (about 8% overall) but a slightly greater role in total word types (about 12%) for all three subjects. Across subjects there are more three-or-more-syllable words than there are morphologically derived words both in types and tokens. In both cases, however, proportions of both three-or-more-syllable and derived words in total word counts/word types are similar for science and social studies (15%-16% for three-or-more-syllable words, 11%-12% for derived words), but the percentages are smaller in mathematics (9% for three-or-more syllable words, 4% for derived words).

Overall, there are more unique clause connectors (types) in science and social studies than in mathematics, but all three subjects have some frequently occurring connectors in common, such as *and, when, if,* and *but.* Nominalizations appear infrequently across subjects. In science and social studies selections, they account for about 2% of total word counts and 3% of word types, and in mathematics they account for less than 1% of total words.

In general, the mathematics texts we analyzed were quite different from both science and social studies texts; science texts had the highest proportion of general and specialized academic words; social studies texts were the most complex in terms of demanding vocabulary (e.g., highest lexical diversity ratio, highest proportions of content-related proper nouns, three-or-more-syllable words, derived words, and a number of different types of clause connectors). The relatively uniform findings across the different topics within subjects for most of the lexical features we examined support the use of these features for later subject-area generalizations in test development (e.g., selecting texts that mirror these lexical characteristics).

Within the total corpus, some words were used rarely and others occurred with high frequency across all three subject areas (e.g., certain prepositions, determiners, and conjunctions). From a test development perspective, we might attempt to avoid words that are rarely used if the construct we wish to measure is general academic use of language, focusing instead on the vocabulary that forms a core of "must-know" words. Given that derived word forms occur in relatively low numbers across the subjects, we should attempt to avoid the selection of texts with disproportionate numbers of such words for use in test development because they do not represent the norm. However, it should be noted that derived forms best account for words identified as academic vocabulary in all subjects, impressively so in the areas of science and social studies. Derivational formation of words can, therefore, help to identify academic vocabulary more systematically than any of the other lexical features we examined here, at least at the fifth-grade level.

The relatively few similarities in academic words used across subject areas (just 15 academic words in common), especially the infrequent use of general academic vocabulary, suggest the need to pay close attention to the individual characteristics of each subject area and to the particularities of individual texts. Curriculum and test developers are thus faced with striking a balance between the adoption of a census approach (i.e., assess every feature) in order to capture the full range of vocabulary in all academic settings, and the sampling of a restricted number of general academic words shared across subject areas in much greater depth.

## Grammatical Features

The majority of sentence types across subjects are simple sentences, followed by complex sentences. Mathematics has the highest percentage of simple sentences (81%), whereas in science and social studies about 60% of the sentences are simple sentences. Across subjects approximately 26%-29% of total clauses are identified as dependent clauses.

Use of passive-voice verb forms in general and passive constructions with "by" varies by subject, with less than one passive form per sentence on average across subjects. Passive constructions in mathematics are almost nonexistent, whereas passive-voice verb forms occur with higher frequency in science (.24 per sentence) than in social studies (.16).

With regard to prepositional phrases, the usage is the same across subjects, with the average number per sentence being one. The average length of prepositional phrases is approximately four words per phrase across subjects. The average number of noun phrases per sentence is three for all subjects. There are few participial modifiers of any kind (e.g., past or present) in the fifth-grade text selections analyzed; however, there are more in science and social studies (16 and 17 per 100 sentences, respectively) than in mathematics (3 per 100 sentences).

The grammatical analyses reported here were selected based on our previous exploratory work (Butler, Lord, et al., 2004) and the literature that identified a number of grammatical features (e.g., passive-voice verb forms) to be hallmarks of academic texts. Some of the analyses, however, may have been focused at too demanding a language level for typical fifth-grade textbooks in that use of passive-voice verb forms and past and present participial modifiers, for example, was minimal in the selections in all three subject areas. While these features should not be a focus at this level, tracking their presence is important for establishing an academic language trajectory. At the level of the clause and sentence, on the other hand, a small number of measures of length and frequency suggests important differences and commonalties across subjects that will need to be taken into account for test development purposes.

While all subject-area texts in this study have a greater number of simple sentences than complex sentences, the mathematics texts consist almost exclusively of simple sentences, with science and social studies texts containing closer to a 60/40 split between simple and complex sentences. Texts selected for use on academic language proficiency reading tests or in curricula should reflect these tendencies. Sentences in the three subjects are composed of the same number of phrase types: both prepositional and noun phrases are distributed comparably in mathematics, science, and social studies, with each sentence containing just one prepositional phrase and three noun phrases on average. Similarities also extend to the length of these phrase types. That lengthier sentences are more often found in the science and social studies texts is likely attributable to other grammatical structures that increase sentence length, such as embedded clauses (e.g., relative clauses). Finer discrimination among clause types should be included in future linguistic analyses of texts.

## Discourse Features

We observed many contrasts across subjects at each level of analysis. First, the rhetorical mode varies across subjects according to the purpose of the writing. The primary purpose of mathematics word problems is to provide problem-solving contexts. The word problems are typically limited in length and thus do not provide the extended discourse necessary for establishing rhetorical mode. Therefore, this feature could not be identified in the mathematics selections. Science and social studies both follow an expository form to present information; however, their rhetorical modes differ slightly: science selections use a more traditional, straightforward expository form, whereas social studies selections employ a storytelling narrative form.

Ultimately, the organization of texts pulls the other analyses mentioned above together under the same umbrella because most features, whether grammatical or lexical, interact within the organizational structure of texts. The implications of this are multifold, beginning with the need to link relevant features with text organization features; for example, students must recognize comparative adjectives in order to understand that a comparison is being made. In addition, the different features must be tested in their contexts of use. For example, many supporting organizational features are embedded within dominant features occurring mostly at the sentence level; however, the most frequently occurring supporting features (*comparison, sequencing*) occur in a greater variety of contexts. Establishing the relationships between grammatical and lexical features, as well as understanding the typical contexts of use for features at a particular grade level and subject area, enables test developers to organize the content of tests in meaningful ways. Indeed, test organization should reflect language in use, not discrete points of language divorced from context.

Specific areas of concern for test developers include the differences in text organization across subject areas. In our research we found that science and social studies texts make broader use of a range of organizational features than mathematics, reflecting, to some extent, the formulaic nature of the mathematics word problem genre.[8] Frequently used features shared by these two subject areas must be considered for general tests of academic language proficiency, since these subject areas reflect a more substantial portion of students' reading loads, as opposed to mathematics word problems. Conversely, areas of overlap across the three subject areas indicate core features that students must be able to recognize and interpret in the texts they read across subject areas. These features include *comparison, description, enumeration, paraphrase,* and *sequencing.* Texts selected for either curriculum or test development should reflect these features, and test items should tap students' abilities to grasp the meaning and purpose of the features in a given text. Our research also points to the complexity of many of the organizational features; for example, *definition* is provided in multiple ways: through traditional *definition* (*A dog is a type of animal*), through *labeling* (*One type of popular domestic animal is called a dog*), through *paraphrase* (*Dogs, popular pets, can be found in most American homes*), and through *classification* (*A chihuahua, a cocker spaniel, and a boxer are all dogs*). Comparisons are made for the purpose of describing, explaining, and exemplifying. Test developers should consider the multiple layers of occurrence with text features when creating test specifications and subsequently when writing test items. Many of these complexities in language represent levels of language proficiency, (i.e., some subtleties of the features may be understood and produced more frequently at lower levels of proficiency, while others may be more commonly used by advanced level ELLs).

Another area of interest for test developers identified in the current research is the frequent use of features that assist students with their reading (e.g., *paraphrase, providing instruction or guidance,* and *references to other text or visuals*). Similar features, akin to the use of scaffolding, were noted in the first study as typical of those used in oral classroom contexts as well by teachers when they present and explain academic material. Therefore, test developers could consider the inclusion of items that tap students' ability to understand when assistance is being offered and whether students are able to use that assistance effectively.

## Statistical Comparison of Linguistic Features across Subject Areas

Key features from descriptive, lexical, and grammatical text analyses were chosen for statistical analysis based on the degree of contrast they displayed across the three subjects, as shown in table 5.4 above. The univariate ANOVA procedure was conducted to test the significance in mean differences across subjects using, as appropriate, either the mean percentage of a given text feature (i.e., differences in the mean number of sentences per paragraph) or a standardized mean value (i.e., mean ratio of number of unique word types to total number of word tokens).

In every case, because we compare percentages or other standardized values, the contrasts we analyze across subject areas are meaningful despite differences in the overall number of words in each selection. The ANOVAs were conducted with Bonferroni corrections (a conservative adjustment) due to the larger number of multiple comparisons that could have resulted in significant findings by sheer chance. We therefore graphed confidence interval (CI) bands for each of the individual subject-area bars in figures 5.2 and 5.3.[9] These CIs are set at $p < .05$, that is, there is a 95% chance that the mean values for a given language feature fall within the band around the mean. Some of these bands are quite wide (e.g., percentage of participial modifiers per sentence in social studies), which reflects the large degree of variation across the 12 selections within a subject. The CI bands allow us to interpret the ANOVA results more conservatively: where subject means for a given text feature are found to be significantly different and CI bands are nonoverlapping, we can be more confident that any differences detected across subjects truly exist.

Figure 5.2 presents the CI bands for the descriptive and lexical profiles. In five contrasts: *number of sentences, number of words, specialized academic words, percentage of three-or-more-syllable words,* and *percentage of derived words,* mathematics texts have significantly lower means than either science or social studies texts. ANOVA post hoc comparisons are significant at $p < .001$ for all but the contrast between mathematics and social studies for *specialized academic*

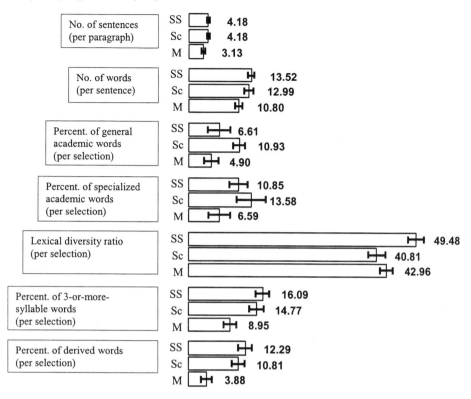

Figure 5.2. Linguistic profiles of fifth-grade social studies (SS), science (Sc), and mathematics (M) text selections: Subject-matter averages for descriptive and lexical data, adapted from Butler, Bailey et al., 2004. Copyright 2004 by CRESST. Reprinted with permission.

*words,* which is significant at $p < .05$ only and has overlapping CI bands that suggest the difference in means in this comparison should be interpreted with caution. Science has significantly more *general academic words* than either mathematics (post hoc comparison $p < .001$) or social studies (post hoc comparisons $p < .01$), although the latter two do not differ significantly from each other. On just one feature, the *lexical diversity ratio,* social studies texts have a significantly higher ratio of word types to word tokens than either mathematics or science texts (post hoc comparisons $p < .001$). *Lexical diversity ratios* for mathematics and science do not differ significantly.

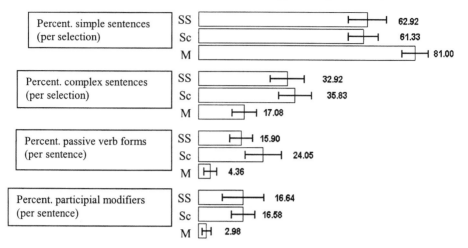

Figure 5.3. Linguistic profiles of fifth-grade social studies (SS), science (Sc), and mathematics (M) text selections: Subject-matter averages for grammatical data, from Butler, Bailey et al., 2004. Copyright 2004 by CRESST. Reprinted with permission.

In terms of findings in the grammatical data (see figure 5.3), in one key contrast (*percentage of simple sentences*), mathematics texts have a significantly higher mean than either science or social studies texts (post hoc comparisons $p < .001$). Conversely, mathematics has far fewer *complex sentences* per selection on average than either science or social studies (post hoc comparisons $p < .001$). Neither science nor social studies texts differ from one another on these sentence structure features. Mathematics has a considerably lower mean percentage of *passive-voice verb forms* and *participial modifiers per sentence* than the other two subject areas (post hoc comparisons between mathematics and social studies for *passive-voice verb forms* $p < .01$; between mathematics and social studies for *participial modifiers* $p < .001$; between mathematics and science for both *passive-voice verb forms* and *participial modifiers* $p < .001$). On average, social studies texts also have significantly fewer *passive-voice verb forms* than science texts (post hoc comparison $p < .05$), but the higher $p$-value and overlapping CI bands strongly suggest caution when interpreting this finding.

Overall, these analyses show that there are statistically significant differences between the subjects in several areas, although some of the results should be interpreted with caution given the small number (12 selections per subject area) of text selections. However, any results at the sentence and paragraph levels are meaningful, as the total number of sentences and paragraphs is more substantial (or in the case of mathematics, where the total number of word problems is 212).

## Implications

### *Prototype Academic English Task Development*

Since textbooks are an integral part of classroom learning, the data generated in this report can be used to determine which linguistic features of textbooks are typical at the fifth-grade level for each subject area and also to help establish trajectories of language complexity across grade levels for each subject area. While the analyses performed in the current research are not exhaustive, they provide evidence of the prevalence of a range of features at the fifth-grade level upon which test development in the future can base item and task development decisions. These features include: (1) nominalizations; (2) frequently used clause connectors; (3) types and frequency of academic vocabulary; (4) passive constructions; (5) prepositional phrases; (6) noun phrases; (7) participial modifiers; and (8) frequently used dominant and supporting discourse features. Table 5.5 provides a sample content framework for developing assessments of academic language proficiency, which lists a selection of the vocabulary, grammar, and text organization features investigated in the current research down the left and the three subject areas across the top.

If we use table 5.5 as a guide for determining test content, we might select high-frequency nonacademic and general academic vocabulary, prepositional phrases, and *comparison, description,* and *sequencing* for inclusion on a general assessment of academic language proficiency. For assessments of subject-specific language proficiency, like the specialized advanced placement and subject-area tests high school students often take before going to college, we might instead focus on measurement words for mathematics and science, and participial modifiers, passive-voice verb forms, and *definition* and *labeling* for science and social studies. Even finer

**Table 5.5 Content Framework for Developing an Assessment of Academic Language Proficiency**

| Linguistics Features | Mathematics | Science | Social Studies |
|---|:---:|:---:|:---:|
| Vocabulary | | | |
|   Non-academic vocabulary | √ | √ | √ |
|   Academic vocabulary (AV) | | | |
|     General AV (high-frequency) | √ | √ | √ |
|     Specialized AV (defined in context) | — | √ | √ |
|     Measurement words | √ | √ | — |
|     Proper nouns | — | — | √ |
|   Clause connectors | √ | √ | √ |
|   Nominalizations | — | √ | √ |
| Grammar | | | |
|   Noun phrases | √ | √ | √ |
|   Participial modifiers | — | √ | √ |
|   Passive voice verb forms | — | √ | √ |
|   Prepositional phrases | √ | √ | √ |
| Organization of Text | | | |
|   Comparison | √ | √ | √ |
|   Definition | — | √ | √ |
|   Description | √ | √ | √ |
|   Enumeration | √ | √ | √ |
|   Exemplification | — | √ | √ |
|   Explanation | — | √ | √ |
|   Labeling | — | √ | √ |
|   Paraphrase | √ | √ | √ |
|   Scenario | √ | — | — |
|   Sequencing | √ | √ | √ |

Source: *Butler et al., 2004. Copyright 2004 by CRESST. Reprinted with permission.*

distinctions can be made if all of the features investigated in this research were to be included in such a framework, (e.g., the text organization feature *quotation, for example,* is not included in the framework because we found it only in social studies texts). This is a strong candidate for inclusion in a test of specialized academic language knowledge in social studies.

The information presented in table 5.5 has been sequenced in the order it was presented throughout the chapter. For actual test development, the features may be reorganized into different categories; for example, grammatical features of text are embedded in the text organization and do not occur discretely. Therefore, students must be able to make meaning out of vocabulary and grammar in order to understand the main and supporting ideas in a text (e.g., students must comprehend comparative adjectives in order to understand that a comparison or contrast is being made; knowledge of adverbial connectors is critical to understanding a sequencing of events).

Once it has been determined that a text and associated tasks match the parameters established in the current research, they can undergo both internal and external reviews by curriculum and/or language experts and subject-area teachers. External reviews will provide a combination of focus-group data and questionnaire data and will include a sensitivity review (to detect biases in terms of gender, race, etc.), a text and item review to assure that the texts and items are topically and linguistically representative of the types that teachers typically use in their classrooms, and a language review to catch any additional linguistic anomalies or concerns that may exist. Based on this feedback, items can be retained, rejected, or modified.

## Extension to Additional Grade Levels

The results of the analyses have implications for applications of the research methodology to different grade levels or grade clusters, particularly higher grade levels where textbooks may include far greater amounts of such lexico-grammatical features as nominalizations, greater numbers of and diversity in clausal connectors, passive verb constructions, prepositional phrases, and participial modifiers. For example, we expect that the use of passive-voice verb forms will increase with each grade level; however, currently we do not have empirical evidence showing at which grade the comprehension and use of passive voice becomes critical for young readers, as well as whether there are frequency differences among subclassifications of passive constructions at different grade levels. Research such as this will lead to the identification of trajectories of language use by grade level and in each subject area, valuable not only in testing but also in materials and curriculum development and professional development.

## *Teaching and Testing Academic Language as a Second Language*

Taken together, the two studies described here further our understanding of what the upper elementary grades demand of all students in terms of language use and understanding. In the analysis of teacher talk in the first study, there was great variability in the degree to which teachers held students accountable for verbalization of their knowledge, with only some teachers, for example, requiring students to provide fully elaborated explanations for their scientific claims. This source of variation in teacher discourse style has implications for student learning and assessment and is documented for other subject areas (e.g., mathematical discourse) as well (e.g., Kazemi, 1999). Overt instruction of subject-area vocabulary (i.e., specialized academic vocabulary) was frequently made, however, primarily relying on examples rather than on formal definitions, and occurring more often than overt instruction of general academic vocabulary.[10]

The results of the second study provide new information about content-specific language demands that will inform the discussion of the nature of academic language. The study also invested considerable effort in the creation of a methodology for conducting comprehensive linguistic analyses of texts. The academic vocabulary and discourse analyses in particular were iterative in that the processes for conducting analyses were developed, piloted, and revised as part of the study.

Implicit in these studies is the belief that academic language development is or should be within the purview of content-area teachers as well as language arts teachers and, in the case of ELLs, ESL specialists. Future work describing academic language should be extended to other grades and other content areas. As future research builds on the base established here, it will be possible to identify academic language features that cut across content areas and those that are specific to a particular content area. Curriculum development and the development of language test specifications that focus on both oral and written academic language could then follow.

ELLs are particularly in need of instruction that focuses on academic language development. If the language taught in the ESL classroom is overly simplified or does not include academic language, ELLs will be less able to successfully transition out of ESL services to mainstream classrooms. Also, the creation of academic language proficiency assessments will help prevent ELLs from exiting ESL services until they have sufficient academic language skill to negotiate grade-level content material and assessments.

## Notes

The research assistance of Christine Ong and Charmien LaFramenta for the sections on teacher oral language is gratefully acknowledged, as is the assistance of Becky Huang, Malka Borrego, Priya Abeywickrama, and Frank Herrera for the sections on textbook language.

1. These results are part of a larger study of science classroom interactions conducted at the National Center for Research on Evaluation, Standards, and Student Testing (CRESST) (see Bailey, Butler, La Framenta, and Ong, 2001/4).
2. In the examples, material in square brackets was added by the researchers to provide contextual information and was not part of the actual teacher/student talk. Information in parenthesis describes physical actions or classroom activities included in the original transcript.
3. K-W-L: What we *know,* what we *want* to know, what we *learned* (e.g., Ogle, 1986).
4. The results of this study are part of a larger study of textbook language demands conducted at CRESST (see Butler, Bailey, Stevens, Huang, and Lord, 2004).
5. Guidelines were developed specifically for each type of analysis and seven researchers were trained for the different analyses, with pairs of researchers focusing on descriptive, lexical, grammatical, and discourse features, respectively.
6. Low frequency was operationalized as less than or equal to 10 occurrences per million words, which equals a SFI (frequency index score) of 50 or lower in Zeno et al. (1995).
7. The texts were Badders et al., 2000; Banks et al., 2001; Boehm et al., 2002; Frank et al., 2000; Greenes et al., 2002; Maletsky et al., 2001; Moyer, Hackett, Baptiste, Stryker, and Vasquez, 2001; and Willoughby, Bereiter, Hilton, and Rubinstein, 2003.
8. The absence of some organizational features in mathematics textbooks may unfortunately be consistent with the recent concerns of mathematicians who have called for the greater use of *generalization* and inclusion of proofs in mathematics education (e.g., Schoenfeld, 1994). Word problems would seem to be particularly well positioned to allow for the generalization of mathematical concepts across contexts, and it

is hoped that textbook writers (following reformed content standards) could make use of this opportunity in the future.

9. The calculations for these CIs were based on the 12 text selections of each subject area (each subject area conducted independently) in order to be more conservative. We did this rather than rely on the less stringent CIs based on the combined total of 36 selections across subject areas that are automatically produced by the ANOVA procedure.

10. These findings deserve more study since there were only 21 observations in a total of 10 classrooms in Southern California; there could be regional differences, socioeconomic differences, and so on in the way teachers interact with their students.

## References

Abedi, J., Lord, C., and Plummer, J. R. (1997). *Final report of language background as a variable in NAEP mathematics performance* (CSE Tech. Rep. No. 429). Los Angeles: University of California, National Center for Research on Evaluation, Standards, and Student Testing (CRESST).

Abunahleh, L., Allen, S., Arthur, B., Beals, S., Butler, M., Drenzer, B., et al. (1982). Coping with problems of understanding: Repair sequence in conversations between native and non-native speakers. *Interlanguage Studies Bulletin, 6*(1), 112–120.

Adams, G. L., and Engleman, S. (1996). *Research on direct instruction: 25 years beyond DISTAR* (Report No. ISBN-0–675–21014–3). Seattle, WA: Educational Achievement Systems (ERIC Document Reproduction Service No. ED413575)

Austin, J. L. (1962). *How to do things with words.* Oxford: Clarendon Press.

Badders, W., Bethel, L. J., Fu, V., Peck, D., Sumners, C., and Valentino, C. (2000). *Houghton Mifflin science: Discovery works* (California ed., grade 5). Boston: Houghton Mifflin.

Bailey, A. L. (2000/5). Language analysis of standardized achievement tests: Considerations in the assessment of English language learners. In *The validity of administering large-scale content assessments to English language learners: An investigation from three perspectives* (CSE Tech. Rep. No. 663). Los Angeles: University of California, National Center for Research on Evaluation, Standards, and Student Testing (CRESST).

Bailey, A. L. (in press). From Lambie to Lambaste: The conceptualization, operationalization, and use of academic language in the assessment of ELL students. In K. Rolstad (Ed.), *Rethinking school language.* Mahwah, NJ: LEA.

Bailey, A. L., Butler, F. A., LaFramenta, C., and Ong, C. (2001/4). *Towards the characterization of academic language in upper elementary science classrooms* (CSE Tech. Rep. No. 621). Los Angeles: University of California, National Center for Research on Evaluation, Standards, and Student Testing (CRESST).

Bailey, A. L., Stevens, R., Butler, F. A., and Huang, B. (2005). *Using standards and empirical evidence to develop academic English proficiency test items in reading* (Final Deliverable (April) to IES, Contract No. R305139600002). Los Angeles: University of California, National Center for Research on Evaluation, Standards, and Student Testing (CRESST).

Banks, J. A., Beyer, B. K., Contreras, G., Craven, J., Ladson-Billings, G., McFarland, M. A., et al. (2001). *United States adventures in time and place (grade 5).* New York: McGraw-Hill.

Boehm, R. G., Hoone, C., McGowan, T. M., McKinney-Browning, M. C., Miramontes, O. B., and Porter, P. H. (2002). *Harcourt Brace social studies: Early United States.* Orlando, FL: Harcourt Brace.

Butler, F. A., Bailey A. L., Stevens, R., Huang, B., and Lord, C. (2004). *Academic English in fifth-grade mathematics, science, and social studies textbooks* (Final Deliverable to IES, Contract No. R305B960002; CSE Tech. Rep. No. 642). Los Angeles: University of California, National Center for Research on Evaluation, Standards, and Student Testing (CRESST).

Butler, F. A., Lord, C., Stevens, R., Borrego, M., and Bailey, A. L. (2004). *An approach to operationalizing academic language for language test development purposes: Evidence from fifth-grade science and math* (CSE Tech. Rep. No. 626). Los Angeles: University of California, National Center for Research on Evaluation, Standards, and Student Testing (CRESST).

California State Board of Education (1998). *Science content standards for California public schools, kindergarten through grade twelve.* Sacramento: California Department of Education.

Cambridge International Dictionary of English. (2001). Retrieved July 20, 2001, from http://dictionary.cambridge.org

Cazden, C. (1980). The contribution of ethnographic research to bicultural bilingual education. In J. E. Alatis (Ed.), *Georgetown University Round Table on Languages and Linguistics: Current issues in bilingual education, 1980* (pp. 64–80). Washington, DC: Georgetown University.

Cazden, C. (1988). *Classroom discourse: The language of teaching and learning.* Portsmouth, NH: Heinemann.

Cazden, C. (2001). *Classroom discourse: The language of teaching and learning* (2nd ed.). Portsmouth, NH: Heinemann.

Celce-Murcia, M., and Larsen-Freeman, D. (1983). *The grammar book: An ESL/EFL teacher's course.* Rowley, MA: Newbury House.

Chamot, A. U. (2005). The Cognitive Academic Language Learning Approach (CALLA): An update. In P. Richard-Amato and M. A. Snow (Eds.), *Academic success for English language learners* (pp. 87–102). White Plains, NY: Longman.

Chamot, A. U., and O'Malley, J. M. (1994). *The CALLA handbook: Implementing the cognitive academic language learning approach.* Reading, MA: Addison-Wesley.

Chung, T. M., and Nation, P. (2003). Technical vocabulary in specialised texts. *Reading in a Foreign Language, 15*(2), 103–116.

Coelho, E. (1982). Language across the curriculum. *TESL Talk, 13*(3), 56–70.

Cummins, J. (2000). *Language, power, and pedagogy: Bilingual children in the crossfire.* Clevedon, UK: Multilingual Matters.

Dale, T. C., and Cuevas, G. J. (1992). Integrating mathematics and language learning. In P. A. Richard-Amato and M. A. Snow (Eds.), *The multicultural classroom: Reading for content area teachers* (pp. 330–349). White Plains, NY: Longman.

Delpit, L. (1995). *Other people's children: Cultural conflict in the classroom.* New York: New Press.

Echevarria, J., and Graves, A. (1998). *Sheltered content instruction: Teaching English-language learners with diverse abilities.* Needham Heights, MA: Allyn and Bacon.

Erickson, F. (1987). Transformation and school success: The politics and culture of educational achievement. *Anthropology and Education Quarterly, 18*(4), 335–356.

Fradd, S. H., and Lee, O. (1999). Teachers' roles in promoting science inquiry with students from diverse language backgrounds. *Educational Researcher, 28*(6), 4–20.

Frank, M. S., Jones, R. M., Krockover, G. H., Lang, M. P., McLeod, J. C., Valenta, et al. (2000). *Harcourt science* (California ed., grade 5). Orlando, FL: Harcourt.

Gardner, H. (1993). *Multiple intelligences: The theory in practice.* New York: Basic Books.

Gee, J. P. (1996). *Social linguistics and literacies: Ideology in discourse.* London: Falmer Press.

Gersten, R., and Carnine, D. (1986). Direct instruction in reading comprehension. *Educational Leadership, 43*(7), 70–78.

Gibbons, P. (1998). Classroom talk and the learning of new registers in a second language. *Language and Education, 12*(2), 99–118.

Gibbons, J., and Lascar, E. (1998). Operationalizing academic language proficiency in bilingualism research. *Journal of Multilingual and Multicultural Development, 19*(1), 40–50.

Greenes, C., Leiva, M. A., Vogeli, B. R., Larson, M., Shaw, J. M., and Stiff, L. (2002). *Houghton Mifflin mathematics* (California ed., grade 5). Boston: Houghton Mifflin.

Gutiérrez, K. (1995). Unpackaging academic discourse. *Discourse Processes, 19*(1), 21–37.

Halliday, M. A. K., and Hasan, R. (1976). *Cohesion in English.* London: Longman.

Halliday, M. A. K., and Martin, J. R. (1993). *Writing science: Literacy and discursive power.* London and Washington, DC: Falmer Press.

Heath, S. B. (1983). *Ways with words.* Cambridge: Cambridge University Press.

Kaufman, D. (1997). Collaborative approaches in preparing teachers for content-based and language-enhanced settings. In M. A. Snow and D. Brinton (Eds.), *The content-based classroom: Perspectives on integrating language and content* (pp.175–187). New York: Longman.

Kazemi, E. (1999, Spring). Mathematical discourse that promotes conceptual understanding. *Connections.* Los Angeles: UC Regents.

Keys, C. (1999). Revitalizing instruction in scientific genres: Connecting knowledge production with writing to learn in science. *Science Education, 83*(2), 115–130.

Kinsella, K. (1997). Moving from comprehensible input to "learning to learn" in content-based instruction. In M. A. Snow and D. M. Brinton (Eds.), *The content-based classroom: Perspectives on integrating language and content* (pp. 46–68). White Plains, NY: Longman.

Lee, O. (2001). Culture and language in science education: What do we know and what do we need to know? *Journal of Research in Science Teaching, 38*(5), 499–501.

Lemke, J. (1990). *Talking science: Language, learning, and values.* Norwood, NJ: Ablex. (ERIC Document Reproduction Service No. Ed362379)

Lord, C. (2002). Are subordinate clauses more difficult? In J. Bybee and M. Noonan (Eds.), *Subordination in discourse.* Amsterdam: John Benjamins.

MacWhinney, B. (1995). *The CHILDES project: Computational tools for analyzing talk.* Hillsdale, NJ: Erlbaum.

MacWhinney, B., and Snow, C. E. (1990). The child language data exchange: An update. *Journal of Child Language, 17,* 457–472.

Maletsky, E. M., Andrews, A. G., Bennett, J. M., Burton, G. M., Johnson, H. C., Luckie, et al. (2001). *Harcourt math* (grade 5). Orlando, FL: Harcourt.

Martin, J. R. (1991). Nominalization in science and humanities: Distilling knowledge and scaffolding text. In E. Ventola (Ed.), *Functional and systematic linguistics* (pp. 307–337). Berlin: Mouton de Gruyter.

McDonald, R. W., Pressley, M., and Hampston, J. M. (1998). Literacy instruction in nine first-grade classrooms: Teacher characteristics and student achievement. *Elementary School Journal, 99*(2), 101–128.

Moyer, R., Daniel, L., Hackett, J., Baptiste, P., Stryker, P., and Vasquez, J. (2001). *McGraw-Hill science* (California ed., grade 5). New York: McGraw-Hill.

Nation, I. S. P. (2001). *Learning vocabulary in another language.* Cambridge: Cambridge University Press.

Nation, I. S. P., and Coxhead, A. (2001). The specialised vocabulary of English for academic purposes. In J. Flowerdew and M. Peacock (Eds.), *Research perspectives on English for academic purposes* (pp. 252–267). Cambridge: Cambridge University Press.

National Research Council. (1998). *Preventing reading difficulties in young children* (Committee on the Prevention of Reading Difficulties in Young Children, C. E. Snow, M. S. Burns, and P. Griffin, Eds., Commission on Behavioral and Social Sciences and Education). Washington, DC: National Academy Press.

NUD*IST 4.0 [computer software]. (1996–2000). Victoria, Australia: Qualitative Solutions and Research PTY LTD.QSR.

Ogle, D. (1986). K-W-L: A teaching model that develops active reading of expository text. *Reading Teacher, 39,* 564–570.

Pan, B. (1994). Basic measures of child language. In J. L. Sokolov and C. E. Snow (Eds.), *Handbook of research in language development using CHILDES* (pp. 26–49). Mahwah, NJ: Lawrence Erlbaum.

Philips, S. U. (1972). Participant structures and communicative competence: Warm Springs children in community and classroom. In C. B. Cazden, V. P. John, and D. Hymes (Eds.), *Functions of language in the classroom* (pp. 370–394). New York: Teachers College Press.

Phillips, J. R. (1973). Syntax and vocabulary in mothers' speech to young children: Age and sex comparisons. *Child Development, 44,* 182–185.

Piaget, J. (1972). Language and thought from the genetic point of view. In P. Adams (Ed.), *Language in thinking* (pp. 170–179). Middlesex, UK: Penguin Books. (Original work published 1967.)

Piaget, J., and Inhelder, B. (1969). *The psychology of the child* (H. Weaver, Trans). London: Routledge and Kegan Paul.

Pimm, D. (1987). *Speaking mathematically: Communication in mathematics classrooms.* London: Routledge and Kegan Paul.

Pimm, D. (1995). *Symbols and meanings in school mathematics.* London: Routledge.

Polman, J., and Pea, R. (2001). Transformative communication as a cultural tool for guiding inquiry science. *Science Education, 85*(3), 223–38.

RAND. (2002). *Reading for understanding: Toward a research and development program in reading comprehension.* Santa Monica, CA: Rand. Retrieved August 12, 2003, from http://www.rand.org/publications/MR/MR1465/.

Reppen, R. (2001). Register variation in student and adult speech and writing. In S. Conrad and D. Biber (Eds.), *Variation in English: Multidimensional studies* (pp. 187–199). Harlow, UK: Pearson Education.

Richard-Amato, P. A., and Snow, M. A. (1992). Strategies for content-area teachers. In P. A. Richard-Amato and M. A. Snow (Eds.), *The multicul-*

*tural classroom: Reading for content area teachers* (pp. 145–163). White Plains, NY: Longman.

Richard-Amato, P., and Snow, M. A. (2005). Instructional strategies for K-12 mainstream teachers. In P. Richard-Amato and M. A. Snow (Eds.), *Academic success for English language learners* (pp. 197–223). White Plains, NY: Longman.

Richards, B. (1987). Type/token ratios: What do they really tell us? *Journal of Child Language, 14,* 201–209.

Rivard, L., and Straw, S. (2000). The effect of talk and writing on learning science: An exploratory study. *Science Education, 84*(5), 566–593.

Rosenshine, B. (1986). Synthesis of research on explicit teaching. *Educational Leadership, 43,* 60–69.

Rosenshine, B., and Stevens, R. (1986). Teaching functions. In M. Wittrock (Ed.), *Handbook of research on teaching* (3rd ed., pp. 376–391). New York: Macmillan.

Scarcella, R. (2003). *Academic English: A conceptual framework* (Tech. Rep. No. 2003-1). Santa Barbara: UC Linguistic Minority Research Institute.

Schegloff, E. A. (2000). When "others" initiate repair. *Applied linguistics, 21*(2), 205–243.

Schegloff, E. A., Jefferson, G., and Sacks, H. (1977). The preference for self-correction in the organization of repair in conversation. *Language, 53*(2), 361–382.

Schleppegrell, M. (2001). Linguistic features of the language of schooling. *Linguistics and Education, 12*(4), 431–495.

Schleppegrell, M. (2004). *The language of schooling: A functional linguistics perspective.* Mahwah, NJ: Lawrence Erlbaum.

Schoenfeld, A. H. (1994). *Mathematical thinking and problem solving.* Hillsdale, NJ: Lawrence Erlbaum.

Searle, J. R. (1970). *Speech acts.* Cambridge: Cambridge University Press.

Short, D. J. (1993). *Integrating language and culture in middle school American history classes* (Report to OERI). Washington, DC: Center for Applied Linguistics and the National Center for Research on Cultural Diversity and Second Language Learning.

Snow, M.A. (2001). Content-based and immersion models for second and foreign language teaching. In M. Celce-Murcia (Ed.), *Teaching English as a second or foreign language* (3rd ed., pp. 303–318). Boston: Heinle and Heinle.

Snow, M. A., and Brinton, D. (1997). *The content-based classroom: Perspectives on integrating language and content.* New York: Longman.

Solomon, J., and Rhodes, N. (1995). *Conceptualizing academic language* (Research Rep. No. 15). Santa Cruz: University of California, National Center for Research on Cultural Diversity and Second Language Learning.

Templin, M. C. (1957). *Certain language skills in children.* Minneapolis: University of Minnesota Press.

Turner, J. (1997). Creating content-based language tests: Guidelines for teachers. In M. A. Snow and D. Brinton (Eds.), *The content-based classroom: Perspectives on integrating language and content* (pp. 187–200). New York: Longman.

Vygotsky, L. (1962). *Thought and language.* New York: Wiley.

Vygotsky, L. (1978). *Mind in society: The development of higher psychological processes* (M. Cole, Ed.). Cambridge, MA: Harvard University Press.

Willoughby, S. S., Bereiter, C., Hilton, P., and Rubinstein, J. H. (2003). *SRA: Math explorations and applications* (grade 5). Chicago: SRA/McGraw-Hill.

Wong Fillmore, L., and Snow, C. (2000). *What teachers need to know about language.* ERIC Clearinghouse on Languages and Linguistics. Retrieved August 1, 2000, from http://www.cal.org/ericcll.

Zakaluk, B., and Samuels, S. J. (Eds.) (1988). *Readability: Its past, present, and future.* Newark, DE: International Reading Association.

Zeno, S. M., Ivens, S. H., Millard, R. T., and Duvvuri, R. (1995). *The educator's word frequency guide.* New York: Touchstone Applied Science Associates.

# CHAPTER 6

# Making Choices in Academic English Language Testing: Evidence from the Evolution of Test Specifications

FRED DAVIDSON, JUNG TAE KIM, HYEONG-JONG LEE, JINSHU LI, AND ALEXIS A. LÓPEZ

This chapter discusses the evolutionary nature of test development. We propose an "audit trail" of change in a particular type of testing materials, known as "specifications."[1] We suggest that language test developers keep track of changes and of why changes happen. The tracking of such changes is an important element of test validation. We illustrate change tracking through analysis of test specifications from a major national language test development initiative: the WIDA project.[2] Our chapter thus has two major purposes: first, we illustrate and discuss test specifications as a fundamental tool in testing, and second, we discuss one particular role their audits can have in validation.

## Test Specifications

A test specification—or "spec"—is a blueprint for test creation. There are many types of test specs. From a stable, evolved spec, test developers can generate many equivalent test items or tasks. A spec shows test writers how to write tasks such that they measure the same target skill, all the while doing so with different task content. The spec would tell the testing team what kinds of items are acceptable and what items are not permitted.

The concept of test specifications is not new. As early as the 1920s, testers were formulating "rules" for test creation: what to include and what to exclude from items against some criteria (Ruch, 1924). Some canonical understandings have emerged since that time. Specs are routinely advocated in textbooks on testing, and the books present an array of different spec designs. A key decision in spec formulas is whether the particular spec model endorses or does not endorse any certain models of language ability. For example, Davidson and Lynch (2002; following earlier work by W. J. Popham) discuss spec formulas that do not assume any particular view about the material being tested; that is, they suggest that the spec authors (themselves) should identify and explain those beliefs. In contrast, Bachman and Palmer (1996, part 3) align their specs with presumptions about the nature of language as a human trait.

Specs also exist at multiple levels of generality. At the highest level, specs are a set of decisions about what is being tested: how many items on this skill, how many on that, where to get materials, what score weighting to apply to various subtests and how to apply it. This higher level is often called a "table of specifications" (Davidson and Lynch, 2002, p. 66). Alderson, Clapham, and Wall (1995) present another approach to the design of language test specifications that is at such a higher level of generality. At lower levels of generality, specs are written to produce actual test questions. Both the Bachman and Palmer approach and that of Davidson and Lynch are such lower-level specs. In actual use, the level of generality of a spec is itself a design consideration. Language test developers benefit from generative tools all along the spectrum: from highly articulated, closely focused guidelines to produce individual test tasks to very general guidelines about the assembly of an entire test. All such documents are specs, for all serve a fundamentally generative purpose. Lower-level specs—which are the focus of this chapter— ultimately contribute to the production of a higher-level specification table.

In our work on spec-driven language testing, certain principles and concepts continue to emerge and to be refined, beyond the discussion of specs in the literature (e.g., Davidson and Lynch 2002; Lynch and Davidson 1994). To illustrate some recent developments in our work on language test specs and to illustrate the fundamental nature of specs themselves, we would like to review two such recent emergent concepts.

The first is an "archetype." Please read the following generative guiding spec language shown in text box 6.1—this kind of language is very typical in a test specification. Avoid the temptation to turn the page and see the sample item it produces, given as text box 6.2. Try to visualize the item in your mind's eye—read the first text box several times, closing your eyes each time and visualizing the item it will produce.

---

### Text Box 6.1

Generative Guiding Language (for the item given in text box 6.2)

The purpose of this item type is to test a student's ability to read and interpret basic descriptive statistics embedded in a brief text item stem. The statistical report is from some scientific survey or study and refers to common everyday knowledge. The interpretation is assessed through five multiple-choice responses. One choice is correct. The other four choices—the distracters—are wrong because they misinterpret the report in subtle ways. Close reading is required to distinguish between the choices.

The stem will have two sentences. The first sentence of the stem of the item will present a statistical report or result. Typical forms for such reports include proportions (*X out of Y report Z*) and averages (*The typical X has/ does Y*). The second sentence of the stem will always read: "Which *must* be true?" The distracters will be wrong because certain mathematical interpretation is *not* possible given the particular language either included or not included. The correct choice will be that which is true given a strict and limited reading of the stem.

The student will select the intended correct choice in order to get value for the item. In making that selection, the student will (1) apply mathematical principles of statistical analysis; and (2) by close detailed reading, compare and contrast the various interpretations shown in the five choices.

---

The language in text box 6.1 is a description of an actual item, taken from a real high-stakes K-12 ELL exam, which we show in text box 6.2.

If you played along with our experiment here, ask yourself this question: "When reading text box 6.1, what kind of item did I see in my mind's eye? Once I went ahead and read text box 6.2, did it match what I imagined?"

Suppose that it did *not* match. Then ask yourself this question: "Does the mismatch matter?" We suspect that you did not imagine an item precisely like that shown in text box 6.2, but we also suspect that—once you reflect on your vision—your item will feel similar to that we have shown here.

Text box 6.1 presents specification language—what we call "generative guiding language." Text box 6.2 presents an item generated by that language. In specification-driven testing, it is not necessary to match the sample item precisely. Instead, it is necessary to be "congruent."[3]

An archetype is a widely shared common item style to measure a given skill. To test the archetypal nature of this exercise, copy text box 6.1 and text box 6.2 from this chapter. Then, in a group of colleagues, repeat this exercise. Ask your colleagues to write out the item they see—give them copies of text box 6.1. Put your colleagues' samples on overhead or flipcharts—does it seem that everybody in the room is thinking the same thing? There may be an archetype at play. It is very difficult to escape the ways we have always tested things, as it is equally difficult to escape the ways that we have—ourselves—been tested. As a close to the exercise, give them copies of text box 6.2 and ask if they think their items are congruent, among themselves and with the item shown in text box 6.2.[4]

A second notion has become increasingly important to our spec-writing team: reverse engineering. The item shown in text box 6.2 is an available sample test question from a published high-stakes ELL screening exam in our home state (Illinois State Board of Education, 2005). The generative guiding language in text box 6.1 was produced by analysis of the item. That is, text box 6.2 came first. Reverse engineering is the production of guiding language from already existing sample items or tasks.

We believe there are four types of reverse engineering (RE): straight, historical, critical, and test deconstruction.

*Straight RE* is when the spec seeks to replicate the item or task exactly as it is. For example, a test development team may have a test in hand, but the people who developed it have left, taking their memory with them of how and why the test was written as it was. Perhaps the test has gotten old. Maybe there have been security problems. By straight RE, newcomers can figure out the design of the test and attempt to generate new equivalent items. The administrator of such a program can replicate an existing test more quickly

---

**Text Box 6.2**

Sample Item (produced by the guiding language in text
box 6.1)

   Four out of five doctors like Brand X. Which *must* be
true?

   A. Five doctors were surveyed.

   B. Exactly four doctors like Brand X.

   C. More than five doctors had to be surveyed.

   D. Exactly 100 doctors had to be surveyed.

   E. An average of 80% of the doctors surveyed liked
      Brand X.

---

and accurately if he or she first produces specs that describe the existing test.

*Historical RE* is when specs are straight reverse engineered across
many versions of a test in order to better understand how the test
has changed over time. An administrator of a language program
might do straight RE over time across existing but evolving tests in
the program's archives. This would help the administrator understand how the program got to its present state.

*Critical RE* is when the spec replicates and improves the item or
task. For example, the very same administrator might become dis-
satisfied with how testing has evolved at his or her institution. As
the archived tests are better and better understood, the administrator and the staff may see room for improvement. New test specs are
crafted. The new specs share much of the philosophy of the institution but allow the administrator and new teaching staff to effect
change and innovation.

*Test deconstruction*[5] is when the spec is used to better explain the
contexts (social, political, curricular, theoretical) in which the test
operates. The spec is, itself, a way station tool toward a larger analysis. Once again, our administrator—analyzing tests over time—may
come to understand not only how testing was done at that institution at a particular era but why. Perhaps there are some retired staff
members around who can answer questions such as: "Why did you
all do it this way 10 years ago?" The answers to such questions are

invaluable aids not only in test development but also in understanding the larger political ebb and financial flow of any educational waters.

The language in text box 6.1 was produced by straight RE of the
item shown in text box 6.2. As you and your colleagues grapple with
your archetype, we strongly suspect you will become critical of it.
Is this a good way to test reading of text-embedded statistics? For
example, the item stem is actually rather short. Don't real-world
tests of embedded statistics involve longer passages, tables, graphs,
and so on? What grade levels would use such a spec, and why? How
do you decouple reading ability from mathematical ability in a task
such as this? In general, how might you change the item and its
guiding language to make for a better test? Answering these questions is critical RE, because you would refine the spec as you come
to better understand what it is trying to do.

We believe that spec-driven testing is an iterative, feedback-laden,
consensus-driven process. It is also a process of discovery. Text box
6.1 and text box 6.2—in tandem—are a sample of one single spec:
you see the sample item that the spec will generate and the guiding
language that surrounds it. As test development cycles, as feedback
rolls in, and as the team members achieve consensus about what to
change and what not to change, the test grows and evolves and
hopefully improves validity of the decisions to be made based on
test results. Along the way, certain phenomena emerge that should
generalize to other test development settings. We have shared two
in our exposition of specs here: archetypes and reverse engineering;
we have experienced these phenomena many times in different
spec-driven settings. As we audited the WIDA specs (thus far), we
uncovered some additional evolutionary principles of test creation.

## The WIDA Project

The WIDA project is a consortium of 10 states that seeks to develop
ELD tests that are congruent with the new federal mandate embod-
ied in the No Child Left Behind legislation (NCLB, 2001). WIDA
began as a cooperative venture of three states: Wisconsin, Delaware, and Arkansas; hence the shortening of the three state names
to produce the name. (See Bailey, chapter 1 for more information
about the WIDA assessment project.)

Of greatest relevance to our chapter in this book is the specification-driven nature of the WIDA assessment, called "ACCESS for ELLs." As this book goes to press, the WIDA project has been through about four major versions or generations of test specifications. The next spec generation will be straight reverse engineered from the operational test, because the test has itself progressed beyond the current set of specs: the item writers have—in effect—improved on the specs as they actually wrote the test. It is important to do this last step, so that future users of the WIDA tests will have some generative documents from which to train new item writers, to communicate with stakeholders and with test takers, and to observe and track the operational rollout of the exam.

## Traveling the Audit Trail

Text box 6.3 shows the evolution of WIDA specs through version 3.0, up to the point of the November 2004 field tests. Although there are four versions, we number them starting with 0 to emphasize that the first batch of specs were really a thought-generating set of prototypes.

---

### Text Box 6.3

Timeline of WIDA Spec Development

Version 0, summer 2003: 20 prototype specs, four skills, four grade clusters

Version 1.0, early October 2003: 167 specs, three skills (listening, reading, and writing), five grade clusters (kindergarten was broken out)

Version 2.0, late 2003: 90 specs, two skills revised (listening and reading), two grade clusters revised

Version 3.0, spring 2004: 254 specs, four skills, four grade clusters (kindergarten is still broken out but unrevised at this stage)

---

The specs were developed in feedback with the test item writing subcontract team at the Center for Applied Linguistics (CAL) in Washington, D.C. It is important to note that the development of versions 2.0 and 3.0 were guided by the WIDA online item-writing course, in which CAL contracted with a number of teachers to write items and tasks for the operational test.

As of version 3.0, the general information contained in WIDA specs is shown in text box 6.4.

---

### Text Box 6.4

Elements of WIDA Specs

Sample item
Generative guiding language, notably:
    Information to identify the spec (name, number, standard, domain, skill, level, and so forth)
    General information about the test item/task (purpose, content, test procedure, format)
    Information about the stimulus/prompt
    Information about the response that is expected of the test taker
    Information about how the item/task is scored

---

Our audit uncovered nine principle areas of change in the WIDA specs (see text box 6.5).

---

### Text Box 6.5

Areas of Change in WIDA Specs through Version 3.0

Consistency
Authenticity
Alignment
Bias check
Expected responses
Scoring issues
Construct
Decision-making process
The nature of a spec "version"

---

We would like to illustrate three of these areas of discovery further. First is our understanding of "authenticity" of the material to be tested. In the version 2.0 language arts and listening specifications at grades 3–5 and 6–8, the prompt text was written fully by the spec writer. Our feedback from the item writers indicated that real-life samples were essential at these grade levels. In version 3.0, these specs included sample texts from grade-level textbooks. The operational definition of authenticity changed to stipulate any type of materials that are actually used in classrooms.

The passages taken from grade-level textbooks may themselves be of questionable authenticity, of course. The point being made here is that all parties agreed that grade-level text passages seemed more authentic than passages authored by the spec writers. Ultimately, the best solution to this particular dilemma is text analysis such as that advocated by Bailey, Butler, Stevens, and Lord in chapter 5 of this book.

The second area of discovery concerned bias checking. WIDA implemented an industry-standard bias check later in the test development. "Bias" here refers to cultural, gender, age-related, sexist, religious, or other kinds of information that may offend either test takers or score users and that also may cause test-taker performance to "bounce."[6] Along the way, our teams detected and discussed areas of potential bias and tried to resolve them. In several specs at version 1.0, sample items referred to regions or countries in the world that are experiencing or have experienced political conflict. Spec writers had difficulty writing sample items. Should they use real or fake names of countries and regions? We felt that test takers might react to the names used in a negative manner or in some manner that caused their item performance to change, thus reflecting something other than the abilities being tested. The problem seemed most salient if the sample items referred to social or political instability. A discussion was held with the WIDA team on this point and a workaround was found: we would not mention instability at all. The skills assessed were altered so that "instability" was replaced with "political, economic, or historical significance to U.S. or to world history." By version 3.0, specs requiring reference to geographical regions of the world had shifted to avoid a potential bias, and this shift reflected a fundamental reference in the spec (i.e., about economic significance) rather than an attempt at some value judgment about political stability.

Third, a very interesting finding emerged regarding the nature of a "version." As of this writing, there is healthy disagreement among our team as to whether version 3.0 is truly a fourth-generation spec or whether the changes from version 1.0 to version 2.0 are salient enough to merit a new generation. When compared, version 2.0 was effectively a revision of version 1.0, not a major redefinition of the things being measured. Version 3.0 was such a redefinition because we broke out the skills to a much finer-grained array (254 specs). As specs grow and evolve and change, so to do our understandings of the things we are measuring. One way to define the thing we measure is to see whether it separates into a unique spec or whether it collapses with other skills.

The next version of WIDA specs—be they called version 4.0 or 3.0—will be reverse engineered from the operational tests, from notes on bias checking, from pilot and field test results, and from interviews with item writers and other WIDA project staff. Initial feedback along those lines indicates that we are presently at rather a fine-grained level. There are 254 specs for the current version 3.0 spec bank (i.e., a collection of specifications for the generation of new items, analogous to the term *item bank*, from which new, equivalent forms of a test are compiled). The item writers and their supervisors have (already) categorized listening and reading items into what are now called "folders." These folders share many common characteristics, and so draft folder specifications are in preparation. These folder specs should be a more productive level of generality for the operational test—there will be far fewer than the 254 specs seen in version 3.0.

These three sample trails show how we have audited our own work. The functional outcome of the audits is to strengthen our argument that the inferences drawn from the test's results are valid for their intended purposes. Each sample audit seeks to show how a particular decision evolved and to justify the resolution of that decision. As the test goes operational, these decisions may be challenged and may well change. That is as it should be. The audits not only justify the current state of affairs, they also help to anticipate consequences yet to come.

## Making It Work

First, it is clearly a lot of work to track all this information. We have some practical suggestions for both test developers and teachers creating their own classroom-based assessments of AEL based on our experience thus far that may make audit tracking easier:

- Set up a database in which test specs are created and make the tracking an integral part of the database. Spec writers would need to enter into the database not only the new specs but also how they change from previous versions.

- Hold regular meetings at which spec evolution is discussed. It is very important to track and understand how specs evolve and change—doing so is the central argument of this chapter. Such change often happens at team meetings, and it can be recorded.

- Decide on the meaning of a version. Too many versions make too much work and too much tracking. Before tracking changes, the team should agree whether a spec has changed enough (in the first place) to merit contribution to an audit.

- Link your audit analysis of items to the audit analysis of the entire test. Our discussion in this chapter is of low-level fine-grained specs. As you audit the evolution of those documents, you will naturally also audit how they contribute to an overall test. The same benefits ensue at all levels of spec generality.

- Organize your audit analysis. Each of our three example discoveries we presented is a separate audit, in the sense that accountants use the term. Each ends in rationalization for decisions made: in our examples, how to handle bias, whether to author texts, and what we should call a version. Accountants speak of "working papers" as a way to arrange the multiple audit trails when justifying actions in a corporation—so, too, each of our three examples could yield a single working paper that shows the problems faced, versioned spec excerpts to illustrate each problem, and the final resolution of the problem.[7] We have, of necessity, summarized the analyses here; in real use, there would be much more to each trail.

- Finally, look beyond the audits. Test development is more than creating specs and auditing them. It involves a number of traditional steps we do not cover in this chapter, such as piloting, operational maintenance and routine data analysis, and the creation of other documents needed by the testing team (for example, a test administration manual). The specs and their audits can usefully inform, but should not replace, these other test development activities.

What is the tactical use of the information we have obtained? To put the matter bluntly, we are setting up lines of defense against attack on the validity of test results. For instance, if WIDA is challenged about bias in its test items, we can counter with the facts that (1) we did bias checking; and (2) we did it all along the way and documented it. We can claim and support that we anticipated potential problems regarding bias, and we can show how we resolved those problems. Likewise, if we are challenged about authenticity, we can show how we operationally defined that (admittedly) tricky word, at least as regards text selection. Bias and authenticity emerged organically in the creative process of spec writing and revision. Longer-standing principles of spec-driven test creation can also help with test validation. Reverse engineering will help us to produce the next version of specs. And we can use the notion of archetypes when illustrating novel versus traditional item types in the test.

Auditing our specs has shown us, once again, how specs foster creative dialogue and consensus building. Ideally, the audit could be shared with a wider community (e.g., stakeholders in schools, parents, even test takers). It could also foster a more collegial understanding of tests and encourage dialogue and discussion—as advocated by Shohamy (2001).

Test specifications and audits are useful in a wide variety of test settings. They apply not only to large-scale test development (like WIDA) but also to smaller testing needs, like the assessment done in a classroom. Teachers can defend their testing decisions far more easily if they can document how they arrived at those decisions, and the audit permits them to do that. Audited test specs hold principled value—the audit is a decontextualized method to establish and document how any test is anchored to a given domain of content.

## Concluding with a Paper Chase

We presented a fundamental tool in test development: the specification, which is a generative document from which many equivalent testing tasks can be produced. A spec has two basic components: guiding language and sample tasks or items. Together, these components sketch a claim that a particular domain of content is actually being assessed. How does a spec achieve such a claim?

Test specs are not written and done with, straight out of the gate. They evolve, through critical feedback, through trialing, and through consensus. We can track the changes in our conception of the task; to paraphrase the movie *The Paper Chase*, we begin with mush but end up with clarity. Our team has found this to happen, again and again, and we naturally fell upon a method of tracking our transit from mush to clarity: the audit.

The audit shows us how our conceptions emerge and solidify. We gave several such examples in this chapter, such as our evolving grasp of difficult concepts like authenticity or expected responses.

Any spec audit is part of the ongoing problem of validity. Test validity concerns our confidence in the inferences drawn from the results of the test scores; the establishment of validity requires a sound argument (Kane, 1992). The WIDA tests will be used for two primary purposes. One is program redesignation, as when a test taker is moved from one kind of language service program to another. The second is measuring yearly progress to determine if ELLs are progressing in their command of English. These decisions imply serious educational consequences. Auditing specs is a way to force the test team to discuss and encounter problems before they happen, and perhaps even before extensive piloting or tryouts are done. We would prefer to begin our validity argument now than to wait until it is forced upon us.

## Notes

This material is based on work supported by the WIDA Consortium as a subcontract on U.S. Department of Education Grant Award S368A030007. Any opinions, findings, and conclusions or recommendations expressed in this publication are those of the author(s) and do not necessarily reflect the views of the WIDA Consortium.

Portions of this paper were presented by Kim, Lee, Li, and López at the Midwest Association of Language Testers, Dayton, Ohio, October 2004.

1. The term *audit trail* comes from the work of Guba and Lincoln (1989) in qualitative research, as adapted slightly by Davidson and Lynch (2002, p. 9) in their discussion of test validity.

2. WIDA is a consortium of (as of this writing) 10 states representing about 280,000 English language learners (WIDA 2005). The WIDA assessments have been approved by the U.S. Department of Education as compliant with the most recent reauthorization of the Elementary and Secondary Education Act (No Child Left Behind, 2001). The governing standards for WIDA's assessments have been adopted by Teachers of English to Speakers of Other Languages (TESOL) as their recommended national standards. The reader is also encouraged to visit the WIDA website: www.wida.us.

3. An alternate term for this is *fit-to-spec*. Spec authors often speak of items and tasks (generated from specs) as either "fitting" or "not fitting" the spec.
4. This kind of activity is but one—of many—that can be designed to train spec writers and users of specifications. We encourage you to be creative with specs both in their use and in training staff for their use. Davidson and Lynch (2002, appendix 2) discuss the teaching of test specifications.
5. We are grateful to Samira Elatia for this term.
6. I.e., yield unpredictable or erratic results in either analysis of item data or subtotals and totals.
7. One coauthor of this chapter, Jinshu Li, is working on a master's thesis at UIUC in which some formats for such working papers are being explored.

## References

Alderson, J. C., Clapham, C., and Wall, D. (1995). *Language test construction and evaluation*. Cambridge: Cambridge University Press.

Bachman, L. F., and Palmer, A. S. (1996). *Language testing in practice*. Oxford: Oxford University Press.

Davidson, F., and Lynch, B. K. (2002). *Testcraft: A teacher's guide to writing and using language test specifications*. New Haven: Yale University Press.

Guba, E. G., and Lincoln, Y. S. (1989). *Fourth generation evaluation*. Newbury Park, CA: Sage.

Illinois State Board of Education. (2005). *Illinois measure of annual growth in English mathematics sample items, grade 11*. Retrieved January 31, 2005, from http://www.isbe.net/assessment/PDF/IMAGEGrade11.pdf

Kane, M. T. (1992). An argument-based approach to validity. *Psychological Bulletin 112*(3), 527–535.

Lynch, B., and Davidson, F. (1994). Criterion-referenced language test development: Linking curricula, teachers, and tests. *TESOL Quarterly, 28*(4) 727–743.

No Child Left Behind. (2001). Conference Report to Accompany H.R., 1, Rep. No. 107-334, House of Representatives, 107th Congress, 1st Session, December 13.

Ruch, G. M. (1924). *The improvement of the written examination*. Chicago: Scott-Foresman.

Shohamy, E. (2001). *The power of tests: A critical perspective on the uses of language tests*. Harlow, UK: Longman.

WIDA Consortium. (2005). Retrieved January 31, 2005, from http://www.wida.us.

# CHAPTER 7

# Academic English: A View from the Classroom

MARGARET HERITAGE, NORMA SILVA,
AND MARY PIERCE

For students who are English language learners (ELLs), the challenge of schooling is to acquire English while simultaneously constructing new curriculum knowledge. The challenge for teachers of ELLs is to plan instruction that meets the language learning needs of students to ensure that their ability to speak, listen, read, and write in academic subjects across the curriculum does not lag behind that of their peers. To do this requires an accurate grasp of their students' language and content knowledge, a depth of content knowledge and lexico-grammatical knowledge, and a wide knowledge of pedagogy from which teachers can draw to select the appropriate strategy for the learning goals. In this chapter, we will examine the linguistic competencies that students need to have for academic success, present a model of teacher knowledge for students' academic success, and explore the application of the model in the classroom setting. A critical component of our model is teachers' knowledge of students derived from formative and summative assessments. We will discuss the challenges that current assessment practices, both formative and summative, present for teachers in implementing our model of teaching ELL students.

## Competencies for Academic Success

Understanding and using academic registers correlates with academic success (Snow, Cancini, Gonzalez, and Shriberg, 1989). A register is the constellation of lexical and grammatical features that characterize particular uses of language (Halliday and Hasan, 1989; Martin, 1992). Registers vary because language use varies from context to context (Schleppegrell, 2001). Halliday (1994) describes the variables of context as *field,* the topics and actions that language is used to express; *tenor,* the language relationship between users and their purposes; and *mode,* the channel through which the communication is carried out. For example, there is a considerable difference between the field, tenor, and mode of a formal presentation on a topic at a business meeting compared to conversation over dinner with friends in a restaurant. Understanding the field, tenor, and mode of a language context enables language users to draw on their lexico-grammatical knowledge to construct a schema that anticipates a pattern of language use and its associated meanings. Cummins (1986) and Skutnabb-Kangas (1984) showed that minority-language students are less likely to acquire academic registers than their dominant-language peers. Thus, a key consideration for teachers of ELL students is developing their students' abilities to conceptualize and convey meaning in a range of academic registers.

Consider these excerpts from the first-grade writing standards established by the National Center on Education and the Economy and the University of Pittsburgh in 1999 (New Standards Primary Literacy Committee, 1999): "By the end of the year we expect students to: 1) produce narrative accounts in which they demonstrate a growing awareness of author's craft by employing some writing strategies, such as using dialogue, transitions or time cue words . . . 2) produce reports in which they gather information pertinent to a topic, sort information and report on it to others . . . 3) produce functional writings that give instructions . . . and 4) demonstrate an ability to reproduce some of the literary language and styles they hear in the classroom (e.g., metaphor, simile, complex syntax, descriptive detail)."

While many first-grade ELL students acquire sufficient English to engage in social conversations, which to an informal observer might look like proficiency in English (American Educational Research Association, 2004), there are significant differences between informal interactional language and the language demands of these first-grade writing standards.

To produce narrative accounts requires children to develop a sequence of events that flow from an initiating event and to signal the chronology of events through transition words. It requires an appropriate selection of tenses to set different time frames in relation to each other and the ability to differentiate the syntax of the account from the syntax of dialogue, when the tenses may change from present to future. By contrast, the report writing does not require a temporal sequence and is characterized by directly stated sentences, specialized vocabulary related to the topic, and conjunctions of mainly cause or purpose. Functional writing necessitates presenting a goal and relating steps in a process to accomplish the goal and the use of the present tense, imperative verbs, temporal conjunctions, and action verbs. Reproducing literary language involves using distinct syntax that is representative of literary forms, including complex sentences and vocabulary choices that convey a sense of imagery. Additionally, each expectation requires metalinguistic skills (i.e., the ability to reflect on language), including awareness of word selection and syntactic forms.

For their students to develop the language knowledge represented in the first-grade writing standards, teachers will need to provide the opportunity for them to experience, acquire, and practice the vocabulary and syntax associated with a variety of registers in oral and printed language. Moreover, because of the variation in the lexical and grammatical features of academic language in different disciplines (see Bailey, Butler, Stevens, and Lord, chapter 5; Butler, Bailey, Stevens, Huang and Lord, 2004), teachers will have to pay particular attention to the distinctive characteristics of oral and printed language across the curriculum.

## Printed Language

"Learning to read is one of the most important things children accomplish in elementary school because it is the foundation for most of their future academic endeavors. From the middle elementary years through the rest of their lives as students, children spend much of their time reading and learning information presented in text" (Stevens, Slavin, and Farnish, 1991, cited in National Reading Panel, 2000). To be successful in school, therefore, all students need to acquire the skills of learning to read and the skills of reading to learn.

To read to learn, students must have both the reading skills (e.g., word recognition, fluency, comprehension-based processing) and the academic language skills (e.g., syntactic knowledge, lexical knowledge) necessary to acquire information from text. Dutro (2003) highlights the interrelatedness of these skill areas in the example *If we had provided the soil with essential nutrients, the plant would have grown larger.* She notes that to be able to read this text successfully, in addition to effective reading skills, students need knowledge of the conditional mood (*If . . . would have*), knowledge of the past perfect (*had grown*), knowledge of the comparative form of the word large *(larger)*, and background knowledge and vocabulary about plants to understand the words *nutrients* and *soil.*

Gibbons (1998) draws attention to the intertextual relationship of oral language to printed language that exists in a classroom and its significance for language learning. Oral language and printed language have different syntactic characteristics (e.g., Reppen, 2001; Schleppegrell, 2001). Printed language tends to use more complex structures than academic oral language (Bailey, in press). If we take Dutro's printed language example, it is more likely that students (and probably their teachers) will express the relationship between essential nutrients and plant growth in a less complex sentence structure (e.g., *The plant didn't grow larger because we didn't give the soil enough nutrients*). A consideration for teachers of ELL students, therefore, is the link between oral and printed language and how to bridge the "linguistic" gap in their instruction (Gibbons, 1998).

The importance of vocabulary, syntax, and background knowledge for ELLs is underscored when we look at the factors that contribute to noncomprehension of text. Typically, comprehension problems are linked to inadequate understanding of the words used, insufficient background knowledge of the domain represented, a lack of familiarity with the syntactic structures, and an absence of knowledge about the conventions used to achieve the purpose of the text (Lyon, 1998). The experience of one of the authors in a first-grade classroom serves to illustrate how comprehension problems can occur.

The teacher has been teaching the class various reading strategies to decipher unfamiliar words and is now holding an individual conference with an ELL student. She knows that this student has difficulty with reading and tends to avoid reading when he can. Although he has little or no difficulty using his knowledge of English phonics to say the sounds in most of the words in his books, he has difficulty making meaning. The teacher begins the conference by asking the student to tell her about what he has been reading.

*Teacher:*   Can you tell me about what you have been reading today?

*Student:*   I read this book about frogs.

*Teacher:*   Can you tell me about the story? What happens?

The student shrugs his shoulders and flips through the pages. The teacher recognizes that this student is having comprehension problems and wants to know why. She asks the child to read a passage from the text. The student begins to read; it soon becomes apparent to the teacher that, although the student reads many decodable words, he attempts to read other words phonetically, often reading aloud a word that does not make sense, but still going on. The teacher decides that reviewing one of the reading strategies she has taught may help this student increase his level of comprehension of this text.

> *Teacher:* Remember the reading strategies we have been using to make sense of what we are reading? First, listen to yourself read the sentence, then stop and ask yourself "Does what I read make sense?" If not, reread and try again.

The student reads on, stopping occasionally, but continues to miscue and even make up words. He appears to be unaware which are real words in English and which words he has invented to say something for each group of letters he sees on the page. The teacher decides to scaffold this student's learning by reteaching another reading strategy.

> *Teacher:* Let's try another reading strategy. Readers who are unsure of a word can look at the picture and the beginning sound to make a guess about the word. If I wanted to know what this word was, for example (*teacher points to the word "frog"*), I might look at the picture and see a frog. Yes, this word starts with "fr." And "frog" makes sense in the sentence. The word must be "frog." Why don't you try it?

The student looks at the word "toad" on the page and proceeds to look up at the picture. He looks back at the word and says "t-t-t" and then looks back at the picture. He says "Tog?" and looks up questioningly at the teacher. He is unsure if this is a word, but it is his best attempt at the strategy. The teacher recognizes that, even though the child understands the strategy, it still fails to work, because the student does not have the background knowledge about toads nor does he have the word "toad" in his English vocabulary to match the picture he sees.

A further challenge for this student is even when he can decode all the words in the text, if he encounters unfamiliar syntactic structures he is unable to make sense of the words. For example, when he reads the sentence *Today, you look very green, even for a frog,* the subordinate clause of the sentence presents comprehension difficulties. This student needs to build a wider English vocabulary, but he also needs to be explicitly taught the various language structures he will encounter in reading.

## Teaching ELLs

Up to this point we have discussed the competencies that ELL students need for academic success. Next, we present a model of effective instruction for ELLs to meet these competencies (see figure 7.1). This model extends earlier work by Bailey and Heritage (2004) on formative assessment and teacher knowledge.

In this model, we use Shulman's (1986) distinctions of different types of teacher knowledge—content knowledge and pedagogical content knowledge. Content knowledge refers to the understanding of the concepts and skills that need to be taught; pedagogical content knowledge refers to the ability to convey content knowledge through multiple models of teaching for student understanding and achievement. In our model, we separate content knowledge into two interrelated areas. One area of content knowledge concerns domain-specific knowledge. For example, an algebra teacher will have knowledge of exponential and polynomial functions, and she will know when to teach the concepts in the curriculum sequence. Similarly, a history teacher, responsible for developing students' understanding of China's extensive urbanization and commercial expansion between the 10th and 13th centuries, will have knowledge of the expansion of China's external trade with the people of Southeast Asia, and he will know what prior knowledge will benefit students' understanding of the concept.

In our model, we draw from the notion that content knowledge cannot be separated from the linguistic means through which it is presented and understood (Christie, 1985; Schleppegrell and Achugar, 2003). Thus, we include the academic language of the domain as the second component of content knowledge. We suggest that domain content knowledge and knowledge of the domain language (register) are of equal importance. When planning instruction, therefore, teachers need to invoke both knowledge components simultaneously. For example, in order to teach the history of China's trade expansion, not only will the teacher need to have knowledge of the

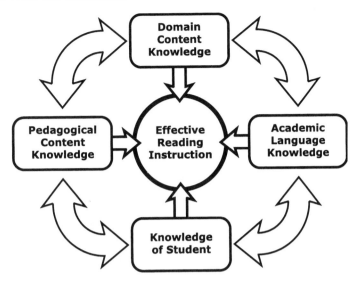

Figure 7.1. Model of effective instruction for ELLs.

specific vocabulary used to describe trade expansion, he must also know the syntactic structures and vocabulary required to analyze and express cause and effect relations. Paralleling this view of instruction, in the Language across the Curriculum model, all teachers undertake language development associated with their individual content areas (Bullock Report, 1975).

Effective instruction for ELLs involves integrating content domain knowledge with academic language knowledge and the interaction of these knowledge areas with pedagogical content knowledge. The pedagogical approach the teacher selects is dependent on what the students are to learn. For example, a science teacher might give students firsthand experiences of classifying rocks to help students learn about the properties of igneous, sedimentary, and metamorphic rocks and the related vocabulary. A mathematics teacher might help students understand the meaning of *product* and *factor* by exploring their etymologies: "a product is something that is produced, or is a result; and a factor is an ingredient or contributor, just as 6 x 9 has the factors, or contributors of 6 and 9 that produce the result or product, 54" (Thompson and Rubenstein, 2000, p. 573).

To invoke these three types of teacher knowledge effectively, teachers need information about their students. Hence, the model includes teachers' knowledge of students, which in our model comprises three domains: content, academic register, and background. Content refers to (1) the students' level of knowledge in a specific content area; (2) their understanding of concepts in the content area (i.e., the degree to which they can make generalizations through a process of abstraction from a number of discrete examples); (3) the skills specific to the content area (i.e., the capacity or competence to perform a task); and (4) the attitudes the students are developing (e.g., the value the students place on the subject, the interest they display, and the students' levels of initiative and self-reliance) (Department of Education and Science [UK], 1985). Academic register refers to the vocabulary and language structures specific to the domain and also to the characteristics of the text types common to the domain (e.g., expository and narrative text). Background refers to knowledge of students' culture, their prior experiences, and their primary language, all of which represent important resources that the teacher can use when planning instruction.

Teachers' knowledge about students will be obtained from a range of assessments, both summative and formative. Summative assessments can inform teachers' decisions about program and school improvement and inform parents, students, and the public about student achievement. However, in our model, we emphasize the role that formative assessment plays in effective instruction. The view of formative assessment is drawn from Black, Harrison, Lee, Marshall, and Wiliam (2003), who state that "for assessment to function formatively, the results had to be used to adjust teaching and learning" (p. 10) and "formative assessment can occur many times in every lesson" (p. 2).

When teachers begin to work with a new group of students they can use summative information to ascertain students' levels of performance in content and academic register as a starting point for their teaching. However, more fine-grained information to guide and modify their teaching will be obtained through ongoing formative assessment during the course of instruction. Listening to students' responses to questions, to their explanations, to their discussions; assessing students' representations of knowledge; and observing behavior are means through which teachers can gain information about students' content knowledge, skills, academic language levels, and attitudes. Furthermore, outside the context of the lesson, parents can be a rich source of information about their children. Information from parents can extend teachers' knowledge of the students' home language, cultural background, prior experiences, and attitude to learning and can be used in a formative sense to adjust teaching and learning.

To implement this model successfully, the classroom culture that teachers establish is a critical consideration. The moral, affective, and behavioral aspects of the classroom have been referred to as the invisible culture (Philips, 1983). The invisible culture is made up of the normative values and standards of the classroom that shape the behavior of the teacher and the students, thus impacting the nature and quality of learning.

Krashen (1981) developed the affective filter hypothesis, which posits there are several affective variables that contribute to success in second language acquisition. These include self-confidence, positive self-image, and low anxiety in the learning environment. The teacher's role is to explicitly address these elements by creating an invisible culture in which all students feel they are respected and valued and that they have an important contribution to make. This will necessarily involve building a community of learners, which is characterized by a recognition and appreciation of individual differences. Classroom norms of listening respectfully to each other, responding positively and constructively, valuing each other's cultural and language backgrounds, and appreciating the different skill levels among peers will enable all students to feel safe in the learning environment. A safe environment allows students to take risks, to make mistakes, to develop self-confidence and a positive-self image, and to learn with and from each other.

In addition to selecting pedagogical approaches that are responsive to the students' cultural and language backgrounds and specifically "teaching to" the prosocial behaviors described above, teachers will need to model the "safety" norms of the classroom in their own behavior. As Sizer and Sizer (1999) remind us, students "watch us all the time. They listen to us sometimes. They learn from all that watching and listening" (p. xvii).

In our model of teaching ELLs, content knowledge (which involves the two interrelated areas of domain content and domain academic language knowledge), pedagogical content knowledge, and student knowledge are invoked in a mutually dependent and dynamic interaction within a constructive and supportive classroom culture. The pedagogical approach will be determined by the content, the language demands of the students, and the knowledge of students. The content and language demands will be determined by the teachers' knowledge of the students, the content, and the language through which the students can both communicate and think about the content. Given their dynamic nature, the interaction of these components will likely change during the course of an instructional sequence. Next, we turn to how the interaction of the components of our model can change as teachers make on-the-spot decisions based on the formative assessments they are conducting throughout the lesson.

## Formative Assessment and Teacher Decisions

Assessment is essential to effective teaching and learning. Black and Wiliam (2004) stress the importance of formative assessment, which holds the promotion of student learning as its primary purpose, therefore distinguishing it from assessments that are designed for student accountability or ranking. Formative assessment is within the control of the teacher. It can occur several times in a variety of ways during a lesson, and it is used to adapt teaching to meet the needs of students (Black et al., 2003). A crucial aspect of formative assessment is listening to students. As Erickson (2003) wrote, "teachers must listen in order to know how to act pedagogically at the right times" (p. x).

Before a lesson, teachers will have made plans about what they want their students to learn and the pedagogical approach they will adopt to achieve their learning goals. However, they are likely to adjust their pedagogy depending on the information they acquire from observing and especially from listening to their students. Research suggests that effective teachers maintain the flexibility to pursue topics that arise from discussions, or they insert minilessons if they perceive the need for them in the course of the original lesson (Wharton-McDonald, Pressley, and Hampston, 1998). Although the overall learning goal will not necessarily change, the pathway to it, including intermediate learning goals, may be altered.

In figure 7.2, we present a model of how formative assessment can change the interaction of the components of our model and, hence, the pathway of the lesson.

The teacher begins the lesson with the learning activity that has been selected. There may come a point in the lesson when, based on

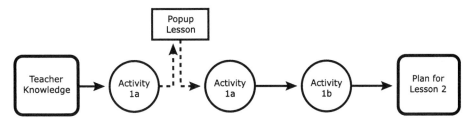

Figure 7.2. Model of lesson pathway.

her formative assessment, she decides to make a change in the instructional plan. For example, a math teacher might become aware that some of her ELL students do not understand the term *inverse*, or she might find that a number of her ELL students have not acquired the comparative structures *greater than* and *less than*. At this point, she will decide that a "pop-up" is needed to teach the language to assist conceptual understanding. Thus, when the teacher's knowledge of her students changes, she draws on her areas of interdependent knowledge simultaneously—knowledge of students, content and language knowledge, pedagogical knowledge—to recalibrate the instruction to address the immediate learning need.

Now the teacher has the added pedagogical challenge of teaching something that the other students in the class may already know. Additionally, she has to pull a strategy from her pedagogical content knowledge that will address the language needs of some of the ELL students while ensuring that the other students, who do not have the same language needs, are also benefiting from the lesson. One possibility here is to ask other students to explain what *inverse* means in an everyday context and to illustrate the concept *inverse* in a mathematical context. Similarly, the students could explain and illustrate the language *greater than* and *less than*. She could also present a task to the students in small groups so they have a chance to acquire and practice these language terms in cooperative structures. The length of the pop-up segment will vary and depend on the task at hand. Once the pop-up is concluded, the teacher can resume the originally planned instructional sequence, although another pop-up may be needed at some point in the lesson. At the end of the lesson, the teacher can evaluate the learning that has occurred and draw upon the areas of teacher knowledge described in figure 7.1 to plan subsequent lessons. In subsequent lessons, the same teacher might decide on pop-ups in a different sequence or may decide, based on her ongoing assessment, that a pop-up segment is not necessary at any point.

Moreover, while adapting teaching to learning needs is important for all students, it is especially critical for ELLs, who have the dual demands of acquiring knowledge of content and knowledge of language simultaneously. Teachers' formative assessments, therefore, will need to attend to both aspects of learning, and the focus of the pop-up segments will be based on either one or both aspects.

## Language and Thinking

The work of Vygostky, among others, has led to an increased recognition of the role that language plays in the development of social and cognitive processes. Vygotsky's view is that language and thinking develop simultaneously through everyday sociocultural experiences, and that the development of thinking occurs through scaffolded interaction with more expert others. Martin (1999) refers to scaffolding as "guidance through interaction in the context of shared experience" (p. 126). Vygotsky makes a distinction between the learning that happens in everyday life—"everyday" concepts—and the learning that takes place in more structured experiences—"scientific" concepts. He argues that both kinds of learning occur when the scaffolding is conducted within the learners' zone of proximal development, in which learners can perform at levels they would not be able to achieve independently (Vygotsky, 1978).

Much of the knowledge that schools aim to develop is not available through a student's interaction in everyday experiences. "School" knowledge needs to be articulated in ways that abstract from everyday events while students engage in structured experiences (Schleppegrell, 2004). A clear understanding of the role language plays in the development of cognition requires analysis of the structure and uses of language itself, yet language is the "element of learning that is most unanalyzed and least often explicitly addressed" (Schleppegrell, 2004, p. 23). Drawing from Halliday's work on the developments in grammar that are needed for students to construe more complex kinds of meaning as they learn, Schleppegrell proposes a functional linguistic approach as a means to understand the language needs in learning content. Using the notion of linguistic *register*, (i.e., the lexico-grammatical choices that construe meanings in different contexts), this approach can show how structuring new kinds of knowledge is dependent on new ways of learning language and can identify the features of the language that enable students' cognitive development. Simply put, learning new ways of using language is learning new ways of thinking. Furthermore, Schleppegrell emphasizes that both Halliday and Vygotsky view learning language as integral to, not separate from or prior to, the development of thinking. Thus, the activities that students engage in during their time in school "result in the development of knowledge and language related to the goals of those activities" (p. 23).

The model we propose here is premised on the perspective that language is integral to the development of thinking. Content knowledge is not distinct from the linguistic means through which the knowledge is acquired and expressed. The demands of content knowledge are not privileged above the demands of linguistic resources, nor vice versa. Thus, the classroom becomes a place where students are engaged in the integrated learning of content and language through meaningful experiences in conjunction with scaffolding by teachers and peers of the features of academic language, both spoken and written, that are needed to construe meaning. In our model, language and content function interdependently in the context of mainstream classrooms. Hence, all teachers need to be both content teachers and language teachers.

## Instructional Approaches

Since the early 1980s, many instructional programs for ELLs have been strongly influenced by Krashen's (1981) *intake* hypothesis. Krashen derives the intake hypothesis from the characteristics of "caretaker" speech, which contains a high proportion of intake, and he explicates, "intake is first of all *input* that is *understood*" (p. 102). *Understood or comprehensible input* is normally pitched at a slightly higher level than language learners' existing language competence and is, consequently, within their zone of proximal development (Vygotsky, 1978). This is achieved through assistance from the extralinguistic context and from experience and knowledge of the world. Krashen stresses the role of vocabulary in intake and emphasizes the acquisition of vocabulary as a means to foster the acquisition of syntax. In his view, "knowing the words, even without knowing the syntax, provides the listener with enough information so that a great deal can be understood. With comprehension . . . syntax will come" (p. 109). Moreover, he contends that comprehension precedes speech production; when acquiring a second language, children have a "silent period." during which time they develop language competence through intake.

The implications of Krashen's hypothesis for instructional approaches for ELLs are threefold. First, teachers need to provide comprehensible input for their language-learning students. Next, they should focus on relevant and interesting topics rather than grammatical sequences. Last, they should accommodate phases of language development, beginning with a preproduction phase or silent period (Gillet and Temple, 2000).

A widespread instructional approach focusing on comprehensible input is content-based, sheltered instruction, known in California as Specially Designed Academic Instruction in English (SDAIE). SDAIE incorporates strategies for teachers to adjust their talk so as to maximize its value as "comprehensible input." These strategies include slowing the rate of speech; using a controlled vocabulary and sentence length (i.e., simplifying the linguistic input); using realia, artifacts, and models; checking frequently for understanding; using semantic maps; employing cooperative learning group activities; gesturing; brainstorming; and summarizing. All of these strategies are intended to assist students to access content knowledge.

In SDAIE methodology, the focus is on teaching particular vocabulary related to the content. Because of the emphasis on the natural language acquisition approach, there is no explicit teaching of syntactic structures in which the vocabulary is embedded, nor of any functional language (e.g., prepositions, conjunctions). More typically, these forms of language are taught in separate English language development (ELD) lessons and not as part of the content lessons, with the implicit expectation that there will be a transfer of the language structures into the content areas. Language development programs like *Into English* (Hampton Brown, 2004) provide teachers with decontextualized language development units, which may not always correspond to the content areas under study. Thus, ELL students are not developing language skills and content knowledge simultaneously.

A more recent approach to supporting ELLs in accessing content is "frontloading" (Dutro, 2003). Frontloading strategies are used in addition to SDAIE and in conjunction with a systematic English language development program. Furthermore, this approach involves teaching the language demands that are likely to be encountered in content lessons. The frontloading strategy includes preteaching vocabulary and grammatical structures of the language needed to develop and communicate content understanding before engaging with specific content. Frontloading does not develop academic register in the context of content learning. Rather, in this method the language skills are taught "in an upfront investment of time to render the content understandable to the student" (p. 6).

In the Cognitive Academic Language Learning Approach (CALLA), high-priority content is the primary focus of instruction in English as a second language (ESL) classes, and academic language skills are developed when the need arises from the content. Additionally, CALLA includes explicit instruction in learning strategies for delivering content-ESL instruction (Chamot and O'Malley, 1994). Conceived of initially as a program for upper-elementary and secondary ESL students, CALLA is targeted at (1) students who have developed social communicative skills but not grade-level academic language competence; (2) students who have acquired academic language in their native language but not in English; and (3) bilingual English-dominant students who have not developed academic language in either of their languages (Chamot and O'Malley, 1994). The expectation is that students will be able to acquire both content and academic language in the ESL classes and successfully transfer to the mainstream classroom. More recently, CALLA has been implemented with young children and with students at the beginning level of English proficiency (Chamot, 2005). Reed and Railsback (2003) provide descriptions of other instructional approaches, which lie outside the remit of this chapter, that utilize the students' native language to varying degrees.

The model we present differs from the approaches described above. The academic register is taught in the context of content lessons, and the model stresses the integral nature of conceptual development and the language in which it is understood and conveyed. The language is not pretaught, and vocabulary and syntax issues are attended to simultaneously with content during the course of instruction. In our model for ELL instruction, the content understanding and the language through which it is understood and expressed are integrated to form the objectives of the lesson, and the pedagogical approach is selected to teach both simultaneously. From the outset, the content and language objectives are dynamically interacting with pedagogical knowledge. It should be noted that we are not advocating lessons in grammar. Rather, our perspective centers on the ability of the teacher to systematically identify the vocabulary and syntactic demands of the domain and to assist students to acquire the academic register through scaffolding in a situation of context-embedded learning, where the learner receives support from the physical and visual environment.

Fillmore (1982, 1991) identified certain conditions that need to be in place for ELLs to acquire English. A key condition is frequent interaction with others who are sufficiently knowledgeable in order to model how the language works and how it can be used. In interactions with ELLs, students who were proficient English speakers provided access to the language at the appropriate level. Proficient English speakers provided clues about how to use units of language to communicate ideas, and they gave feedback to clarify meanings. In line with these conclusions, we propose that our model be used in mainstream classrooms where native speakers and ELLs are learning together.

Moreover, we propose that the development of academic language can be undertaken at the same time as social language, beginning in kindergarten. In the authors' experience, a number of teachers have been surprised to learn that ELL kindergartners and first graders can use specific vocabulary such as *pistil, stamen,* and *pollination;* teachers assumed the ELL students would need a certain level of social language before acquiring academic language. However, if students are learning about plants and pollination in an experiential learning environment in which the language learning is context embedded, acquiring the precise vocabulary becomes a natural activity.

Teaching ELLs and native speakers together demands a high level of skill on the part of the teacher. In addition to a thorough knowledge of content and language structures, a vital skill is a teacher's ability to interpret formative assessment information in light of his or her content and language knowledge. Once the teacher has interpreted the information, pedagogical skills to differentiate instruction effectively will be a critical determinant of how well the range of students' needs is met. The teacher has to be able to open multiple entry points to a lesson to provide access for all learners, and the teacher must be able to scaffold the lesson at different levels so that the needs of individual students can be met.

## Implementing the Model

Now we turn to some specific examples of how this model can be implemented in two content areas of the curriculum, mathematics and science.

### *Mathematics*

The language of mathematics is precise, uses highly specialized vocabulary, and is very different from the language spoken in everyday activities, making it difficult for students to use this language in other contexts (Chamot and O'Malley, 1994). An added complexity is that besides the specific vocabulary in mathematics, such as *addend* and *quotient*, more familiar words, like *function* and *round* (as in "rounding up"), have specialized meanings (Cuevas, 1984).

In addition to the vocabulary demands, the syntactic constructions of mathematics can present difficulties for ELL students. Spanos, Rhodes, Dale, and Crandall (1988) identified five syntactic features of the language of mathematics: (1) comparatives (e.g., *greater/less than, as . . . as*); (2) prepositions (e.g., *divided into, divided by*); (3) passive voice (e.g., *x is defined as*); (4) reversals (e.g., the number *a* is five less than *b*); and (5) logical connectors (e.g., *if . . . then*). These features are likely to be encountered in textbooks, which are not typically written for ELL students and lack the scaffolding to assist comprehension (Chamot and O'Malley, 1994). To enable their students to develop and communicate mathematical understanding, mathematics teachers will need to ensure that their ELL students are acquiring the mathematics register.

The following is an actual mathematics lesson taught at the beginning of the year in eighth grade re-created as two lessons to take account of academic language and content needs of two groups of students, both of which have mixed language abilities (i.e., some students speak only English [EOs], some are fully bilingual, and some are ELLs). While both teachers are working toward the same goal, a foundational knowledge for Algebra I, based on the ongoing formative assessment, their decision making creates different pathways toward the learning goal.

The first objective the teachers have is to ensure the students understand the simplification of complex division. The teachers decide to begin the lesson by eliciting prior knowledge through an activity that will allow them to *listen to* the language produced by the students and to assess their understanding of the concept of division in a formative way before undertaking the simplification of complex division. Both teachers decide to start by asking students "What does division mean?" The students' responses to the question will form the basis for the lesson. The teachers' intention is to co-construct the students' conceptual understanding and their academic register.

In their respective classrooms, the teachers begin the lesson by asking the question "What does division mean?" They then direct the students to discuss fifteen-fifths and to represent their collective understanding in cooperative groups. In mixed groups of ELLs and EOs, the students begin their discussions. Each teacher asks each group to report to the whole class in turn, and she charts the responses and the visual representation of their definitions.

In classroom A, students respond with the following:

*Group 1:* Division is how many times a number could go into another number. Like in fifteen-fifths, five goes into fifteen three times. There are three groups of five in fifteen.

*Group 2:* Division is taking equal groups from a larger number. It's like finding out how many times you had to take five away from fifteen to get to zero. Five was taken away three times.

*Group 3:* Division is repeated subtractions from a number. The number of times you subtracted the number is the answer. Then you find out how many groups you had to subtract. Fifteen divided by five equals three. Fifteen minus five, ten minus five, five minus five equals zero. Three groups of five were taken away.

*Teacher:* Each of your examples describes the process of division. Now can you tell me what is the simplest way of expressing fifteen-fifths?

*Student 1:* Fifteen-fifths is asking "How many groups of five are there in fifteen?" So the simplest way of saying fifteen-fifths is three.

*Student 2:* The answer is there are three groups of five in fifteen.

*Teacher:* Great job, everyone!

The teacher decides that the definitions the students produce show that she can move forward with the lesson on simplification of complex division.

The classroom B teacher has a different set of responses, ranging from silence to:

*Group 1:*   Division of fifteen-fifths means a fraction or a division. Fifteen divided by five is three.

*Group 2:*   Division means dividing some numbers and make it to a smaller number. Fifteen-fifths is fifteen divided by five. That makes three.

*Group 3:*   Division is opposite of multiplication. Fifteen-fifths is like five goes into fifteen and that makes three because three times five is fifteen.

*Group 4:*   Division is when you flip the number when you divide and when you multiply. Fifteen-fifths is like five times something is fifteen, so the answer is three.

*Group 5:*   Division is dividing one number by another to solve the problem. Like fifteen-fifths is X, so then five times X equals three.

It becomes clear to the classroom B teacher that the students are familiar with an algorithm but are struggling with conveying their understanding of division. She concludes that this could be because they either do not understand the concepts sufficiently well or they lack the vocabulary and syntax to express their understanding.

A quick analysis of their responses leads the teacher in classroom B to the decision of delivering a pop-up segment. Based on her *domain content knowledge,* the classroom B teacher decides the students must be able to recognize that division is not only the opposite of multiplication but also a series of subtractions of equal group size. From her academic language knowledge, she knows that the vocabulary *subtraction, group,* and *repeated* will need to be taught. Accordingly, the classroom B teacher draws upon her pedagogical knowledge to recalibrate the instruction to give a quick pop-up segment designed to help students define division as a series of subtractions of groups.

The classroom B teacher locates math manipulatives, essential for ELLs and extremely useful for EOs, to provide extralinguistic support and to enable the students to physically break down the fraction fifteen-fifths (e.g., fifteen minus five equals ten, ten minus five equals five, five minus five equals zero). The classroom B teacher ensures that she uses the precise vocabulary in conjunction with the manipulatives so that students are hearing the process of division defined by the phrases *subtraction of groups* and *repeated subtraction.*

After her demonstration, the teacher invites the students to use the manipulatives to do other division examples of their choice. All the while, she walks around the classroom, engaging with each group to ensure that the students are using the precise language to define what they are doing.

At the end of the group session, the teacher calls on an ELL student to define division:

> *Student:* Fifteen-thirds means that we have to find out how many groups of three are in fifteen. So, if we subtract three and do the subtraction again and again, we will find out how many groups of three there are in fifteen.
>
> *Teacher:* That's it! Do you remember the word we used to mean to do the subtraction again and again?

The student cannot remember and the teacher asks another student whom she has heard use the word *repeated* in the small-group activity.

The mathematics teachers continue with the sequence of planned activities to guide students to the next step in recognizing a complex division problem. In the next phase of the lesson, both teachers use manipulative rods on an overhead projector to demonstrate six wholes.

> *Teacher:* How can we say six wholes in thirds?

Students are given sets of rods and are asked to work in pairs in a think/pair/share activity. The teachers of classrooms A and B walk around their classrooms and *listen to* the students as they use their rods to demonstrate their understanding of the fraction. The students take six whole rods and place three-thirds rods beside each whole rod to represent how six is equal to three-thirds, three-thirds, three-thirds, three-thirds, three-thirds, three-thirds. The teachers bring their classes back together and ask:

> *Teachers:* If fifteen-fifths asks, "How many groups of five are there in fifteen," then what does six two-thirds mean?
>
> *Students:* How many groups of two-thirds are there in six?
>
> *Teachers:* Super! How can we show this? Use your rods to show this.

The teachers walk around and watch as students use the manipulatives to demonstrate their understanding. The teachers ask students to show and tell how they represented the division using the rods on the overhead projector. In classroom A, a student explains what he is doing:

> *Student:* I could take groups into two-thirds until I get to six. So I subtract two-thirds with repeated subtraction. Like this: two-thirds, two-thirds, two-thirds equals six-thirds equals two; two-thirds, two-thirds, two-thirds equals six-thirds equals two; two-thirds, two-thirds, two-thirds equals six-thirds equals two. So I have nine groups into two-thirds in six. So six two-thirds equals nine.

The classroom A teacher recognizes that the student understands the concept but is using the preposition *into* instead of *of* when referring to groups, whereas in classroom B the students use *groups of* correctly. A quick pop-up could clarify the point for classroom A. Because the classroom learning environment is set up to be cooperative in nature, lowering the "affective filter," the teacher asks if someone might be able to explain the difference in Spanish. Another Spanish speaking student suggests that it is easy to confuse the two (showing sensitivity to the classmate), but "groups of" is the same as "grupos de."

> *Teacher:* So what do you have?
>
> *Student:* So I have nine *groups of* two-thirds in six. So six two-thirds equals nine.
>
> *Teacher:* Fabulous! Let's work on a few more problems. As you do this in pairs, explain your process to your partner.

As the teachers walk around in their respective classrooms and listen to the students talk about what they are doing, they recognize that some EOs and many ELLs are not using the precise mathematical language of *numerator* and *denominator*. Both teachers make a decision to focus on these terms and decide to scaffold the students' language by giving a quick pop-up segment using the precise mathematical lexicon. The teachers tell the students that they are going to focus on talking like mathematicians, and they do several complex division problems emphasizing the specific vocabulary of numerator and denominator. They also reinforce sequential language and deliberately use the terms *first, second, then,* and *finally* during the pop-up segment. The teachers ask the students to continue with a division problem and to make sure that they are talk-

ing like mathematicians. At the end of the work session, the teacher
in classroom A comments:

> *Teacher:*   As I walked around the classroom, I noticed you were
>              using the labels *numerator* and *denominator* as you ex-
>              plained the process. I also heard some students using the
>              words *first, second, then,* and *finally.* You used sequential
>              language to explain your process. Great work!

The teachers ask the students to record in their algebra logs six
two-thirds equals nine and to describe the process of division using
the vocabulary they have learned.

It should be noted that although the two teachers had the same
objectives and introduced their lessons from the same starting point,
the development of their lessons differed. Throughout the lessons,
both teachers were formatively assessing their students, and the differences in their lessons were because they adjusted their teaching
in response to the information they gained from their assessments
of the students. Yet, the lessons had many similarities. Both teachers provided a structure for using the logical connectors *if . . . then*
and modeled the structure in the process of division. The teachers
explained to the students that the structure was one that they would
be using a lot in algebra. The students recorded the model in their
logs. The teachers finished the lesson by leaving the students with a
question to think about for the following day's lesson. They asked
the students to look at all their complex division problems and to
try to find a mathematical rule for them. They suggested using the
structure *if . . . then* to explain the mathematical rule and let the
students know that they will begin tomorrow's lesson by sharing
ideas. Thus, they both reached the same end point and concluded
the lesson in the same way.

In these lessons, the teachers are addressing both mathematics
concepts and the academic register simultaneously in classrooms
that include ELLs and EOs together. To assess the students' conceptual understanding and mathematical language, they use pedagogical strategies that elicit prior knowledge, and they listen carefully to the students' use of language. They identify the precise
vocabulary and syntax that the students need, and they "teach to"
both in the course of the lesson and in the context of concept development. Throughout the lesson they are continuously assessing
their students, and they recalibrate their instruction when neces-

sary through the use of pop-up segments. The teachers offer opportunities for extra linguistic support with the use of representations and manipulatives. The collaborative group work permits students to enter the activity at different levels, provides for extended discourse, and allows ELL students, in particular, to hear models of English. The teachers scaffold the students' language and thinking in meaningful experiences. They have also created an environment in which it is the norm for students to work together, to listen to each other, and where the Spanish language is valued as a resource for scaffolding English language learning.

## Science

Lemke (1990) suggests that "learning science means learning to *talk* science" and "talking science means observing, describing, comparing, classifying, analyzing, discussing, hypothesizing, theorizing, questioning, challenging, designing experiments, following procedures, judging, evaluating, deciding, concluding, generalizing and reporting" (p. 1). To successfully engage in these processes, students need to have an understanding of the concepts, know the related vocabulary, and be able to use the required language structures (Laplante, 1997). When learning science, ELLs, in particular, face complex language demands, which requires teachers to integrate language learning with content learning (Spanos, 1989).

The following is a lesson one of the authors taught to a multiage kindergarten and first-grade class comprising EOs and ELLs at Seeds University Elementary School at UCLA. The teacher is making plans to teach a unit of study to develop the concept of the life cycle. To plan the lessons, the teacher refers to the goals for the study that she has identified from her domain content knowledge. These goals include (1) understanding that plants and animals have life cycles that include being born, developing into adults, reproducing, and eventually dying; (2) knowing that the details of this life cycle are different for different organisms; and (3) understanding that many characteristics of an organism are inherited from the parents.

The teacher plans to introduce the students to the life cycle of a caterpillar as a first step in developing the understanding that organisms have stages of life and that the sequence of the cycle differs among organisms. She draws from her academic language knowledge to identify the specifics of the academic register that her students will need to use to talk like scientists about the life cycle of a caterpillar. She determines that the students will need the vocabulary and syntax to observe, describe, compare, question, sequence, and report. Some of the specific vocabulary that children need to acquire includes the nouns *caterpillar, chrysalis,* and *larva;* the verbs *grow, change, transform,* and *reproduce;* and the prepositions *on, over, under, through, inside,* and *outside.* To be able to make comparisons between different organisms, they will need to use words such as *like, same as, similar,* and *different.* Additionally, to be able to report their observations and to describe a sequence of events, the children will need to use these words in declarative sentences, and they will need to develop interrogative structures so they can ask questions.

The teacher knows that this is the first time in the school's science curriculum that the students will be introduced to the life cycle, but at this point, she does not know if their previous experiences outside the school have included some knowledge of caterpillars and the life cycle. She knows, from the language assessments and from working with the students, that there is a range of language production levels in the class. She is aware some students will be able to produce single words or short phrases such as "caterpillar" or "It is a caterpillar" and other children are capable of producing more complex sentences in written and oral language.

She plans to increase students' vocabularies and to progress from "It's a caterpillar" to using more complex sentence structures like "The fuzzy black caterpillar is crawling over the leaf," "The caterpillar has grown larger each day," and "After several days, the fuzzy black caterpillar began to spin a cocoon of silky thread around itself." She wants to ensure that all the students acquire the specific domain vocabulary, and she wants her ELL students, specifically, to develop the abilities to use different verb tenses, to apply comparative structures, and to expand their use of pronouns, adverbs, and prepositional phrases.

She draws from her pedagogical knowledge to select an approach that will best build on the students' current level of understanding and help them learn the concepts and language simultaneously. This teacher believes that the best way to build children's understanding of the world is through the process of inquiry. She also believes that children are most engaged when they are working firsthand with materials and making their own observations rather than simply reading the material in a book. She knows all children benefit from context-embedded language learning and providing extralinguistic support for ELLs is crucial. Therefore, the teacher plans to develop the concepts and language by providing students with first-hand experience of caterpillars. She decides to have secondhand materials (e.g., charts and books) about caterpillars available for reference and to expose children to the structures of expository text.

The teacher begins the lesson by telling the children that they are going to be studying a particular creature.

> *Teacher:* I have here creatures that we will be studying for the next few weeks. (*She places several caterpillars at the students' tables around the room.*) In your groups I want you to talk about what creatures you think these are.

Students begin excited discussions about the creature. Many ELL students use their primary language and others use English. To help them identify the creature, some students begin to look through some of materials the teacher has provided. The teacher moves around the room listening to the various conversations. One group of students tries to distinguish whether the creature is a worm or a caterpillar.

> *Juan:* It's a worm.
>
> *Camilla:* I think it's a caterpillar. It looks like this picture (*pointing to a picture of a caterpillar in a book*).
>
> *Emily:* I don't know. I'm not sure what it is.
>
> *Juan:* It's a worm. It wiggles.
>
> *Camilla:* Caterpillars do that, too.
>
> *Emily:* I saw a worm before. It looked different. Is this a different kind of worm?

Eventually, the teacher brings the class together to discuss what each group thinks about the creature:

> *Teacher:* Jason's group thinks that this is a caterpillar. How do we know that this is a caterpillar?"
>
> *Camilla:* Because it is like the one in this book.
>
> *Diego:* I saw a worm like this.
>
> *Teacher:* What did the worm look like?

> Diego:      It did this. (*Diego moves his hands in a wriggling movement.*)
> Teacher:    It wriggled? (*moving her hands in the way Diego did*).
> Diego:      Yes, it wriggled.

After a period of discussion, it is clear that a number of the children think that the caterpillar is a worm. At this point, the teacher tells the students that they will continue their investigation of the creature the next day.

The teacher decides that the children need to expand their content knowledge and brings worms to class the following day so that students can make comparisons between the two creatures. The worms are in a glass case with soil; the caterpillars are in a case with leaves. In a think/pair/share activity, she pairs ELL students with native English speakers and asks the students to observe the two creatures, think about what they are noticing, and discuss their observations with their partner.

> Teacher:    Let's talk about what you notice about these creatures, these two animals. How are they moving?
> Emily:      This one [the caterpillar] is bunching up and moving over the leaf.
> Diego:      This one [the worm] is in the dirt!
> Teacher:    This creature is going *under* the ground, and this creature is moving *over* the leaf. What else did you notice?
> Juan:       This one [the caterpillar] is on the top.
> Teacher:    Good job! The lid is on top of the case (*she points to the lid*) and you noticed that the creature is clinging to the underside of the lid (*she points to the underside of the lid*). Did you see the other creature cling to the underside of the lid?
> Class:      (*in unison*) No!

The teacher decides that the students have enough information about the creature to be able to determine what it is. She reads two short paragraphs from the books available that describe the characteristics of a worm and a caterpillar. The class decides that it is a caterpillar.

The teacher tells the children that they will be closely observing the caterpillar over the next few weeks and that they will be recording the changes they observe in their science journal. She tells them they are collecting data about the caterpillar and that is what scientists do. The teacher uses a think-aloud exercise to model the declarative structures that the students will first use for their observations.

*Teacher:* When I observe the caterpillar, I notice that it is doing various things. This is the way I would describe what I see the caterpillar doing right now.

*(The teacher looks closely at the caterpillar for a few moments.)* The caterpillar is crawling slowly over the leaf.

The teacher repeats the sentence. She directs the students to work in pairs to describe what the caterpillars are doing. She listens to the children and supports their language production when necessary.

Next, she asks the students to enter their first observation in their journal. For the ELLs, the teacher provides a support structure in the first few pages of the journal: "The caterpillar is _____." She will continue to scaffold the children's writing to increase syntactic complexity as the study progresses.

When the children study the behaviors and movements of the caterpillar, the teacher plans to directly teach the vocabulary and structures students will need to accurately describe what they observe. On one occasion, she listens to a group of students discussing their observations in their primary language.

*Alfonso:* La oruga es como una larva. Es como un gusano porque los dos son larvas. [The caterpillar is like a larva. It is like a worm because they are both larvae.]

*Laura:* Pero yo creo que se va a convertir en una mariposa. Los gusanos no se hacen mariposas. Se va a tapar con algo y va a salir una mariposa. [I think it will become a butterfly. Worms don't turn into butterflies. It will cover itself and a butterfly will come out.]

*Nico:* Se hace una crisalida. Me lo dijo mi mama. [It makes a chrysalis. My mom told me that.]

Although the teacher does not speak Spanish, she recognizes the words *crisalida, mariposa,* and *larva.* Furthermore, she realizes that these students already have some conceptual knowledge about the life cycle, as well as an academic vocabulary in their primary language. She decides to use the students' knowledge to benefit the entire class and includes a pop-up segment during the period of observation to make a quick list of cognates. With class participation, she creates a chart of these Spanish and English cognates, which can be used as a reference in speaking and writing. The pop-up segment helps to increase the English vocabulary for students who have prior conceptual knowledge, introduces specific vocabulary for the EOs to highlight some of the concepts that they will be learning about, and reinforces that Spanish is a "status" language in the classroom.

In these lessons, the teacher provides context-embedded activities to develop simultaneously the twin goals of academic language and content knowledge. Through firsthand experiences, she activates the students' background knowledge about worms and caterpillars, providing schema for them to access new information. The students' firsthand observations and the use of secondhand materials enable the children to determine the differences between worms and caterpillars. The teacher provides many opportunities for students to participate orally in the lesson through peer to peer and teacher to student discussions, and she listens carefully to what the students are saying. Before the pair discussions, the teacher models sentence structures to provide support for ELLs. The open-ended nature of the pair discussions also encourages students who are proficient in English to use a range of language structures. She adds new elements to her discussions that are within the students' zone of proximal development (e.g., *clinging to the underside of the lid*) to help students stretch toward higher levels of language proficiency. She uses target words (e.g., *over* and *under*) when summarizing students' feedback. In the science journals, she provides a structure to bridge oral and written language. Even though she does not speak Spanish, the teacher listens carefully when the students are discussing the caterpillars in Spanish, and she is able to use their academic language in their primary language as a resource for all the students in the class.

## Instructional Planning

What might be approaches to instructional planning where students are engaged in purposeful tasks that enable them to develop new language resources to explore and create meaning? Next, we present a framework and a lesson plan template, developed by the authors, for instructional planning that supports both language learning and learning content through language.

As a first step, teachers engage in a process of backward planning and "unpack" the standards for which they are responsible. This involves an analysis of all subconcepts that a student will need to learn in order to meet the standards. Then teachers decide which subconcept needs to be addressed first; what knowledge, skills, and register need to be developed; which pedagogical strategies and resources will be employed; and what evidence they will use to determine the level of students' language and content understanding. Consider our examples of the mathematics lessons. The teachers had unpacked the standards for Algebra I and decided that they wanted to lay a foundational knowledge beginning with the concept of division as repeated subtraction of equal groups. The teachers used the following template to plan the lesson on this concept (see figure 7.3).

Recall that in their lessons both teachers spent some time focusing on the vocabulary *numerator* and *denominator*, which do not appear on their written plans. By listening carefully to the students' discussions, they became aware that this vocabulary was not being used and decided to emphasize the words and have the students practice using them in the correct context.

Throughout the lesson, because the teachers had determined in their plans what they would focus on to assess students' conceptual understanding and linguistic resources and had decided on the pedagogical strategies they would use, they were easily able to adjust their pedagogy to respond to the evidence they were receiving from their students in the course of the lesson.

The approach we have described gives teachers a tool for long- and short-term planning that will enable them to analyze the elements of learning both content and language for the effective teaching of both. Next, we consider a system of assessment constructed on a continuum of content and language learning that would make such an approach to planning and assessing students' learning a realistic option for all teachers, regardless of grade or subject.

## A System of Assessment

Current accountability systems and the No Child Left Behind Act (2001) rely on annual, large-scale achievement tests as a means of school improvement. Test results in mathematics, language arts, and (by 2006) science are expected to inform educators about stu-

**Grade:** 8                                                                    **Date:** 9/12/04

| Concept(s) |
| --- |
| Division as a series of subtractions of equal groups<br><br>Fractions as parts of unit wholes and as divisions of whole numbers |

| Knowledge | Skills |
| --- | --- |
| Process of division<br><br>Simplification of complex division | Explain strategies using precise mathematical language (oral and written)<br><br>Use sequential constructions<br><br>Apply knowledge of simple division to complex division<br><br>Generalize mathematical rule from experiences |

| Register |
| --- |
| **Vocabulary:** division, subtract, subtracting, subtracted, subtraction, repeated, group, fraction, first, second, third, then, finally<br><br>**Syntax:** I have subtracted...from...;  I am subtracting...from...;<br>Division represents the number of repeated subtractions of equal groups;<br>X divided into...groups;  X divided by...;  There are...groups of...in...;<br>First, I did...second I did...then, I did...and finally I...;  If...then... |

| Strategies |
| --- |
| Elicit prior knowledge with question "What does division mean?"<br><br>Collaborative, mixed-language group discussion: extended discourse<br><br>Students report back to share strategies<br><br>Chart and evaluate responses | Modeling using manipulatives (rods) and language structures<br><br>Students represent division with rods<br><br>Listen to students in group activities<br><br>Think/pair/share activities |

| Resources | Assessment |
| --- | --- |
| Rods for each group<br><br>Overhead projector | Student representations showing subtraction of equal groups<br><br>Explanations that use precise language of lesson plan |

Figure 7.3. Template for instructional planning.

dent performance on state standards and about how to improve student academic achievement. Additionally, NCLB requires annual assessment of ELLs in their English oral language reading and writing.

The limitations of large-scale tests as tools to improve student achievement are well captured by Smithson and Porter (2004); they observe that the results from the statewide accountability measures tell teachers how well the students did on the test, but they give limited information about what the students did well on, and even less information about why they did well. Moreover, the effectiveness of large-scale measures is also limited by their infrequency. The interval between when the test is administered and when teachers receive the results is too long. Additionally, the tests cover too large a period of instruction to provide the kind of "online," detailed information necessary for instructional planning.

In *Knowing What Students Know* (National Research Council, 2001), a committee of the National Research Council described an ambitious vision for a coordinated system of assessment that includes assessments to support classroom instructional decisions and assessments to provide system-level evidence of achievement for policy purposes. The committee advocated three principles on which to base this system.

*Comprehensiveness.* To create a comprehensive system of assessment, a range of measurement approaches is required to provide the evidence for educational decision making. Multiple measures give students various ways and opportunities to demonstrate their competence, thereby enhancing the validity and fairness of the inferences drawn.

*Coherence.* To be coherent, a system combining large-scale and classroom-based assessments must be built on the same underlying model of learning. Shepard (2004, p. 239) adds that these models of learning "are more exacting than the description of learning outcomes represented in today's content standards because they also describe the pathways by which students develop proficiency."

*Continuity.* To be coherent, system assessments must measure students' progress over time and provide a continuous stream of evidence about performance. For this to occur, maps of progress in a subject domain need to underlie the assessments. Multiple measures of performance would be linked to the map, providing a range of evidence of students' progress along a continuum of learning.

Consider this vision as it applies to the assessment and instruction of ELL students. Large-scale and classroom-based assessments link to a learning continuum, which describes the pathway to proficiency in content domains, and the academic register of the domain would provide teachers with the ongoing information they need to guide instructional planning. Multiple measures of performance in each aspect of the domain would afford students the opportunity to show what they know in a variety of ways, thereby enhancing the accuracy of the teachers' judgment about the levels of students' language and content knowledge. (See Genesee and Upshur, 1996 for a similar vision in classroom-based second language assessment.)

The model of instruction we have presented in this chapter calls for teacher knowledge in three areas that would be directly impacted by the application of the *Knowing What Students Know* (National Research Council, 2001) vision. First, a clearly defined continuum of learning, which describes the skills, understanding, and knowledge in each content area and the sequence in which they typically develop, would provide teachers with a map of progression in the domain. This would enable systematic planning and would provide an infrastructure for guiding observations and for listening to the students during the course of their learning. Second, a progress map of academic language linked to the each step of the content continuum would enable teachers to identify the academic language demands and to plan and assess students' learning in content and language simultaneously. Third, the progress maps would serve as the basis for assessments for both accountability and formative purposes; since they are constructed on the same model of learning, formative classroom-based assessments would be a fine-grained version of the more coarse-grained, large-scale assessments used for accountability purposes. Reliable and valid classroom-based assessments mapped onto the continuum of learning would afford teachers diagnostic information about students' language and content knowledge to guide their instructional planning and to monitor student progress.

The fourth component of our model, pedagogical knowledge, would be impacted by the information that teachers derive from the progress maps and their classroom-based assessments, including observation and listening to students. What to teach is a factor in how to teach. Within this system of assessment, teachers would have the advantage of being able to draw from deeper knowledge of the progression in content and academic language and of the students' performance in order to select the most effective pedagogical approaches.

In contrast to this vision, current assessments fall short of providing teachers with diagnostic information on content and language. Statewide efforts have been made to assess students' language proficiency to redress the previous dearth of language assessments; nonetheless, the information from these assessments does not provide timely diagnostic data for teachers.

Nationwide, school districts are attempting to provide teachers with content and English language development assessments. However, the content and the language assessments are conceived of as separate, and an assessment of content does not necessarily shed light on language and vice versa. Moreover, some of the language assessments are too broad in scope (e.g., the Student Oral Language Observation Matrix) to provide day-to-day information for instructional planning. Others (e.g., language portfolios) are overly demanding of teachers and require a considerable amount of detailed knowledge about language, which many teachers do not have (Filmore and Snow, 2005). Thus, the potential for using information from these assessments for instructional planning is diminished.

Commercial English language development programs typically provide end-of-unit assessments, but these are not always related to the instructional content of mainstream classrooms. Further, because of the commercial advantage of such programs being implemented across the country, the assessments may not be aligned to state standards in the content areas and in language development, limiting their utility as tools for instructional planning. Finally, these assessments are not built on the same model of progression in the content and language domains and do not provide teachers with multiple measures of student performance mapped onto a clearly defined continuum of learning.

In sum, teachers are not well served in the current state of assessment practices, nor by the design of standards. They lack a clearly defined pathway of learning that intertwines conceptual development and academic register from which they can plan and assess learning. Further, they do not have access to valid and reliable diagnostic assessments of student performance that are directly related to the twin goals of developing content knowledge and academic register.

## Conclusion

In this chapter, we have presented an approach to formative assessment of, and effective instruction in, content and academic language of ELLs in mainstream classrooms. This approach combines four components of teacher knowledge in a dynamic, interactive network. The implementation of this approach is dependent on a number of factors. First, it is dependent on the depth of teacher knowledge of the development of student learning in the interrelated domains of content and academic register. Second, it relies on a coordinated system of assessments whereby large-scale and classroom-based assessments are constructed on the same model of learning, with classroom assessments providing ongoing diagnostic information about students' learning in both language and content. Third, it requires teachers to draw accurate inferences from the assessment information and to translate the information into teaching and learning goals and actions. Fourth, it demands high levels of skill on the part of teachers to create a "safe" classroom environment and to differentiate and scaffold instruction to meet the cognitive and language learning needs of a wide range of students.

In addition to requiring significant changes in the design of current assessment systems and in current descriptions of content and language learning, our approach requires teachers to be language teachers as well as content-area teachers. While many teachers, especially those in middle and high schools, will have a considerable content knowledge, few will have knowledge of language structures, the development of language, knowledge of second language acquisition and the factors affecting it, how language and language learning figure in content learning, and the grammatical and lexical knowledge required for text understanding. Typically, neither professional preparation nor professional development focuses on these aspects of language; therefore, teachers are all too often underprepared to teach academic language in the content areas.

Also needed is an extensive repertoire of pedagogical strategies that can be deployed to teach academic register and content simultaneously. For example:

- providing context-embedded experiences for concept development and language learning (Cummins, 2005)
- providing opportunities for extended talk in the curriculum (e.g., Barnes, 1976; Britton, 1970; Bruner, 1978)—that is, student to student and teacher to student
- paraphrasing (Bailey, in press)
- strategic questioning to scaffold the development of students' thinking and language production
- anticipation guide to support reading (Readence, Bean, and Baldwin, 1981)
- creating bridges for learners between personal ways of knowing and public discourse (Gibbons, 1998)
- language analysis for history texts (Schleppegrell and Achugar, 2003)

All of these are strategies that can be used to support both content and language learning simultaneously. Indeed, these strategies are not only helpful to ELLs—they can be equally beneficial to support the learning of native English speakers.

For all teachers to be language teachers will require changes in pre-service and in-service professional development. Currently, the teaching force in the United States is not equipped to help students who speak little or no English on arrival at school (Fillmore and Snow, 2005). The challenge that is presented for professional development is to provide teachers with content, lexico-grammatical, assessment, and pedagogical knowledge to assist their ELL students in acquiring both content knowledge and the necessary academic register to comprehend and produce increasingly complex and sophisticated expressions of content understanding orally and in text.

Despite the burgeoning content of teacher education programs, Fillmore and Snow (2005) argue that not enough time is spent on crucial matters, namely the development of language. They contend that, because of policy and societal demands for competence in English, issues related to language (and literacy) are at the heart of educating students more than ever, and they argue for increased attention in teacher education programs to be given to language learning.

However, everything a teacher needs to know cannot be learned in pre-service education. Continued professional development is crucial to the development of knowledge and skills needed to be an effective teacher. Increasingly, there is agreement that professional development is most beneficial when it is long term, school based, collaborative, and focused on students' learning (e.g., Darling-Hammond and Sykes, 1999; Garet, Porter, Desimone, Birman, and Yoon, 2001; National Staff Development Council, 2001). Based on this consensus, Hiebert, Gallimore, and Stigler (2002) present a model for professional development that involves teachers' generating a professional knowledge base that is derived from sharing practitioner knowledge in collaborative structures. They suggest that daily lessons form the unit of analysis for teachers to focus on the "many elements that make up the flow of teaching" (p. 8). This practice parallels the lesson study group model that is widespread among teachers in Japan.

Imagine the following situation: teachers have a strong foundational knowledge of content and language from their pre-service education; throughout their careers they are involved in collaborative study to refine different approaches to content and language development; they take the time to analyze why certain approaches are more effective than others, and they learn from mistakes. In such a scenario all teachers would be language teachers as well as content teachers. In planning instruction, according to our framework, analyzing and explicitly addressing language elements, along with the other elements of learning (concepts, knowledge, and skills), could become second nature. Classes where students receive ESL instruction outside the mainstream classroom would become a thing of the past in all schools. Can there be any doubt that in this scenario *all* teachers would be better equipped to meet the needs of their ELL students and that the ELL students would be better served by their teachers?

## References

American Educational Research Association. (2004, Winter). English language learners: Boosting academic achievement. *Research Points, 2*(1). Retrieved January 31, 2005, from http://www.aera.net/publications/ ?id=314.

Bailey, A. L. (in press). From Lambie to Lambaste: The conceptualization, operationalization, and use of academic language in the assessment of ELL students. In K. Rolstad (Ed.), *Rethinking school language.* Mahwah, NJ: Lawrence Erlbaum.

Bailey, A. L., and Heritage, H. M. (2004, September) *Developing comprehensive evidence-based reading comprehension: A view of the construct and assessment model.* Paper presented at the annual conference of the National Center for Research on Evaluation, Standards, and Student Testing at the University of California, Los Angeles.

Barnes, D. (1976). *From communication to curriculum.* Harmondsworth, UK: Penguin.

Black, P., Harrison, C., Lee, C., Marshall, B., and Wiliam, D. (2003). *Assessment for learning: Putting it into practice.* New York: Open University Press.

Black, P., and Wiliam, D. (2004). The formative purpose: Assessment must first promote learning. In M. Wilson (Ed.), *Towards coherence between classroom assessment and accountability, part II: 103rd yearbook of the National Society for the Study of Education* (pp. 20–50). Chicago: University of Chicago Press.

Britton, J. (1970). *Language and learning.* Harmondsworth, UK: Penguin.

Bruner, J. (1978). The role of dialogue in language acquisition. In A. Sinclair, R. Jarvella, and W. Levelt (Eds.), *Knowing, learning, and instruction.* Hillsdale, NJ: Lawrence Erlbaum.

Bullock Report. (1975). *A language for life: Report of the Committee of Inquiry appointed by the Secretary of State for Education and Science under the chairmanship of Sir Alan Bullock.* London: Her Majesty's Stationery Office.

Butler, F. A., Bailey A. L., Stevens, R., Huang, B., and Lord, C. (2004). Academic English in fifth-grade mathematics, science, and social studies textbooks (Final Deliverable to IES, Contract No. R305B960002; currently available as CSE Tech. Rep. No. 642). Los Angeles: University of California, National Center for Research on Evaluation, Standards, and Student Testing (CRESST).

Chamot, A. U. (2005). The Cognitive Academic Language Learning Approach (CALLA): An update. In P. A. Richard-Amato and M. A. Snow (Eds.), *Academic success for English language learners* (pp. 87–102). White Plains, NY: Longman.

Chamot, A. U., and O'Malley, J. M. (1994). *The CALLA handbook: Implementing the cognitive academic language learning approach.* New York: Longman.

Christie, F. (1985). Language and schooling. In S. Tchudi (Ed.), *Language, schooling, and society* (pp. 21–40). Upper Montclair, NJ: Boynton/Cook.

Cuevas, G. J. (1984). Mathematics learning in English as a second language. *Journal of Research in Mathematics Education, 15*(2), 134–144.

Cummins, J. (1986). *Bilingualism and special education: Issues in assessment and pedagogy.* Clevedon, UK: Multilingual Matters.

Cummins, J. (2005). Language proficiency, bilingualism, and academic achievement. In P. A. Richard-Amato and M. A. Snow (Eds.), *Academic success for English language learners* (pp. 76–86). White Plains, NY: Longman.

Darling-Hammond, L., and Sykes, G. (Eds.). (1999). *Teaching as the learning profession: Handbook of policy and practice.* San Francisco: Jossey-Bass.

Department of Education and Science. (1985). *The curriculum from 5 to 16.* Curriculum Matters 2, an HMI Series. London: Her Majesty's Stationery Office.

Dutro, S. (2003). *An introduction to a focused approach to English language instruction.* Paper presented at the California Reading Association Conference. San Diego: California Reading and Literature Project.

Erickson, F. (2003). Foreword to *Listening: A framework for teaching across differences* by K. Schultz. New York: Teachers College Press.

Fillmore, L. W. (1982). Instructional language as linguistic input: Second language learning in classrooms. In L. C. Wilkinson (Ed.), *Communication in the classroom.* New York: Academic Press.

Fillmore, L. W. (1991). Second language learning in children: A model of language learning in social context. In E. Bialystok (Ed.), *Language processing by bilingual children.* New York: Cambridge University Press.

Fillmore, L. W., and Snow, C. E. (2005). What teachers need to know about language. In P. A. Richard-Amato and M. A. Snow (Eds.), *Academic success for English language learners* (pp. 47–75). White Plains, NY: Longman.

Garet, M. S., Porter, A. C., Desimone, L., Birman, B. F., and Yoon, K. S. (2001). What makes professional development effective? Results from a national sample of teachers. *American Educational Research Journal, 38*, 915–945.

Genesee, F., and Upshur, J. A. (1996). *Classroom-based evaluation in second language education.* Cambridge: Cambridge University Press.

Gibbons, P. (1998). Classroom talk and the learning of new registers in a second language. *Language and Education, 12*(2), 99–118.

Gillet, J. W., and Temple, C. (2000). *Understanding reading problems: Assessment and instruction* (5th ed.). New York: Longman.

Halliday, M. A. K., (1994). *An introduction to functional grammar* (2nd ed.). London: Edward Arnold.

Halliday, M. A. K., and Hasan, R. (1989). *Language, context, and text: Aspects of language in a social-semiotic perspective* (2nd ed.). Oxford: Oxford University Press.

Hampton Brown. (2004). *Into English.* Carmel, CA: Author.

Hiebert, J., Gallimore, R., and Stigler, J. W. (2002). A knowledge base for the teaching profession: What would it look like and how can we get one? *Educational Researcher, 31*(5), 3–15.

Krashen, S. D. (1981). *Second language acquisition and second language learning.* Oxford: Pergamon Press.

Laplante, B. (1997). Teaching science to language minority students in elementary classrooms. *Journal of the New York State Association for Bilingual Education, 12,* 62–83.

Lemke, J. L. (1990). *Talking science: Language, learning, and values.* Norwood, NJ: Ablex.

Lyon, G. R. (1998). Overview of reading and literacy research. In S. Patton and M. Holmes (Eds.), *The keys to literacy* (pp. 8–17). PDF document retrieved October 12, 2004, from the Council for Basic Education (CBE) website: http://www.c-b-e.org/PDF/KeystoLiteracy2002.pdf.

Martin, J. R. (1992). *English text.* Philadelphia: John Benjamins.

Martin, J. R. (1999). Mentoring semogenesis: "Genre-based" literacy pedagogy. In F. Christie (Ed.), *Pedagogy and the shaping of consciousness: Linguistic and social processes* (pp.123–155). London: Continuum

National Reading Panel. (2000). *Teaching children to read: An evidence-based assessment of the scientific research literature on reading and its implications for reading instruction* (NIH Pub. No. 00-4769). Washington, DC: National Institute for Child Health and Development.

National Research Council. (2001). *Knowing what students know: The science and design of educational assessment* (Committee on the Foundations of Assessment, J. Pellegrino, N. Chudowsky, and R. Glaser, Eds.). Washington, DC: National Academies Press.

National Staff Development Council. (2001). *NSDC standards for staff development.* Oxford, OH: Author.

New Standards Primary Literacy Committee. (1999). *Reading and writing grade by grade: Primary literacy standards for kindergarten through third grade.* Washington, DC: National Center on Education and the Economy (NCEE) and the University of Pittsburgh.

Philips, S. U. (1983). *The invisible culture: Communication in classroom and community on the Warm Springs Indian Reservation.* New York: Longman.

Readence, J. E., Bean, T. W., and Baldwin, R. S. (1981). *Content area reading: An integrated approach* (2nd ed.). Dubuque, IA: Kendall/Hunt.

Reed, B., and Railsback, J. (2003). *Strategies and resources for mainstream teachers of English language learners.* Northwest Regional Educational Laboratory. Retrieved January 31, 2005, from http://www.nwrel.org/request/2003may/overview.html.

Reppen, R. (2001). Register variation on student and adult writing. In S. Conrad and D. Biber (Eds.), *Variation in English: Multidimensional studies* (pp. 187–199). Harlow, UK: Pearson Education.

Schleppegrell, M. J. (2001). Linguistic features of the language of schooling. *Linguistics and Education, 12*(4), 431–459.

Schleppegrell, M. J. (2004). *The language of schooling: A functional linguistics perspective.* Mahwah, NJ: Lawrence Erlbaum.

Schleppegrell, M.J., and Achugar, M. (2003). Learning language and learning history: A functional linguistics approach. *TESOL Journal, 12*(2), 21–27.

Shepard, L. A. (2004). Curricular coherence in assessment design. In M. Wilson (Ed.), *Towards coherence between classroom assessment and accountability, part II: 103rd yearbook of the National Society for the Study of Education* (pp. 239–249). Chicago: University of Chicago Press.

Shulman, L. S. (1986). Those who understand: Knowledge growth in teaching. *Educational Researcher, 15*(2), 4–14.

Sizer, T. R., and Sizer, N. F. (1999). *The students are watching: Schools and the moral contract.* Boston: Beacon Press.

Skutnabb-Kangas, T. (1984). *Bilingualism or not: The education of minorities.* Clevedon, UK: Multilingual Matters.

Smithson, J. L., and Porter, A. C. (2004). From policy to practice: The evolution of one approach to describing and using curriculum data. In M. Wilson (Ed.), *Towards coherence between classroom assessment and accountability, part II: 103rd yearbook of the National Society for the Study of Education* (pp. 105–131). Chicago: University of Chicago Press.

Snow, C. E., Cancini, H., Gonzalez, P., and Shriberg, E. (1989). Giving formal definitions: An oral language correlate of school literacy. In D. Bloome (Ed.), *Classrooms and literacy* (pp. 233–249). Norwood, NJ: Ablex.

Spanos, G. (1989). On the interaction of language and content instruction. *Annual Review of Applied Linguistics, 10,* 227–240.

Spanos, G., Rhodes, N. C., Dale, T. C., and Crandall, J. (1988). Linguistic features of mathematical problem solving: Insights and applications. In R. R. Cocking and J. P. Mestre (Eds.), *Linguistic and cultural influences on mathematics* (pp. 221–240). Hillsdale, NJ: Erlbaum.

Stevens, R. J., Slavin, R. E., and Farnish, A. M. (1991). The effects of cooperative learning and direct instruction in reading comprehension strategies on main idea identification. *Journal of Educational Psychology, 83*(1), 8–16.

Thompson, D. R., and Rubenstein, R. N. (2000). Learning mathematics vocabulary: Potential pitfalls and instructional strategies. *Mathematics Teacher, 93*(7), 568–574.

Vygotsky, L. S. (1978). *Mind and society: The development of higher mental processes.* Cambridge, MA: Harvard University Press.

Wharton-McDonald, R., Pressley, M., and Mistretta Hampston, J. (1998). Literacy instruction in nine first-grade classrooms: Teacher characteristics and student achievement. *Elementary School Journal, 99*(2), 101–127.

# CHAPTER 8

# A Research Agenda for the Future of English Language Development

ALISON L. BAILEY

This final chapter lays out an extensive research agenda that will be necessary in the immediate future if we are to continue to move toward building high-quality assessments of academic English at the K-12 level. The agenda highlights some key suggestions as well as important concerns raised by the authors of the chapters in this volume, noting where gaps in our knowledge of the AEL construct still remain and where current ELD assessment policies and teaching practices may need to evolve to meet the needs of ELL students.

(1) Historically, the individual states in the United States have largely adopted ELD standards, content standards, and assessments of ELD at different points in time and frequently in isolation. Some states have derived ELD standards from ELA standards alone. In those instances, the resulting ELD standards do not, we argue, provide a sufficiently broad content base for development of ELD tests. Content-area standards in mathematics and science and empirical evidence should also be used as input for ELD standards and test development to help ensure a thorough operational definition of the language required for success in the academic context (Bailey and Butler, chapter 4).

Under Title III of the No Child Left Behind Act (NCLB, 2001), every state needs to show linkage between state content standards and state ELD standards as input to the development of state English proficiency tests. Specifically, the U.S. Department of Education (2003) released the following draft guidance for this regulation:

B-5. The statute requires English language proficiency standards to be linked to state academic content and achievement standards in reading or language arts and in mathematics beginning in the school year 2002-2003. This is required in order to ensure that LEP students can attain proficiency in both English language and in reading/language arts, math and science. English language proficiency standards should also be linked to the state academic standards in science beginning in the school year 2005-2006. (p. 10)

This has the potential to be an extremely effective direction in which to take ELL assessment and programming because strong alignment between content standards and assessments will enable the states to ensure accurate and meaningful measurement of student achievement (Fast and Hebbler, 2004). Similarly, strong linkage between state content-area and ELD standards will help the states to ensure language learners are given the opportunity to learn the relevant language needed to succeed in school. Documenting these developments with an audit trail as outlined in Davidson, Kim, Lee, Li, and López, chapter 6 will be essential for arguing the benefits and expense of the new assessment efforts.

However, all this rests on the critical assumption that the standards, which play a key role in the AEL framework and contemporary U.S. schooling, have all been validated. This is far from the case. In chapter 4, Bailey and Butler, while noting that the AEL construct can usefully take account of ELD and content-area standards, acknowledged the limitations of relying on such standards documents. As pointed out by McKay (2000), most ELD standards have yet to be subjected to validation studies. Consequently, we call for an ongoing evaluation process of why certain standards are adopted and not others that should be central to any standards-based approach to educational assessment. Given limitations to standards, we may even be wiser to talk of standards-*informed* assessment, not standards-based. Moreover, the ELD standards at the very least should be periodically reevaluated as the AEL construct garners increased specificity as the result of further research on academic language demands.

(2) We call for basic research to outline the trajectory of academic English language demands across the grade levels. Although we recognize that such work will encounter a great deal of variability in current practice, we believe that researchers will be able to identify some qualitative shifts in the language demands that ELL students face as they progress through the curriculum. Complicating the articulation of AEL proficiency by grade or grade clusters is the fact that ELL students may have idiosyncratic exposure experi-

ences, which means their ELD is not age regulated (Corson, 1997). Understanding the progression of AEL demands has implications for curriculum and professional development, not only for assessment development.

Such an undertaking will require the utilization of recent advances in research methods. In order to conceptualize and represent the AEL learning processes and the developmental patterns underlying the outcomes, longitudinal data will be needed, as Mayer points out in chapter 3. The process of AEL development can then be better studied, and individual differences in the rate of growth can be systematically examined using growth modeling techniques (e.g., Muthén, 2001; Muthén, Khoo, Francis, and Boscardin, 2002). Classification of students into subgroups of trajectory starting points based on initial AEL level or by program status (e.g., LEP, IFEP, RFEP) should also be attempted so we learn more about the relationship between student language proficiency and eventual academic achievement.

(3) We call for further research to explicate which academic language competencies are domain specific and which are generally applicable across instructional contexts. While current cognitive theory has increasingly argued that cognition and discourse are often specific to a discipline or context, we suspect some remarkable similarities between the recommended disciplinary discourse for teaching content areas such as mathematics, science, and history that suggests domain-general AEL. The findings we generated from studies of science classrooms (Bailey, Butler, Stevens, and Lord, chapter 5) and social science classrooms (Stevens, Butler, and Castellon-Wellington, 2000) should be subjected to replication and the classroom research expanded across grade levels and across disciplines to determine if the hypothesized general academic discourse practices do indeed play a prominent role at other grades and in other disciplinary contexts. If some discourse practices are indeed shared across disciplines, or there proves to be general academic discourse practices, such findings have the potential to change the ways in which we organize content assessments for use with ELL students.

(4) To address pedagogical factors that may impact rate and ultimate attainment of AEL, we call for research that will characterize variation in classroom instructional and linguistic practices. These include the many ways in which teachers integrate content and academic uses of language as outlined in Heritage, Silva, and Pierce,

chapter 7. Something as straightforward as organizing classrooms for whole-group or small-group discussions may impact student opportunity to be exposed to and acquire AEL and consequently impact content-area learning, too (e.g., Enyedy, Barajas, and Bailey, 2005).

Again, advances in statistical techniques can now address such classroom variation while measuring student achievement. Multilevel growth models, utilizing Hierarchical Linear Modeling (HLM) software, for example, involve both individual student-level variables and classroom-level measures, with students nested within classrooms (Bryk and Raudenbush, 1992).

(5) In conjunction with articulating the language demands placed on ELL students and the gains students may make, we suggest investigation of the resources that students already possess to meet academic challenges. We hypothesize that one major resource will be students' existing competence in social language. However, from existing empirical evidence it is unclear exactly what the relationship is (or could be) between competence in social language and academic language. Some have argued, for example, that the social/academic language dichotomy itself should be challenged, and that completing academic tasks actually involves a wide range of linguistic resources, including those often relegated to the realm of "social" language (Bunch, 2004, 2005, in press; see also MacSwan and Rolstad, 2003; Rivera, 1984; Rolstad, in press). Specifically, there is an absence of conclusive evidence of how social language proficiency impacts AEL in terms of being a precursor to AEL, or even how social language itself continues to develop across the grade levels.

(6) Related to point (5) above, we call for psycholinguistic studies of student representation and understanding of AEL, for example, study of students' overt knowledge of variants in linguistic register: namely, when to use the discourse of formal, academic settings and when to use the discourse of informal, conversational settings. For example, Bunch (2004, 2005, in press) has shown that seventh-grade students, working in small linguistically heterogeneous groups, showed awareness that classroom presentations of their work to their teacher and fellow students involved different linguistic expectations than when discussing that work with each other in small-group settings. This knowledge may be still largely implicit for some students, and if so teachers can help make it ex-

plicit. Certainly this knowledge should be measured at different levels of ELD proficiency, across different age levels, and after different numbers of years in U.S. schooling to better tailor future AEL programming to not only the language development but also the metalinguistic development of ELL students.

Finally, it remains to say only that none of the findings from any of the studies already conducted or proposed here will have any impact unless we take account of those who teach and the skills they will need to implement such an extensive new knowledge base. The most critical of all components of this research agenda will be the translation of this work into teacher professional development, be that in-service programming for current teachers, some finding ELL students in their classrooms for the first time, or training for novice teachers in teacher education programs who are rightfully expectant of innovative and effective new practices for use with the nation's growing population of ELL students.

## References

Bryk, A. S., and Raudenbush, S. W. (1992). *Hierarchical linear models: Application and data analysis methods.* Newbury Park, CA: Sage.

Bunch, G. C. (2004). *"But how do we say that?" Reconceptualizing academic language in linguistically diverse mainstream classrooms.* Unpublished doctoral dissertation, Stanford University, Stanford, CA.

Bunch, G. C. (2005, April). *What can listening to students teach us about "academic language"?* Paper presented at the American Educational Research Association Annual Conference, Montreal, Canada.

Bunch, G. C. (in press). The language of ideas and the language of display: Expanding conceptions of "academic language." In Rolstad, K. (Ed.), *Rethinking school language.* Mahwah, NJ: Lawrence Erlbaum.

Corson, D. (1997). The learning and use of academic English words. *Language Learning, 47*(4), 671–718.

Enyedy, N., Barajas, F., and Bailey, A. L. (2005, April). *Language disconnects between small group problem solving and whole class discussions.* Paper presented at the American Educational Research Association Annual Conference, Montreal, Canada.

Fast, E. F., and Hebbler, S. (2004). *A framework for examining validity in state accountability systems.* Washington, DC: CCSSO.

MacSwan, J., and Rolstad, K. (2003). Linguistic diversity, schooling, and social class: Rethinking our conception of language proficiency in language minority education. In C. B. Paulston and G. R. Tucker (Eds.), *Sociolinguistics: The essential readings* (pp. 329–340). Malden, MA: Blackwell.

McKay, P. (2000). On ESL standards for school-age learners. *Language Testing, 17*(2), 185–214.

Muthén, B. (2001). Latent variable mixture modeling. In G. A. Marcoulides and R. E. Schumacker (Eds.), *New developments and techniques in structural equation modeling* (pp. 1–33). Mahwah, NJ: Lawrence Erlbaum.

Muthén, B., Khoo, S. K., Francis, D., and Boscardin, C. K. (2002). Analysis of reading skills development from kindergarten through first grade: An application of growth mixture modeling to sequential processes. In S. Reise and N. Duan (Eds.), *Multilevel modeling: Methodological advances, issues, and applications.* Mahwah, NJ: Lawrence Erlbaum.

No Child Left Behind Act. (2001). Pub. L. No. 107-110, 115 Stat. 1425, December 13.

Rivera, C. (Ed.). (1984). *Language proficiency and academic achievement.* Clevedon, UK: Multilingual Matters.

Rolstad, K. (Ed.) (in press). *Rethinking school language.* Mahwah: NJ: Lawrence Erlbaum.

Stevens, R. A., Butler, F. A., and Castellon-Wellington, M. (2000). *Academic Language and content assessment: Measuring the progress of ELLs.* (CSE Tech. Rep. No. 552). Los Angeles: University of California, National Center for Research on Evaluation, Standards, and Student Testing (CRESST).

U.S. Department of Education. (2003, February). *Part II—Draft final non-regulatory guidance on the Title III state formula grants program: Standards, assessment, and accountability.* Washington, DC: Office of English Language Acquisition.

# Contributors

**Alison L. Bailey** is associate professor and division head of the Psychological Studies in Education Program in the Department of Education, University of California, Los Angeles (UCLA), in addition to being a faculty associate researcher for the National Center for Research on Evaluation, Standards, and Student Testing (CRESST). A graduate of Harvard University, Dr. Bailey focuses her research primarily on language and literacy development and the English language development and assessment of second language learners. She directs the Academic English Language Proficiency Project at CRESST which, since 1998, has conducted research to provide an empirical basis for the operationalization of the academic language construct for assessment, curriculum, and teacher professional development. Dr. Bailey is coauthor of the new IPT assessment of English language development at the prekindergarten-kindergarten level published by Ballard and Tighe and most recently was made the 2005-6 Fellow of the Sudikoff Family Institute at UCLA to expand public awareness of critical issues related to education and the media.

**Frances A. Butler, Ph.D.,** is currently an independent educational consultant focusing on language assessment and related issues. For 15 years, Dr. Butler was a senior research associate and language testing specialist at CRESST. Known for her research in language testing, especially ESL, she has directed test development projects and research that focused on K-12 language minority populations as well as adult ESL learners.

**Martha Castellon** has had 13 years of experience working on issues related to the needs of English language learners. She worked as a bilingual first-, second- and third-grade teacher for the Long Beach Unified School District. After earning her master's degree in TESL from UCLA in 1998, she joined CRESST. She is currently a doctoral student at Stanford University's School of Education.

**Fred Davidson** is an associate professor of English as an international language at the University of Illinois, where he also holds appointments in educational psychology and in curriculum and instruction. His background and interests focus on language testing, research methods and data management for applied linguistics, and the history and philosophy of educational and psychological measurement. He is the coauthor of *Testcraft: A Teacher's Guide to Writing and Using Language Test Specifications,* published by Yale University Press in 2002.

**Margaret Heritage** is assistant director for professional development at CRESST. Her current work focuses on data use for school improvement supported by technology and on the development of literacy assessment tools. In the United Kingdom she was a classroom teacher, principal of an elementary school, and latterly a county education inspector. In the United States she served as principal of the Corinne A. Seeds University Elementary School, the laboratory school of the Graduate School of Education and Information Studies at UCLA. Margaret Heritage has also held teaching appointments at California State University- Los Angeles, UCLA, and Stanford University.

**Jung Tae Kim** is a doctoral student in the Department of Educational Psychology at the University of Illinois at Urbana-Champaign, where he also obtained his master's degree in TESL. His primary research interests are in language testing using computer and computer-assisted language learning (CALL). His research includes Web-based language test development (currently focusing on speaking) and specification-driven test development and administration encompassing input from test takers with respect to consumer-referenced testing.

**Hyeong-Jong Lee** is a doctoral student in the Department of Educational Psychology at the University of Illinois at Urbana-Champaign with the specialization of language testing and second language acquisition. He completed his MA in ESL at the University of Hawai'i at Manoa in 2000. While his research interest focuses on the reliability and validity issues of both theoretical and applied aspects of language test development, he has been working on statistical modeling in SLA-related studies.

*Jinshu Li* is currently studying in the MA program in TESL at the University of Illinois at Urbana-Champaign. A native of China, she earned her bachelor's degree in English from Beijing Second Language University in June 2001 and worked as an EFL trainer in the State Power Co. of China for two years. She is now serving as a research assistant for the WIDA project. Her main research interests include validity narratives, test spec development, and audit trail studies.

*Alexis A. López* has just completed his doctoral degree in the Department of Curriculum and Instruction at the University of Illinois at Urbana-Champaign. He is a former Fulbright Scholar with an MA in TESL. His main research interests are test development, test specifications, and test impact. Dr. López is currently working as a project manager at Second Language Testing, Inc.

*Carol Lord* is associate professor of teacher education at California State University-Long Beach, where her work includes blending her background in linguistics with an understanding of student and teacher needs in the classroom. For the past several years Dr. Lord has been a coinvestigator at CRESST at UCLA on work that characterizes academic language for a range of educational applications.

*Jan Mayer* began her educational career as a bilingual classroom teacher and later became a school district administrator. She received her doctorate from the University of San Francisco. In the 1990s Dr. Mayer came to the California Department of Education, where she has worked to implement the legal requirements for English learners in schools throughout the state and participated extensively in the development of state and local accountability systems. Dr. Mayer is currently the assistant superintendent of the Learning Support and Partnerships Division at the California Department of Education.

*Mary Pierce,* a national board certified teacher, is currently the assistant principal of Para Los Niños Charter School, which serves low-income students whose primary language is Spanish in downtown Los Angeles. In this capacity she provides professional development to the teachers as well as administrative support. Mary Pierce began her career in the field of education as a teacher in a two-way dual immersion program in the Los Angeles Unified School

District and went on to become a demonstration teacher in the Learning in Two Languages Program at the Corinne A. Seeds University Elementary School, the laboratory school of the Graduate School of Education and Information Studies at UCLA.

***Norma Silva*** is the principal at Para Los Niños Charter School, which serves a population of English language learners in downtown Los Angeles. Her experience includes over 20 years of teaching in bilingual education. Previously Norma Silva was director of student and family affairs and the summer school principal at Corinne A. Seeds University Elementary School, UCLA. Her current interests center on the development of primary language literacy for fluent Spanish speakers and on creating teacher professional development programs that focus on cognitive and academic language development in science, social studies, and mathematics for English anguage learners.

***Robin Stevens*** is a language services consultant, specializing in language testing and project management. Formerly a public administration analyst at the Center for the Study of Evaluation/CRESST at UCLA, she is a graduate of San Jose State University and the Monterey Institute of International Studies. Her research at UCLA has focused on the standardized test performance of K-12 English language learners and on research and development of academic English language proficiency assessments.

# Index

Abedi, J., 72–73, 74

academic achievement, 4,16, 50, 52, 55–56, 65–66, 213; assessment of, 4–5, 27, 37, 84, 201

academic English language (AEL): acquisition of, 4, 16, 213–14; assessment of (*see* assessment: AEL); common core, 10, 69–70; construct of, 1–2, 6–9, 12, 68–69, 71, 80, 104, 127, 211–12; content area-specific, 10, 69–70, 134, 213; discourse features of, 15–16, 96, 130–31, 140–42, 145; exposure to, 5, 16, 69, 94, 214; framework for educational applications of, 68, 82–93; functions of, 107 (*see also* language functions); lexical features of, 12–14, 96, 127–29, 136–38, 147, 171, 173; operationalization of, 6, 8, 12, 68, 71–82, 86, 103; proficiency assessments for (*see* English Language Development [ELD]: proficiency assessments for); proficiency in, 70, 72, 94, 212; proficiency tasks, 71, 87–90; school success and, 75, 85; standards, 79, 82–84, 94, 212; student understanding of, 214–15; syntactic (grammatical) features of, 14–15, 96, 130, 134, 138–40, 147, 171, 173; teaching of, 9, 80, 92–93, 95–96, 213

Academic Language Exposure Checklist (ALEC), 112–13

accommodations: language and, 94–95; test performance and, 94; test procedures and, 95

accountability: assessment and, 106, 202; policies, 3–4, 50, 55, 57, 66; students and, 186, 201; systems, 27, 51, 53, 55, 65–66, 83, 199

AEL. *See* academic English language

ALADIN, 91

Alderson, J. C., 158

ALEC. *See* Academic Language Exposure Checklist

assessment: academic achievement and (*see* academic achievement: assessment of); accountability (*see* accountability: assessment and); AEL, 6, 16–17, 79, 82, 85–86, 91, 157, 166; authenticity and, 164–65, 168, 169; content (*see* content assessment); development of, 2, 82–83, 213; educational, 212; ELD proficiency and (*see* English Language Development [ELD]: proficiency assessments for); ELLs and, 74, 93, 212; English language proficiency testing, 6, 27; formative, 176, 178, 180–82, 186–87, 204; high-stakes testing, 55, 159, 160; inclusion, 3–5, 28, 56, 62, 83–84, 106; language demands of, 71; language portfolio, 203; large-scale, 28; primary language, 55; readiness, 5, 35, 46, 64, 70, 85; Sheltered Instruction Observation Protocol (SIOP), 92; spec-driven language testing (*see* test development); specifications (*see* test development: test specifications); standardized, 28, 30, 36, 46, 126; summative, 91, 171,